CRITICAL INSIGHTS

Raymond Carver

CRITICAL
INSIGHTS

Raymond Carver

Editor
James Plath
Illinois Wesleyan University

SALEM PRESS
A Division of EBSCO Publishing
Ipswich, Massachusetts

GREY HOUSE PUBLISHING

Cover Photo: © Sophie Bassouls/Sygma/Corbis

Editor's text © 2013 by James Plath

Copyright © 2013, by Salem Press, A Division of EBSCO Publishing, Inc.

Critical Insights: Raymond Carver, 2013, published by Grey House Publishing, Inc., Amenia, NY, under exclusive license from EBSCO Publishing, Inc.

∞ The paper used in these volumes conforms to the American National Standard for Permanence of Paper for Printed Library Materials, Z39.48-1992 (R1997).

Library of Congress Cataloging-in-Publication Data

Raymond Carver / editor, James Plath, Illinois Wesleyan University.
    pages cm. -- (Critical Insights)
  Includes bibliographical references and index.
  ISBN 978-1-4298-3830-6 (hardcover)
  1. Carver, Raymond, 1938-1988--Criticism and interpretation. I. Plath, James, editor of compilation.
  PS3553.A7894Z83 2013
  813'.54--dc23
                                                                    2013009467

ebook ISBN: 978-1-4298-3846-7

PRINTED IN THE UNITED STATES OF AMERICA

Contents_____

About This Volume

James Plath

Raymond Carver was highly regarded at the time of his death, hailed as America's Chekhov by the London *Guardian* and *Sunday Times,* and had been given the lion's share of credit for reviving the short story genre in the 1980s. His work inspired widespread imitations and numerous critical essays, books, and memoirs. Surprisingly, though, there has been only one collection of original essays published prior to this one: *New Paths to Raymond Carver: Critical Essays on His Life, Fiction, and Poetry*, edited by Sandra Lee Kleppe and Robert Miltner. The thirteen new offerings in *Critical Insights: Raymond Carver* add to the critical dialogue, further defining Carver's world and methodology, summarizing Carver's distinct place in American literature, and examining the major issues surrounding Carver criticism. The essays also explore new territory, and it is worth noting that the contributions come from well-known Carver scholars in six different countries—underscoring how truly international Carver's reputation has become.

The section on Career, Life, and Influence begins with my essay "On Raymond Carver," in which I discuss how Carver, more than any other twentieth-century American writer, was tied in spirit and publication to the world of small literary magazines and presses, even after he was "discovered" by *Esquire* editor Gordon Lish and published by a major house. Most critics were enthralled by what they read, with many comparing his spare style to Hemingway's. Carver, meanwhile, was candid about his influences—chief among them, his children, he later claimed—no doubt because he was able to move beyond them and carve a niche for himself. He seems destined to endure in the American literary canon because of the uniqueness and universality of his work, certainly, but also ironically, because of critics' insistence that he's a "minimalist"—a term he resisted—and because he's one of our few major writers whose background and subject matter is consistently blue collar.

Chad Wriglesworth talks about that blue-collar element in greater detail in his essay on how the Pacific Northwest shaped Carver's vision of the world and his fictional aesthetic. Like his father before him, Carver worked in a sawmill, and that hard life led to hard drinking. As Wriglesworth observes, "behind the failures and successes of this memorable writer resides the voice of someone whose life and work was shaped by the scenic power and socioeconomic history of the Pacific Northwest." Wriglesworth discusses Carver's fiction and poetry in that context, noting that even after Carver left the area and returned years later, he reconnected with the Pacific Northwest and resumed writing poetry that was inspired by the "landscape and the water."

In the Critical Contexts section, William L. Stull and Maureen P. Carroll offer not just an overview of the critical reception to Carver's work, but also a sense of the critical confusion that resulted from Lish's heavy editorial hand and how it affected a decade of Carver criticism until one journalist–scholar delved into the Lish archive at Indiana University and began to sort things out. Stull and Carroll also discuss the controversy over the 2009 publication of *Beginners*, a collection of seventeen of Carver's original and unedited stories, and the multiple versions of Carver stories that were previously published, with "minimalist" stories often followed by "corrected" versions that were more expansive, when in reality the later publications were often Carver's unedited originals.

Enrico Monti further explores Carver's association with minimalism in the essay that follows, detailing how the Lish-Carver relationship began and how Lish re-shaped stories but eventually lost his influence over Carver. From the beginning of his career, Carver was associated with minimalism, a literary movement and label that he always resisted. Heralded as the literary descendant of Hemingway, he wrote in a style that reduced language and narrative to the simplest yet most effective structure. Monti's essay situates Carver in the context of Hemingway, minimalism, Lish's influence, and various detractors.

A number of reviewers and critics have remarked that Carver's short stories are heavily pictorial, and in my essay on Carver and painter Edward Hopper I discuss how the two men shared a number of affinities that becomes strikingly evident when their works are compared. Carver's fiction and Hopper's stark canvases both depict isolated, often downcast Americans in near-static tableaus. That sense of isolation and inaction is exacerbated by Carver's deliberate decision to begin many of his stories not at some point during the rising action, as writers typically do, but after the main climax has already occurred.

Like so many American authors, Carver was an alcoholic. Unlike most of them, he wrote honestly and matter-of-factly about alcoholism and the long hard road to recovery. It's an inescapable part of his characters' lives and part of the reading experience. Kirk Nesset discusses alcoholism as it surfaces in Carver's fiction and poetry, in relation to Carver's own struggle with the disease, and as described by Carver and some of his closest friends. At his lowest point, "in the last year before he stopped drinking," Carver knew that he "was finished as a writer and as a viable, functioning adult male. It was over for me. That's why I can speak of two lives, that life and this life."

In his essay on "Middle-Age Crazy: Men Behaving Badly in the Fiction of Raymond Carver and John Updike," Matthew Shipe compares the fiction of two writers whose creative and personal lives couldn't be more different. Yet, Carver and Updike, whose *New Yorker* background and stories reflect a life that's more privileged, find a point of intersection in that their male characters tend to behave badly—especially in relation to the women in their lives and in matters of responsibility. Characters often give in to their impulses, putting themselves first no matter how much they seem to care about the others in their lives. Shipe explores the writers' male characters and also reveals other points of intersection between them.

Although Carver does employ female narrators and points of view in his stories, to the average reader his world seems mostly male. In her essay, Claire Fabre, who wrote the introduction to a special issue on "Carver and Feminism" for the *Raymond Carver Review*, considers the stages of development that feminism and gender studies have undergone in the context of Carver's fiction, focusing especially on the stories narrated by a woman or told from a female point of view. Fabre posits that the most recent wave of gender criticism has enabled readers to reconsider Carver's work "as one that disrupts formulaic representations of gender dividing lines," and that Carver's "treatment of marital tragedies and the constraints imposed on women within a patriarchal world suggest his awareness of most of the issues addressed by feminist criticism."

The Critical Readings section begins with an essay on Carver's poetry, with Robert Miltner convinced that while Carver's legacy as a fiction writer is certain, "his legacy as a poet continues to grow." Miltner illustrates how "Carver's poetry was interlaced and concurrent with his fiction" from the beginning of his writing career and identifies three phases in Carver's poetry—an understanding of which may help readers better appreciate the fiction.

Randolph Runyon offers a study of the three major Carver collections—*Will You Please Be Quiet, Please?*, *What We Talk About When We Talk About Love*, and *Cathedral*—and identifies patterns that enhance our reading of the texts. Even more, Runyon argues that the presence of such patterns invites readers to "collaborate in the work" of putting the text together. Runyon points to the arrangement of stories within each collection and highlights several specific alterations to original publications as enhancing "the esthetic qualities of the collection [while possibly] reducing the emotional charge of the individual stories."

Vasiliki Fachard argues that Carver was aware of the limits of representation "and of the fact that writing is a means of probing—as opposed to copying—reality." She suggests that the power and originality of Carver's fiction stems from being poised between two traditions: realism and "a new fiction that purports to give voice to the unconscious by forcing it to crop out of the surface of a text." As readers consider Fachard's essay, they may find themselves thinking back to what John Updike had to say in Shipe's essay about Carver's "highly polished" work. It may feel like a transcription of reality, but as Carver told interviewers in 1984, "just telling it like it is bores me . . . If you look carefully at my stories, I don't think you'll find people talking the way people do in real life."[1]

In her essay "Small Good Things: Symbols and Descriptive Details in Carver's Short Fiction," Ayala Amir gives a brief history of the symbol and explores the methodology that Carver uses to layer his stories with meaning. There is a deep connection between form and content in Carver's work. Using some of Carver's most famous and frequently anthologized stories as examples, Amir discusses the dynamic that underlies "both the symbolic reading of [Carver's] stories and the attempts of contact and communication undertaken by his characters."

Many people entered Raymond Carver's world for the first time through Robert Altman's *Short Cuts*, a film that was inspired by nine stories and one poem by Carver. In his essay, Peter J. Bailey examines *Short Cuts* in the context of Carver's works and the film's critical reception. Set in Los Angeles, rather than Carver's Pacific Northwest, *Short Cuts* deals with a different socioeconomic class and, as noted film critic Roger Ebert observes, "all the film really has in common with its source is a feeling for people who are disconnected—from relatives, church, tradition—and support themselves with jobs that never seem quite real."[2] Bailey posits that while Altman's "shifting the social strata of the characters while intertwining their narratives leaves not much of Carver's essence behind," it's possible to appreciate how "Carver's and Altman's divergent visions dictated that the resulting movie veers far from Carver's stories when Altman is invoking issues closest to his heart."

Finally, Raymond Carver is generally thought to be a part of the realist tradition, but as Françoise Sammarcelli explains in her essay, there is a "playful metafictional dimension" in Carver's work, with elements of intertextuality, parody, and "ruptures on the surface of the text" that draw attention to the way that meaning is constructed—all of which are associated with so-called postmodern fiction. Carver's short stories are far more complex, Sammarcelli argues, "than many critics focused on the return to representation and realism would have us believe."

The stories and poems that Raymond Carver wrote may appear to be simple, but as these essays collectively show, there are complex techniques at work and equally complex issues that underlie even the shortest story or the plainest poem. The hope is that these essays will not only provide a basic introduction to Raymond Carver and his works, but will also inspire students and scholars to continue the critical dialogue in new and different ways while reinforcing what an important writer Carver remains in twentieth-century American literature.

Notes

1. From Gentry, Marshall Bruce, and William L. Stull, eds. *Conversations with Raymond Carver*. Jackson: UP of Mississippi, 1990. 113. Print.
2. Ebert, Roger. *rogerebert.com*. Chicago Sun-Times, 21 Nov. 2006. Web. 13 Feb. 2013.

CAREER, LIFE, AND INFLUENCE

On Raymond Carver

James Plath

In 1987 an Italian publication described Raymond Carver as "perhaps the most 'mythic'" of contemporary American writers—"the recognized master of that literary renaissance that is producing legions of fiction writers barely out of adolescence . . . the alchemist who has distilled, at an incomparable level of perfection, the quintessence of a genre that only ten years ago seemed in inexorable decline" (Gentry and Stull 192). They were talking about the short story, which had been in remission until Carver's distinctive narratives of blue-collar struggles captivated the reading public and breathed new life into the genre. Just as Hemingway—a writer Carver admired—inspired an earlier generation of would-be writers to try their hand at what looked like deceptively simple and direct fiction, Carver too became an influence. Like Hemingway, he wrote with narrative objectivity, using short sentences and dialogue that, while stylized, appeared to capture the cadences of real speech. Students in master's of fine arts programs were so infatuated with his bare-bones fiction—which had much in common with a reductive style of writing critics were calling "minimalism"— that they flooded literary magazines with imitations. As former *Esquire* fiction editor Tom Jenks confirmed, during the late 1970s and early 1980s "[the] style most often attempted by young writers is one marked by short, hard-edged sentences, like those of Ray Carver, and the subject matter often brushes up against Carver's as well—representative of what I would call a downside neo-realism" (qtd. in Gentry and Stull 85).

Although Carver wrote seven books of poetry, numerous essays, and several plays, he's best known and most celebrated for his short fiction. We know now that the stories in Carver's second major press collection, *What We Talk About When We Talk About Love* (1981), were significantly altered by his editor, who cut the stories severely and ended them more abruptly and elliptically; however, later published versions that were really Carver's originals—but just as powerful as the pared-down ones—proved that sentence length and narrative omissions might not have been as defining as some critics previously thought. In fact, an early reviewer for the *New York Review of Books* presciently observed, "Carver's remarkable talent for short fiction proves itself in the movement of his stories from beginning to end, and not in their enigmatic outcomes" (Edwards 36). More than the much-ballyhooed style or cryptic endings, it was Carver's blue-collar content, a still-stark storytelling sensibility, an understated emotional core, and his empathic treatment of characters that made his fiction distinctive. As rare-book dealer Ken Lopez noted in his introduction to a catalog of Carver offerings, what most set Carver apart from the rest was his "moral vision," as also had been the case with Hemingway. "No one was more acutely aware of the foibles of his characters than Raymond Carver; their quirks, self-deceptions and weaknesses were exposed with surgical precision," Lopez observed. "Yet he never condescended to them or exalted himself or the reader at their expense." By writing sympathetically about his characters, like the artists and writers before him who introduced lower-class elements into the realm of so-called "high art," Carver expanded the fictional world and, as one critic summarized, "was credited with giving us access to a neglected part of the social landscape in which people were indeed living 'minimal' lives" (Scobie 273).

Interestingly, in 1984 Carver told the *New York Times Magazine*, "Until I started reading these reviews of my work, praising me, I never felt the people I was writing about were so bad off. You know what I mean? The waitress, the bus driver, the mechanic, the hotel keeper. God, the country is filled with these people. They're good people. People doing the best they could" (Gentry and Stull 92). Carver knew such people and was the son of such people: born May 25, 1938, in tiny Clatskanie, Oregon, to a father who worked in a sawmill and drank too much and a mother who waitressed and held odd jobs to supplement the family income. It was a hand-to-mouth, paycheck-to-paycheck existence that forced the Carvers to relocate wherever work was available and the housing affordable. That pattern was established while Carver was still in the womb, with Clevie Raymond ("C. R.") and Ella Carver moving to Clatskanie so C. R. could work as a saw filer, a dangerous but better paying job than the standard mill worker. When Carver was three years old the family moved to Yakima in south-central Washington—the site of C. R.'s new job with Cascade Lumber—and nine years later the family would move again, this time to a nicer neighborhood in Yakima to a house with an indoor toilet. After another five years, as their income increased, the family moved to an even more upscale part of Yakima— but the trade-off was that they had to pay rent again instead of owning.

That year, Carver, whose difficult childhood was balanced by the idylls of hunting and fishing in a Pacific Northwest paradise, met a fourteen-year-old counter girl named Maryann Burk at the Spudnut donut shop where his mother waitressed. Three years later—after he graduated from Yakima High School and briefly followed his family to Chester, California, to join his father in the sawmills—he would marry her and become the father of two by the time he was twenty. Out of necessity, Carver also worked his share of "crap jobs" (Gentry and Stull 13), among them hospital janitor, pharmacy deliveryman, sawmill worker, tulip picker, and service station attendant. As newlyweds he and Maryann lived in a basement apartment owned by a physician, cleaning the doctor's office at nights in exchange for rent. Years later they would work for lodging again as they managed a motel that would surface in "Gazebo," his short story about a husband and wife at the end of their ropes. During the tough early years when they lived mostly in northern California, Carver and Maryann took turns working and watching the children, with Carver resenting "that the life I was in was vastly different from the lives of the writers I most admired" (Carver, *Call* 99) In his autobiographical reflection *Fires*, he cited his children—Christine (born December 2, 1957) and Vance (born October 19, 1958)—as the biggest influence on his writing, explaining that their constant needs and interruptions forced him to work in short forms like poetry and short fiction, rather than tackling a novel (Carver, *Call* 97).

As Carver revealed with the same unflinching honesty that characterizes his fiction, "from beginning to end of our habitation under the same roof—some nineteen years in all—there wasn't any area of my life where their heavy and often baleful influence didn't reach" (Carver, *Call* 97). Friends would later recall how he seemed overwhelmed and withdrawn. In 1970, after the Carvers had been married for thirteen years and their children were twelve and thirteen, fellow writer William Kittredge described Carver as someone who "felt very isolated" (Halpert, *Raymond Carver* 16) because, as Carver later explained, "I was too young to be a father with much too much responsibility to keep the family going" (74), Carver said. Yet his own young family's frequent moves—five times in their first four years of marriage—along with the demands of fatherhood, an assortment of low-paying jobs, money problems, family crises, and an accelerated drinking problem, gave him plenty to write about. When asked about the sense of menace that readers perceive in his fiction, Carver told interviewers that they ought to "try living on the other side of the tracks for a while. Menace is there, and it's palpable" (102). To another he explained, "Certainly I think that loneliness and isolation and physical exhaustion are true of my people, or many of them anyway. It was true for me during a period of my life, and . . . these things could not help but find their way into my stories" (163–64).

Carver and Maryann aspired to rise above their menial jobs and hardscrabble lives. They were both readers, and Carver knew by age fifteen—when he enrolled in a creative writing correspondence course his father paid for—that he wanted to be a writer. As a boy, he had often walked to the Yakima Public Library each week, and he remained an inveterate reader throughout his life. For her part, Maryann was convinced that education was the key to improving their lot, and she had no qualms about taking out student loans or quitting jobs to prioritize school. They both took classes during the first ten years of their marriage, and Maryann even received a fellowship to study in Israel, with Ray accompanying her for what turned out to be an unhappy experience for him because the accommodations were less than advertised. But two things changed Carver's life: a fortuitous drug store delivery that he made during which a "lovely old gentleman" gave him copies of two small-press publications, *Poetry* and a *Little Review Anthology* (Stull and Carroll 959) and a creative writing course at California State University (CSU)–Chico, which was taught by John Gardner, who one day brought a box of literary magazines to class and said that this was where 90 percent of the best fiction and 98 percent of the best poetry in the country was being published. "It was a terrific discovery for me," Carver later said (Gentry and Stull 153).

Just as Hemingway was advised by the older and more established author Sherwood Anderson to stop trying to publish in popular magazines such as *Argosy* and *Redbook* and instead write for the little literary magazines (Reynolds 240), Carver learned from this anonymous old man and his intense professor, fresh out of Iowa's famed Writer's Workshop, that the popular magazines weren't the way to go. It was the "littles" that showcased all of the innovative and experimental writing, all the serious writing, all the noncommercial writing that really mattered. That still holds true. Usually published by a single individual or a college student organization, little literary magazines often have on average a small circulation of fifty to three thousand subscribers and a short lifespan of three years or less. More than half of them are nonprofit, and more than half have budgets of ten thousand dollars or less. Between 1912 and 1946, some six hundred literary magazines were published in the United States, and the little magazines that thrived during Hemingway's time were also the best place for serious new writers to break into print when Carver was taking classes and firing off submissions to various literary magazines. "They kept me alive during the 1960s," Carver said. "Getting an occasional poem accepted in a magazine, getting an occasional short story accepted" in magazines "like *Akros, Western Humanities* [*Review*], and *Carolina Quarterly*" (Gentry and Stull 19) gave him an audience and validation as a writer. Carver was also invested in the little magazines as an editor. At

CSU–Chico, where he took classes between 1959 and 1960, he and fellow student Nancy Parke cofounded the literary magazine *Selection*, and three years after transferring to Humboldt State College in the fall of 1960, he became the editor of *Toyon*, an already-established campus literary magazine. More than a decade later, as a visiting lecturer at the University of California, Santa Cruz, Carver became the founding advisory editor of a magazine that survives now as *Quarry West*.

The first of Carver's stories to be published was "The Furious Seasons," which in 1961 appeared in *Selection*. A year later the little magazine *Targets* would publish Carver's first poem, "The Brass Ring." *Toyon* published his second story ("The Father"), and as a *Toyon* editor facing a drought of submissions in 1963, Carver published three of his own stories: "The Aficionados," a Hemingway parody; "The Hair"; and "Poseidon and Company." His story "Pastoral" was published in the higher-circulation *Western Humanities Review* that same year, as was a revised version of "Furious Seasons" in *December*, edited by Curtis L. Johnson, who, like so many little-magazine and small-press editors Carver encountered, would become a friend.

Nearly every major American writer since Hemingway was first published in the little literary magazines, which the *Oxford Guide to American Literature* admits "justified themselves by providing a medium for all kinds of aesthetic experimentation and innovative and unpopular beliefs," despite having printed "a good deal of insignificant or bizarre work" (Hart 436). What sets Carver apart is that, unlike those who used the little magazines merely as a springboard to a professional writing career, he never abandoned them once he was "discovered." He wasn't afraid to get his hands dirty and even famously helped collate *Near Klamath*, his own twenty-six-poem chapbook that was published by The English Club of Sacramento State College in 1968. A year later he would work the trimming machine at *Kayak* editor George Hitchcock's collating parties—a gesture that was rewarded when Hitchcock later published *Winter Insomnia* (1970), Carver's first full-length book of poems. Even after Gordon Lish—who was introduced to Carver in

1967 by small-press entrepreneur Johnson—published "Neighbors" in *Esquire* in 1971 when he was the fiction editor there, and even after Lish engineered the 1976 publication of Carver's first collection of short stories by a major press (*Will You Please Be Quiet, Please?*, Mc-Graw-Hill), Carver remained faithful to the literary magazine world that gave him his start. Of the sixty-six short stories published during his lifetime, forty-seven first appeared in little literary magazines. Most of those magazines paid in contributor's copies, and the ones that rewarded writers with cash offered mostly token amounts. Still, the stories found a wide readership if they were good enough to make it into one of the popular annual anthologies that had major distribution, and Carver's certainly were.

The two main commercial anthologies—*The Best American Short Stories* and *O. Henry Prize Stories* series—considered fiction from the small press world as well as from major magazine outlets, while the *Pushcart Prize* anthologies *only* included the best fiction and poetry published in the little magazines during a calendar year. They all received major newspaper and magazine coverage, and Carver instantly became a fixture in them with "The Furious Seasons" appearing in *The Best American Short Stories 1964*, "Will You Please Be Quiet, Please?" in *The Best American Short Stories 1967*, "What Is It?" in *O. Henry Prize Stories 1973*, "Put Yourself in My Shoes" in *O. Henry Prize Stories 1974*, "Are You a Doctor" in *O. Henry Prize Stories 1975*, "So Much Water So Close to Home" in the *Pushcart Prize I* anthology (1976), "What We Talk About When We Talk About Love" in *Pushcart Prize VI* (1981), "Cathedral" in *The Best American Short Stories 1982*, "The Bath" in both *O. Henry Prize Stories 1983* and *Pushcart Prize VIII* (1983), "Where I'm Calling From" in *The Best American Short Stories 1983*, "Careful" in *Pushcart Prize IX* (1984), "Boxes" in *The Best American Short Stories 1987*, and "Errand" appearing in both *O. Henry Prize Stories 1988* and *The Best American Short Stories 1988*. Early recognition led to a grant from the National Endowment for the Arts (NEA) and visiting lecturer appointments at the University of California, Santa Barbara; the University of California, Santa Cruz; the University of California, Berkeley; and the Iowa Writers' Workshop, where, because of Gardner's encouragement, he once attended as a student.

Carver would continue his lifelong association with little magazines and small presses by not only publishing stories and poems with them, but also by allowing his work to be printed in limited editions and "broadsides," which were illustrated, ready-to-frame presentations of his poetry. Such editions became a means of sustenance for small publishers like Capra Press—which produced hardcover and softcover versions of the first "book" of fiction by Carver, *Put Yourself in My Shoes*, a single story that was printed in signed limited editions—or Herb Yellin's Lord John Press and William B. Ewert, each of whom published a number of Carver limited editions and broadsides. It's worth noting that Noel Young's tiny Capra Press published Carver's second short story collection, *Furious Seasons and Other Stories* (1977), just one year after *Will You Please Be Quiet, Please?* thrust Carver into the national spotlight, earning positive reviews and comparisons. Writing for the *Christian Science Monitor*, Nancy Gail Reed gushed, "In their stark simplicity, their rhythmic patterns of everyday, working-class speech, these stories are reminiscent of the best of Hemingway" (20). Before *Will You Please Be Quiet, Please?* Carver was a literary star only in the firmament of little magazines and presses. Once that book was published to wide acclaim, he could have sent every story thereafter to high-paying, high-circulation popular magazines—but didn't, though often Carver managed to have it both ways. In 1975, for example, he sent "So Much Water So Close to Home" to a little magazine called *Spectrum*, and a year later he mailed an abridged version to *Playgirl*.

Carver's reputation really took off in 1981 with *What We Talk About When We Talk About Love*, which Gordon Lish heavily edited for Knopf, cutting Carver's original seventeen-story manuscript by 55 percent (Stull and Carroll 991). Carver went along with it because he trusted Lish and he was distracted by his drinking and the problems that resulted from it, including a trial for providing false statements so that he could collect unemployment (Sklenicka 281–82). That same year, Carver placed his first story with the *New Yorker* ("Chef's House," 30 November 1981), but he still sent his short fiction to literary magazines—admittedly *top tier* literary magazines like the *North American Review*, *Granta*, *Ploughshares*, *Antaeus*, *Grand Street*, and the *Paris Review*—but little magazines nonetheless. Of *What We Talk About*, the *New York Review of Books* remarked, "This is a world whose people worry about whether their old cars will start, where unemployment or personal bankruptcy are present dangers, where a good time consists of smoking pot with the neighbors, with a little cream soda and M&M's on the side" (Edwards 35). *Newsweek* lauded his stories for their ability to "convey images of loss, of rupture and of loneliness within and just after marriage that are both cautionary and chillingly resonant" (Prescott). The most lavish praise came from Michael Koepf, who wrote the in *San Francisco Review of Books*, "This latest collection of Mr. Carver's short stories and the clear, contemporary vision it gives of the American soul is at once chilling and unforgettably powerful," offering stories that feature a "Chekhovian clarity . . . but a Kafkaesque sense that something is terribly wrong behind the scenes" (Koepf 16).

There *was* something terribly wrong behind the scenes—at least in the often-tumultuous past that Carver used as inspiration for his stories. Life had taken a toll on Carver and Maryann, and there were infidelities, chief among them a 1972 affair that Carver had in Montana with a graduate student and university employee whom he met at a birthday party for fellow writer William Kittredge. That was also when Carver's drinking began to spiral out of control. Maryann wrote in her memoir, "Ultimately our marriage went down because of this liaison, though it took several years" (276), but one suspects the Carvers might have made it were it not for his alcoholism, which became more acute and often led to his becoming violent with Maryann. In 1983, after he had been sober for six years—Carver had finally quit drinking for good on

June 2, 1977—he told the *Paris Review*, "It's strange. You never start out in life with the intention of becoming a bankrupt or an alcoholic or a cheat and a thief. Or a liar," but he admitted to being all of those things. Pressed for details, he replied, "Let's just say, on occasion, the police were involved and emergency rooms and courtrooms" (Gentry and Stull 37–38). In 1976, the year that his breakthrough collection was published, Carver was hospitalized four different times for acute alcoholism, and his debilitating condition and erratic behavior led to the separation from Maryann that turned out to be permanent.

Friends refer to that period as the "Bad Ray" years when Carver was drinking so much that, drunk and hung over at the same time, he was experiencing frequent blackouts. Maryanne was also drinking, but nothing like Carver, who got physical with her on more than one occasion. Novelist Chuck Kinder, who met Carver in 1972 when Carver was juggling a Wallace E. Stegner Fellowship at Stanford with a visiting lecturer's appointment at University of California, Berkeley, recalled one time when Carver hit Maryann on the head with a bottle and an ambulance had to be called. Later, Carver had no memory of it (Halpert, *When We* 44–45). "We'd have situations when there'd be a shattering of glass and yells and screams and howls in the night, and the next minute they'd be ordering pizza," Kinder recalled. That was mirrored in the Carvers' many separations and reconciliations (123–24), no doubt because Maryann remembered happier years before Carver's drinking got out of hand: "Oh, but we had a tremendous amount of fun. We were popular people, we had lots of friends, and we entertained a lot. We were young, and we loved good times" (85). By all accounts, Carver was a shy but also very funny man, though soon his drinking took center stage. When he was at Berkeley, Carver got sick drunk with Charles Bukowski, and students would later tell, with amazement, how incredibly much Carver drank (Sklenicka 208–09). At Iowa City, when he was teaching at the Iowa Writer's Workshop with fellow writer and alcoholic John Cheever, the two men would sit in the parking lot of the local liquor store, waiting for it to open

(Gentry and Stull 40)—two renowned men of letters who spent more time drinking than they did teaching or writing. Often, episodes found their way into the fiction, as when Carver ruined a family Christmas by throwing an entire box of logs into the fireplace and almost burned the house down (Sklenicka 306).

The year he quit drinking for good, Carver met Tess Gallagher, a nationally known poet who had in common with Carver a Pacific Northwest upbringing and who would become his muse and share the rest of his life with him—a miraculous second chance that Carver referred to in a poem as "Gravy":

> No other word will do. For that's what it was. Gravy
> Gravy, these past ten years.
> Alive, sober, working, loving and
> Being loved by a good woman. Eleven years
> Ago he was told he had six months to live
> At the rate he was going. And he was going
> Nowhere but down. So he changed his ways. (*All of Us* 292)

"Instead of dying from alcohol, Raymond Carver chose to live," Gallagher told a conference on intoxication in 2006. "I would meet him five months after this choice, so I never knew the Ray who drank, except by report and through the characters and actions of his stories and poems." Maryann, whose education had led to a job teaching high school, had read and critiqued Carver's drafts, but in Gallagher he found a kindred spirit. Gallagher, who received a Guggenheim and two NEA fellowships for her poetry, also put writing first in her life. She became Carver's first reader and he, hers. They understood each other and what it takes for a writer to thrive, even to the point of establishing two houses in Washington State years into their relationship so that each could have a workspace and complete solitude. Together they read Chekhov—a writer Carver was introduced to at Humboldt State by professor Thelwell Proctor—and they collaborated on projects such as *Dostoevsky: A Screenplay* (1985). She also shared his love of small presses and little literary magazines, having received the Elliston Award for best book of poetry published by a small press the year before she and Carver met.

In 1982, two years after Carver and Gallagher moved to Syracuse, New York—where Gallagher began work as coordinator of Syracuse University's creative writing program and Carver was an appointed professor of English—Carver and Maryann divorced. The following year, *Cathedral*, his third fiction collection by a major press, would be published to generally wide acclaim. It also sparked a reconsideration of his work. "By now Carver has perfected the art of reproducing the signs of emotional paralysis and terror," Dorothy Wickenden wrote in a review for the *New Republic*. "But the stories in *Cathedral* are more complicated than his monochromatic earlier work, in which it is hard to tell one exhausted narrator from another" (38). In a front-page review in the *New York Times Book Review*, Irving Howe observed, "Behind Mr. Carver's stories there are strong American literary traditions. Formally, they summon remembrances of Hemingway and perhaps Stephen Crane, masters of tightly packed fiction. In subject matter they draw upon the American voice of loneliness and stoicism, the native soul locked in this continent's space." Though Howe acknowledged several stories "can already be counted among the masterpieces of American fiction," he took exception with others that, for him, displayed an "emotional meagerness." A reviewer for *Time* magazine, meanwhile, noted how "Carver's art masquerades as accident, scraps of information that might have been overheard at the supermarket check-out counter or the local beer joint. His most memorable people live on the edge: of poverty, alcoholic self-destruction, loneliness," he observed, concluding, "To describe him as a minimalist seems fair but misleading. His stories appear much slighter than they really are. They exist, no matter how casual or slangy their surfaces, in exactly the same spot as the best of their predecessors: the point of the fulcrum where inference tips toward importance" (Gray).

Cathedral, which includes such frequently anthologized stories as "Cathedral," "Feathers," and "A Small Good Thing," solidified Carver's place in the canon, and Carver and Gallagher became one of America's most celebrated literary couples—so much so that when they shared a house in Syracuse they often had to display a sign that read "writers at work" to get any privacy. Still, the awards and successes kept coming. Carver, who had received another NEA grant in 1980, was one of the first two recipients of the Mildred and Harold Strauss Livings awards, which provided Carver and fellow short story writer Cynthia Ozick with $35,000 per year, tax free, for five years. The only restriction was that he could not continue to teach, but that freed him up to move around. In 1984, Carver and Gallagher commuted back and forth between Syracuse and Port Angeles, Washington, where Gallagher had built Sky House on the Olympic Peninsula. Carver bought a house nearby so they could have separate workplaces. He influenced her to take up fiction writing, which led to the publication of two collections: *The Lover of Horses and Other Stories* (1986) and *At the Owl Woman Saloon* (1997); she and the couple's move to the Pacific Northwest inspired his return to writing poetry, a first love that he'd neglected in recent years. In 1985 he published *Where Water Comes Together with Other Water*, which was quickly followed by *Ultramarine* (1986).

Everything seemed idyllic, especially following a trip to Europe that Carver and Gallagher took during the spring and summer of 1987. But in September, Carver was diagnosed with lung cancer—the result of a lifetime of smoking so heavily that he once described himself as "a cigarette with a body attached to it" (Gentry and Stull x). Despite surgery to remove two-thirds of one lung, six months later the cancer returned in the form of a brain tumor. After more treatments, it would resurface again in his lungs. Carver and Gallagher decided to make the most of their remaining time, marrying in Reno on June 17, 1988, and living together at Sky House. Carver died on August 2, 1988, at the age of fifty and was buried at Ocean View Cemetery in Port Angeles with this simple inscription on his headstone, in an order that he specified: Poet, Short Story Writer, Essayist.

The day Carver died, his small-press publisher and editor friends called *their* editor friends, who called other editor and writer friends— many of whom taught, and announced it to their classes—until word of his death spread even before it was reported in newspapers. It was a shock, because the world of little literary magazines had lost a friend to many, and a beloved icon.

Although the curmudgeonly critic Harold Bloom feels that Carver has been "overpraised," there is much to suggest that Carver's work will endure every bit as much as D. H. Lawrence, whom Bloom thought superior. Upon Carver's death, the London papers mourned his loss, calling him "America's Chekhov." The comparison is appropriate, and not just because "Errand," the last story in Carver's last published collection, paid tribute to the Russian short story master. "Years ago I read something in a letter by Chekhov that impressed me," Carver told an interviewer. "It was a piece of advice to one of his many correspondents, and it went something like this: Friend, you don't have to write about extraordinary people who accomplish extraordinary and memorable deeds," and "reading what Chekhov had to say in that letter, and in other letters of his as well, and reading his stories, made me see things differently than I had before" (Gentry and Stull 47).

In a letter to his brother dated May 10, 1886, Chekhov outlined six principles he believed to be crucial in creating a good short story: ("1) no politico-economico-social verbal effusions; (2) objectivity throughout; (3) truth in the description of characters and things; (4) extreme brevity; (5) audacity and originality; (6) warmheartedness" (Chekhov 37). Though the last one is replaced by Carver's obvious empathy, the rest of those qualities exist in Carver's short stories, and twenty-five years after his death Carver's reputation is as strong as ever. Contemporary readers may not be able to identify with his characters or even *like* them, but his stories have a raw, astonishing power that reflects his "no tricks" approach to literature that resonates with honesty and insight into the human condition. While the history of American literature is full of alcoholic writers, none of them has written so openly and honestly about the struggles of an alcoholic than Carver—perhaps because Carver "came back from the grave" and was brave enough to face the blank page without alcohol, enjoying those ten more years as a recovering alcoholic.

"When I read and am moved by a story by Chekhov it's similar to listening to a piece of music by Mozart and being moved by that . . . . When something can reach across languages, and hundreds of years even, and move you, that's all you can ask," Carver once remarked (Gentry and Stull 143).

Carver's stories have the same effect, though, ironically, his place in American literary history seems most assured because from the very beginning he was associated with the literary movement known as "minimalism"— a term which Carver vehemently resisted. "It's been used to tag a number of excellent writers at work today, but I think that's all it is, a tag" (Gentry and Stull 153). In "Fires," Carver tried to qualify the similarities, writing that he had an extremely poor memory and that there were places he'd lived and people he'd known that he couldn't recall at all. Out of necessity, he explained, what he put into his fiction was far less detailed than many writers provide. He speculated, "Perhaps this is why it's sometimes been said that my stories are unadorned, stripped down, even 'minimalist.' But maybe it's nothing more than a working marriage of necessity and convenience that has brought me to writing the kind of stories I do in the way that I do" (Carver, *Call* 95–96).

Works Cited

Bloom, Harold. Introduction. *Bloom's Major Short Story Writers: Raymond Carver*. Ed. Bloom. Broomall: Chelsea, 2002. Print.

Carver, Maryann Burk. *What It Used to Be Like: A Portrait of My Marriage to Raymond Carver*. New York: St. Martin's, 2007. Print.

Carver, Raymond. *All of Us: The Collected Poems*. New York: Knopf, 1998. Print.

___. *Call If You Need Me: The Uncollected Fiction and Other Prose*. Ed. William L. Stull. New York: Vintage, 2001. Print.

Chekhov, Anton. *Letters of Anton Chekhov*. Ed. Avrahm Yarmolinksy. New York: Viking, 1973. Print.

Edwards, Thomas R. "The Short View." Rev. of *Will You Please Be Quiet, Please?* by Raymond Carver. *New York Review of Books* 1 Apr. 1976: 36. Print.

Gallagher, Tess. "Instead of Dying." *Lectures*. Literature Wales, 2006. Web. 5 Feb. 2013.

Gentry, Marshall Bruce, and William L. Stull, eds. *Conversations with Raymond Carver*. Jackson: UP of Mississippi, 1990. Print.

Gray, Paul. "More Art from Less Matter." Rev. of *Cathedral* by Raymond Carver. *Time* 19 Sep. 1983: 127. Print.

Halpert, Sam. *Raymond Carver: An Oral Biography*. Iowa City: U of Iowa P, 1995. Print.

Halpert, Sam, ed. *When We Talk about Raymond Carver*. Layton: G. Smith, 1991. Print.

Hart, James D. *The Oxford Companion to American Literature*. 5th ed. New York: Oxford UP, 1983. Print.

Howe, Irving. "Stories of Our Loneliness." Rev. of *Cathedral* by Raymond Carver. *New York Times Book Review* 11 Sep. 1983, late city final ed., sec. 7: 1. Print.

Koepf, Michael. "The Collapse of Love: What We Talk About When We Talk About Love." *San Francisco Review of Books* May–June 1981: 16. Print.

Lopez, Ken. "Raymond Carver, Introduction." *LopezBooks*. Ken Lopez Bookseller, 2007. Web. 5 Feb. 2013.

Prescott, Peter S. "Lost and Found: What We Talk About When We Talk About Love." *Newsweek* 27 Apr. 1981: 96. Print.

Reed, Nancy Gail. "Short Fiction: Two Writers Getting Under Surfaces." *Christian Science Monitor* 1 Apr. 1976: 20. Print.

Reynolds, Michael. *The Young Hemingway*. New York: Blackwell, 1986. Print.

Scobie, Brian. "Carver Country." *Forked Tongues? Comparing Twentieth-Century British and American Literature*. Eds. Ann Massa and Alistair Stead. London: Longman, 1994. 273–85. Print.

Sklenicka, Carol. *Raymond Carver: A Writer's Life*. New York: Scribner, 2009. Print.

Stull, William L., and Maureen P. Carroll, eds. "Chronology." *Raymond Carver: Collected Stories*. New York: Lib. of Amer., 2009. Print.

Wickenden, Dorothy. "Old Darkness, New Light." Rev. of *Cathedral* by Raymond Carver. *New Republic* 14 Nov. 1983: 38–39. Print.

Raymond Carver and the Shaping Power of the Pacific Northwest

Chad Wriglesworth

Considering Raymond Carver's life and work in relationship to place and, more specifically, to the Pacific Northwest, is a fairly recent scholarly impulse. Carver spent much of his life in small towns throughout Oregon, Washington, and northern California; however, when his writing became popular in the 1970s and 1980s, critics were so preoccupied with his so-called minimalistic style that they overlooked the shaping power of place in his work. In 1981, for example, critic Donald Newlove reviewed *What We Talk About When We Talk About Love* and called it a collection of "tales from Hopelessville," giving readers the impression that Carver's stories are set in generic locations and void of geographic significance (77). The tendency to disassociate Carver's fiction, in particular, from the places he lived and worked has overshadowed scholarly conversations about the author for nearly thirty years. This remains evident in Nicholas O'Connell's book *On Sacred Ground: The Spirit of Place in Pacific Northwest Literature* (2003), which barely mentions Carver's name in relation to the region, and John M. Findlay's 2006 article, "Something in the Soil?: Literature and Regional Identity in the 20th-Century Pacific Northwest," which dismisses Carver's work from the Pacific Northwest on the basis that his stories "tend not to be set in any recognizable Northwest" (180). If it is true—and it may or may not be—that Carver's well-known fiction offers readers little insight into matters of place and regional histories, then moving beyond his most anthologized works toward lesser known stories, poetry, and essays can provide new contexts for discussing Carver's work in relationship to place and, more specifically, to the complex socioeconomic history and transformation of the Pacific Northwest.

"My Father's Life": The Great Depression and Westward Migration

Raymond Carver is among the most influential short-fiction writers of the twentieth century, but his essays and poetry should not be set aside, particularly when it comes to considering his relationship to the Pacific Northwest. In an essay titled "My Father's Life," first published in *Esquire* in September 1984, Carver chronicles the westward migration and laboring struggles of his father, a man who arrived in the Northwest from Arkansas during the Great Depression. When Tess Gallagher, Carver's second wife, revisited the essay for its inclusion in the 2001 collection *Call If You Need Me*, she described it as "one of the most moving expressions on record of a son's love for his father" (xii). The essay will continue to stand on its own artistic and relational merit, but when considered alongside recent scholarship such Carol Sklenicka's biography *Raymond Carver: A Writer's Life* (2009), William L. Stull and Maureen P. Carroll's biographical chronology in *Raymond Carver: Collected Stories* (2009), and Bob Adelman and Tess Gallagher's *Carver Country: The World of Raymond Carver* (2011), readers can begin to grasp ways that Carver's identity is deeply embedded in the working-class history of the Pacific Northwest.[1]

In *Raymond Carver: A Writer's Life*, Sklenicka traces Carver's genealogy and the socioeconomic conditions that caused his ancestors to migrate from Arkansas to the Pacific Northwest during the Great Depression. Carver's father, Clevie Carver (1913–67), was born into a family of once-prosperous cotton farmers who had been struggling to endure the socioeconomic reconstruction of the South since the Civil War. Economic reconstruction and heavy floods in the South stripped the Carvers of wealth and land, reducing them to "sharecroppers and lumber mill hands" who could be found "migrating from one sharecropping situation to another" (Sklenicka 5). In the early twentieth century, Clevie's father, Frank, still a teenager at the time, watched his parents, aunts, and uncles lose their land and sink into "further deprivation as the cotton-based Arkansas economy collapsed at the end of World War I" (5). For years, the Carvers pressed on as itinerant laborers, but as Raymond Carver would later explain, by the time the Great Depression hit Arkansas in 1929, his father and extended family were "about to starve down there, and this wasn't meant as a figure of speech" (*Collected* 719). Weary of sharecropping and economic uncertainty, Clevie's older brother, Fred, and his wife headed West, intending to "abandon the economic quagmire of Arkansas" for good (Sklenicka 5). The couple made a cross-country trek to Omak, Washington, where Fred took a job with a lumber company in the Okanogan Valley. When the couple wrote back to Arkansas with stories of "paradise regained," it fell upon Clevie, only sixteen at the time, to load up an "old, black Model-T Ford sedan" and drive his mother, father, sister, brother-in-law, and their new baby to the Pacific Northwest (5–6).

In "My Father's Life," Carver speculates that when his father migrated to the Pacific Northwest he was not "pursing a dream," but was merely "looking for steady work at decent pay" (*Collected Stories* 719). This may only be partially true. During the Great Depression, President Franklin Delano Roosevelt's New Deal reform was stirring dreams of westward migration and economic hope. The Carvers arrived in the Okanogan Valley at an ideal time, just as regional landowners were using the power of irrigation canals and dams to transform the semiarid landscape into rolling orchards of agricultural prosperity. As historian Carlos Schwantes explains, by the 1920s central Washington was struck with "apple fever" and families like the Carvers were among the earliest migrant laborers to reap the benefits of federally sponsored irrigation (171). Clevie also benefited from Roosevelt's commitment to transform the infrastructure of the American West through the construction of massive hydroelectric dams. As Carver explains, after arriving in the Northwest his father "picked apples for a time" but kept an eye out for bigger and better opportunities and soon "landed a construction laborer's job on Grand Coulee Dam" (*Collected Stories* 719).

By 1935, Clevie's economic prospects were stable enough to return to Arkansas, where he married a "tall country girl" named Ella Casey and then moved additional family members out to Omak, Washington (*Collected Stories* 720). Clevie's sense of optimism was understandable. President Roosevelt had allotted New Deal funds in excess of sixty-three million dollars for the construction of Grand Coulee Dam. By the time Clevie and Ella settled down in Omak, in a place "not much bigger than a cabin," this massive dam was beginning to rise from the dust just fifty miles southeast of their home (*Collected Stories* 720). Clevie, who became part of a team of more than twelve thousand laborers, was present at the dam in 1937 when Roosevelt visited the site with words of progress and encouragement. Journalist Richard Neuberger recalls how the president was the "hero of at least three-fourths of the laborers" at Grand Coulee, men who kept his posters, newspaper clippings, and buttons on display in their bunkhouses (69). Interestingly, Clevie was part of a critical minority who "never bragged about his own work at the dam" (Sklenicka 8). According to Carver, his father was embittered that the president "never mentioned those guys who died building the dam . . . men from Arkansas, Oklahoma, and Missouri" (*Collected* 720).

Despite the dangers and ambivalence that came with working on Grand Coulee Dam, Clevie had temporarily improved his economic condition by migrating to the Pacific Northwest. Decades later, Carver would capture his father's newfound sense of optimism and purpose in a poem titled "Photograph of My Father in his Twenty-Second Year." Written one year after Clevie's untimely death in 1967 and later included in the essay "My Father's Life," Carver imagines his father's sense of hope through a photograph taken during his early days in Washington State when his father was "still working on the dam" (*Collected* 720). On the surface, the poem depicts Clevie as an optimistic laborer who arrived in the Northwest to reap the benefits of Roosevelt's New Deal. He leans against the fender of a 1934 Ford, a car he purchased with money earned as a "farmhand-turned-construction worker" and offers the photographer a "sheepish grin" while posing with his young bride (720). In one hand, he holds a bottle of Carlsbad beer, the other a stringer of fish—both signs of the good life. He wears a "young man's face" and poses "bluff and hearty for his posterity" with an "old hat cocked over his ear" (726). But this is not the whole story. As Carver explains in "On Writing," there is power in absence, in elements that are "left out, that are implied" to the reader (732). And here, even with the sense of youth and promise in the photograph, there are looming indications of "a sense of menace" working beneath what Carver like to call "the smooth (but sometimes broken and unsettled) surface of things" (732).

In the final stanza, Carver prods beneath the photograph's optimistic surface to expose his father's longing and inability to transcend an expendable working-class identity (*Collected* 732). Despite the appearances of security, Carver states that his father's hands and "eyes give him away." They tell the story of a man who "wanted to be bold" and "would like to pose brave and hearty for his posterity" but was merely performing a temporary dream (726). Using the poem to read the past, Carver imagines the years before his own birth, when his mother and father's dreams would begin to slip away. Shortly after the photograph was taken, Clevie's job at Grand Coulee Dam would end, sending his parents in search of work again. They would head several hundred miles down the Columbia River to Clatskanie, Oregon, where Clevie and his brother would take jobs with the Crossett Western Company, part of an Arkansas based timber conglomerate. That same year, Raymond Carver would be born in that "little town along the Columbia River" (720). And as Sklenicka suggests, it would be the region's rivers, orchards, and industries that would shape the young writer's life for decades to come:

> Living near the [Columbia River] and remembering the hardships at Grand Coulee, the Carvers could see the paradoxes inherent in the economic development of the Northwest. In light of such knowledge, Raymond Junior's birth by the side of the great northwestern river seems auspicious. The salmon and the dams, the forests and sawmills, the orchards and the fragile human settlements of the Columbia Basin would shape this boy just as Arkansas had shaped his parents. (9)

The Carvers moved again in 1941, this time to Yakima, Washington, where Clevie and his brother took jobs as saw filers with Boise-Cascade Lumber Company and the women worked in the orchards and fruit-packing plants of the Yakima Valley. With that move, the Carvers set roots in a landscape that would shape a young boy's mind for years to come.

"Nobody Said Anything": Growing up in the Yakima Valley

Raymond Carver lived in Yakima, Washington, from 1941 until his graduation from Yakima Senior High School in 1956. The rivers and irrigated valleys of the region inspired early stories such as "Furious Seasons" and "Sixty Acres" as well as poems such as "Bobber" and "Prosser," imaginative re-creations of youthful days spent fishing and hunting. When reflecting on his early work, Carver explained that "that's what excited me in those days, hunting and fishing. That's what made a dent in my emotional life and that's what I wanted to write about" (Gentry and Stull 33). Yakima was also the place where Carver fell in love with Maryann Burk, his first wife and mother of their two children. However, growing up Yakima was not always so carefree. In 1986, for example, when pressed about the ways Yakima had shaped his youth, Carver became reticent and evaded the question by stating, "I don't know what else to say about Yakima. I'm glad I left" (Gentry and Stull 135). The region had "its own particular beauty," but Carver insisted that "it was much too small a place" and that he had to leave in order to become a writer (Gentry and Stull 135). It is this tension between affection and the need for escape that emerges in much of Carver's work about the Yakima Valley.

When Clevie and Ella moved to Yakima in 1941, they rented a house in the Fairview District, a section of town that was identifiable by its rundown condition and outdoor toilets. Many of Carver's relatives were finding economic stability at the Boise-Cascade lumber company, but according to Ella, "money burned a hole" in her husband's pocket and it was not long until "everybody was better off" than they were (*Collected* 721). The family went without a car for years, until Clevie came home with the "oldest car in town" that Carver remembers "threw a rod the first week" they had it (722). Carver's memories of youth often indicate feelings of shame about his family's social class and living conditions, as well as his anxiousness about his father's drinking, particularly nights of drunkenness when his mother poured "whiskey down the sink" (721).

In the 1986 poem "Shiftless," Carver recalls and critiques the circumstances that led to the sometimes embarrassing poverty of his youth. However, rather than promoting societal advancement through physical work, the child narrator resists the vision of prosperity that his mother and father hoped to inherit by migrating to the Pacific Northwest. Instead of planning to work in timber mills with his father, the boy vows "always / to be shiftless" (*All of Us* 175). In the boy's mind, everything around him is disposable:

> The people who were better than us were *comfortable*.
> They lived in painted houses with flush toilets.
> Drove cars whose year and make were recognizable.
> The ones worse off were sorry and didn't work.
> Their strange cars sat on blocks in dusty yards.
> The years go by and everything and everyone
> gets replaced. (175)

The boy persona explains that his "goal" is not to attain comfort, but to remain "shiftless" since everything will be replaced in time (175). Rather than inheriting the socioeconomic status of his mother and father, the boy embraces an alternative path, one that favors leisure and introspection over industrial progress:

> I liked the idea of sitting in a chair
> in front of your house for hours, doing nothing
> but wearing a hat and drinking cola.

What's wrong with that?
Drawing on a cigarette from time to time.
Spitting. Making things out of wood with a knife.
Where's the harm there? Now and then calling
the dogs to hunt rabbits. Try it sometime. (175–76)

Carver's youthful remembrance and critique of life in the Yakima Valley extends into his fiction as well. As in the poetry, his stories recall a
contradictory place that provided him with a winsome freedom to explore, fish, and wander the community, while also keeping his family
and the larger working class economically oppressed.

In a short story called "Nobody Said Anything," which was first
published in 1973 as "The Summer Steelhead" and collected in *Will
You Please Be Quiet, Please?* (1976), a young narrator skips school
and heads out on a fishing trip to nearby Birch Creek. While walking,
the boy gives explicit directions on how to navigate the rural neighborhood in order to reach the creek. In a letter to his friend, photographer
Bob Adelman, Carver tells how the town in "Nobody Said Anything"
is geographically modeled on Yakima and that walking to Birch Creek
is reminiscent of Carver's "growing years" when he used "to walk to
the fishing holes at Bachelor Creek" (25). The boy narrator sets out for
the creek and provides a telling commentary on the unspoken secrets
of his small town. It is a significant passage that provides readers with
the title line to the story, as well as the emotional contradictions that
Carver experienced while growing up in Yakima, a national seat of
agriculture that promoted itself as the "fruit bowl of the nation" (Burk
9). Carver's narrator remembers:

It was nice out. It was fall. But it wasn't cold yet except at night. At night
they would light the smudgepots in the orchards and you would wake up
in the morning with a black ring of stuff in your nose. But nobody said
anything. They said the smudging kept the young pears from freezing, so
it was all right. (*Collected* 38)

The image of smudgepots to prevent pear trees from freezing left the child narrator with a dirty sense of unspoken defilement. In this regard, the division between what is said and unsaid, known and unknown in Yakima, haunts the larger mood of the story, which, according to Sklenicka, speaks of the narrator as a "divided child and divided self" (27). In the overall story, nobody says anything—nothing about the child skipping school, his own sense of sexual curiosity and guilt, his desire to reconcile his parents' downward-spiraling marriage—all of these anxieties are suppressed to make everything appear as though "it was all right" (*Collected* 38). However, the sensation of dirty secrets swirling through the narrator's youth is not merely a backdrop designed to create atmosphere. It is also an important commentary on the socioeconomic secrets of Yakima, a place that was envisioned to be a promised land of agricultural prosperity, but for some became a socioeconomic nightmare that trapped its inhabitants into a marginalized existence.

"Sixty Acres," an early story written in 1969, follows directly after "Nobody Said Anything" in *Will You Please Be Quiet, Please?* It is perhaps Carver's most critical narrative of life in the Yakima Valley. It addresses economic and environmental injustices from the perspective of Lee Waite, a marginalized and struggling Yakama Indian farmer.[2] In order to comprehend the *weight* that Lee Waite carries, it is necessary to have some knowledge of the history of the region. When the Yakima Valley was settled by Euro-Americans in the early twentieth century, the federal government targeted the region as a site of agricultural prosperity and began transforming local watersheds for irrigation and settlement. The federal reconstruction of the valley began much earlier, in 1855, when the United States government negotiated treaties with Mid-Columbia River tribes, including the Yakama Nation, a confederation of fourteen tribes and bands that have inhabited the Columbia Plateau for millennia. After relegating the tribes to a federally managed reservation, the engineering efforts of the federal government transformed the Yakima Valley into one of the most heavily irrigated and agriculturally productive regions of the United States.

This required retaining and diverting water away from the Yakama Reservation and toward towns made prosperous by irrigation—places such as Yakima, Prosser, and Grandview.

In "Sixty Acres," the agrarian vision of federal irrigation certainly benefits some, but it proves to be bankrupting for Yakama Indians such as Lee Waite. Carver communicates the socioeconomic disparity between the Yakama Nation and other, presumably white, farmers by focusing on the size and stature of Waite's house, land, and farming equipment—possessions that suggest anything but prosperity. Carver describes Waite as "a small thin man with a thin face" who lives in a small house with a crowded porch (*Collected* 49). Neighboring white farmers have invested in modern agricultural technologies, but Waite farms with "old yokes and harnesses" and "a row of rusted hand tools" (49–50). Waite's problems are compounded by the fact that his farm and constraining house barely meet the needs of his growing family. Two children sleep in one room, while Waite and his wife share an attached room with his mother. When Waite surveys his land, he sees only the "wavy flatness of sugar-beet fields" and "an inch or two of grainy snow," all of which give a mocking and "foolish look to the stripped rows of beanpoles in front of the house" (*Collected Stories* 51). As Waite struggles to manage his federal allotment of reservation property, Carver leaves his readers with a vision of a man on the verge of a mental breakdown, a man who is finding it impossible to make an adequate living on the Yakama Reservation.

This sense of constriction and the need for escape ultimately shaped Carver's decision to leave Yakima in search of an identity and a career as a writer. After graduating from high school in 1956, Carver tested the waters of millwork for six months, but hated it and knew he "didn't want to do that for the rest of [his] life" (Gentry and Stull 34). A year later, he married Maryann Burk, a sixteen-year-old girl from Yakima who was carrying their first child. Carver, only three years older than Burk, knew one thing for certain: He wanted to be a writer. And this meant getting out of Yakima and away from timber mills and orchards. Burk was tired of working at the local fruit-packing plant, stacking "rows of little cherries just so," and Carver, already sick of millwork, was certain that no one in Yakima knew much about writing (Burk 82). So, with little more than dreams in their pockets, the young family set out to find their own version of paradise by leaving Yakima behind them.

Returning to the Pacific Northwest: *Where Water Comes Together with Other Water*

In 1983, Raymond Carver was awarded a Mildred and Harold Strauss Living Award, a renewable five-year fellowship intended to support the full-time writing of fiction. At that point, Carver resigned from a teaching position at Syracuse University and moved to Port Angeles, Washington, to take up residence with Tess Gallagher, the woman who would become Carver's second wife. Upon his return to the Pacific Northwest, Carver went back to writing poetry. The collection *Where Water Comes Together with Other Water* (1985) was completed in only six weeks and was followed by *Ultramarine* (1986), *In a Marine Light* (1987), and the posthumously published *A New Path to the Waterfall* (1989). When asked about the outpouring of poetry he wrote in the 1980s, Carver was unable to articulate how or why the poems came so quickly. He suspected, however, that "it had something to do" with his return to the "landscape and the water" of the Pacific Northwest, as though the region itself was revising the style and content of his work (Gentry and Stull 170). Upon returning, Carver noticed that his life and work were reconnecting to place. When asked about the newfound optimism and resurgence of natural imagery in his poetry, Carver explained:

> The water has been coming into these poems, and the moon, and the mountains and the sky. I'm sure this will make a lot of people in Manhattan laugh! Talk of the tides and the trees, whether the fish are biting or not biting. These things are going to worth their way back into my fiction. I feel directly in touch with my surroundings not in a way that I haven't felt in years. (Gentry and Stull 116)

Carver's preoccupation with images of water was far more than an aesthetic exploration. His return to the Pacific Northwest also marked the poet's reengagement with questions of place, spirituality, labor, and the socioeconomic plight of the working class.

As a first-generation migrant laborer in the Pacific Northwest, Clevie Carver experienced nature through physical labor. He made a living near water, working at the Grand Coulee Dam and mill towns such as Clatskanie, Oregon; Klamath, California; and Yakima, Washington. As a second-generation inhabitant of the region, Raymond Carver's expressions of work also came through water as evidenced by his numerous books of poetry influenced by water. The comparison is provocative to consider. When Carver's father was employed as a construction worker at Grand Coulee Dam, the federal government was committed to rerouting and restraining western waterways in order to create jobs, irrigate crops, and generate hydroelectricity. In *Where Water Comes Together with Other Water*, Carver also performs the work of reclamation, only here the poems gather together the life-narratives of people with binding socioeconomic pasts in order to release those histories into a revised vision of health and generosity. This is particularly evident in "My Dad's Wallet" and "The Trestle," two poems about Carver's father that appear in *Where Water Comes Together with Other Water*.

"My Dad's Wallet" is certainly Carver's darkest poem about his father's working-class existence in the Pacific Northwest. Interestingly, before its publication in *Where Water Comes Together with Other Water*, the poem appeared alongside journalist Bruce Weber's memorable 1984 *New York Times Magazine* article "Raymond Carver: A Chronicler of Blue-Collar Despair." The poem situates Carver's father in Klamath, California, right after he has died while making a last-ditch attempt to find economic stability as a saw filer in a timber mill. In the poem, Carver and his mother, Ella, have arrived in a dark and dusty mortuary to grant Clevie a final wish: "to lie close / to his parents" in Yakima, Washington, and near those who migrated with him to the

Pacific Northwest. Carver and Ella were aware of Clevie's last wish, but as Carver states:

> when the breath
> left his lungs and all signs of life
> had faded, he found himself in a town
> 512 miles away from where he wanted most to be. (*All of Us* 89)

In order to grant Clevie his final journey home, mother and son must enter into the game of capital exchange concerning the economics of death. Upon hearing the family's request to return the body to Yakima, the mortician says he can "arrange it, not to worry." However, as critic Arthur Bethea observes, once the undertaker proceeds to pull out his pad and pen, his calculations for food, lodging, and fuel indicate that he is "more concerned about his fee for transporting the corpse than the bereavers' feelings" (Bethea 242). According to Maryann Burk, Carver's first wife, the events depicted in the poem are closely based on actual events. As she remembers, after the funeral the family followed the mortician's hearse from northern California to Yakima. Shortly after they left town, the undertaker "stopped at a drive in" to eat. "Not only did that give us a sad start, but for Ray, the writer and elder son, it was a dramatic, ironic experience to travel across three states, on the same route with his dad's coffin. He kept saying, in tears, 'I just wish I could go take my dad and bury him'" (qtd. in Sklenicka 135).

In "My Dad's Wallet," while Ella and Carver wait for the mortician to return from the back room, Carver describes waiting in an office lit with "poor light" that fell on a "poor place on / the dusty floor," highlighting a condition that is indicative not only of setting, but the dire economic circumstances that this mother and son face (*All of Us* 98–99). The mortician calculates the cost of a journey from Klamath to Yakima and presents the Carvers with an uncompromising scenario:

He took out his pad and pen and began
to write. First, the preparation charges.
Then he figured the transportation
of the remains at 22 cents a mile.
But this was a round–trip for the undertaker,
don't forget. Plus, say, six meals
and two nights in a motel. He figured
some more. Add a surcharge of
$210 for his time and trouble,
and there you have it. (*All of Us* 90)

After hearing the cost, Carver writes that the undertaker "thought we might argue," but instead—out of socioeconomic habit—Ella complies with the conditions set forth on the table. She nods in agreement with all of the calculations, although her son knows that "none of it had made sense to her, beginning with the time she left home / with my dad. She only knew / that whatever was happening / was going to take money" (*All of Us* 90). In an attempt to fulfill her husband's last wish, Ella pulls Clevie's "old and rent and soiled" wallet from her purse. At that moment, the mortician and Carver "stared at the wallet for minute," but said nothing; they only watch as she "opened / it and looked inside. / Drew out / a handful of money that would go / toward this last, most astounding trip" (91).

The closing lines and sense of finality rendered in "My Dad's Wallet" suggest that Carver has closed the final chapter of his father's hardscrabble life as a laborer in the Pacific Northwest. However, this is not the case. In the final section of *Where Water Comes Together with Other Water*, the life-narratives of many people from Carver's personal history are reclaimed from socioeconomic and spiritual drought and gathered into a revised confluence of optimism, health, and generosity. Clevie Carver is among those whose life is reclaimed and released through images of water.

In a poem titled "The Trestle," Carver uses a railway trestle, a dominant image of western labor and industry, to reconfigure his father's relationship to the watersheds he worked within as a millworker for more than thirty years. The connection between water and work surfaces in the opening lines, when Carver rises one morning to confess that he has "wasted his time" and is ashamed of the lack of work he has completed. The poem shifts to events that happened the night before, when the poet "went to bed . . . thinking about [his] dad" (*All of Us* 136). Falling asleep, he remembered days they worked together at a mill in Chester, California, and how they spent their free time at "a little river [they] used to fish—Butte Creek— / near Lake Almanor" (136). Lulled to sleep by memories of water, work, and companionship, Carver wakes the next morning to remember another time when he was a kid, "sitting on a timber trestle, looking down," watching his father in the water far below. Imagining the days when Clevie arrived at Omak from Arkansas, Carver tells how, from the very beginning, his father "loved / this country where he found himself. The West. / For thirty years it had him around the heart, and then it let him go" (*All of Us* 137).

Through the labor of writing, "The Trestle" is a monument of relational reclamation, a place where Carver can find his wandering father in a state of spiritual and socioeconomic health. Carver explains that even after death he can return "to [his] desk back to childhood. And from there it's not so far to the trestle. / And from the trestle I could look down / and see my dad when I need to see him. My sweet father" (*All of Us* 137). According to Arthur Bethea, this poem, the last one Carver wrote about his father, "imaginatively resurrects his long dead parent," endowing him with "holiness and a sense of emotional rejuvenation" (242). This transformation is particularly evident in the closing lines, when Carver reflects on the triviality of his own line of work—its telephone calls, deadlines, and appointments. In such moments, he imagines his father at the trestle and, through writing about water, joins him in a baptismal form of renewal. Seeking realignment and regeneration to history and place, Carver writes: "I want to plunge my hands in clear water. The way he did. Again and then again" (*All of Us* 137).

Despite an early death in 1988, Raymond Carver lived and worked many places in his life. After growing up as the child of Great Depression laborers in the Pacific Northwest, he left Yakima, Washington, and managed to reside in almost every region of the United States. He worked and taught at places ranging from New York's Syracuse University and the University of Iowa to the University of Texas at El Paso, and the University of California, Santa Cruz. Along the way, while attempting to balance his commitments to family, writing, and teaching alongside the ongoing pressures of alcoholism and looming bankruptcy, Carver's short stories revived public and scholarly interest in an almost forgotten genre. The influence and scope of Carver's prose and poetry certainly transcends the Pacific Northwest, but behind the failures and successes of this memorable writer resides the voice of someone whose life and work was shaped by the scenic power and socioeconomic history of the Pacific Northwest.

Notes

1. In addition to these books, the following articles consider Carver's work in relationship to the Pacific Northwest: Angela Sorby's "Teaching Carver's Voices through Pacific Northwest Music," in Carver Across the Curriculum: Interdisciplinary Approaches to Teaching the Fiction and Poetry of Raymond Carver (2011); Tamas Dobozy's "Raymond Carver in the Viewfinder," Canadian Review of American Studies 41.3 (2011); and Chad Wriglesworth's "Stepping onto the Yakama Reservation: Land and Water Rights in Raymond Carver's 'Sixty Acres,'" Western American Literature 45.1 (2010).

2. In 1994, the Confederated Tribes and Bands of the Yakama Nation officially changed the spelling of their name from Yakima to Yakama. This chapter uses the word Yakima when referring to the city and its surrounding valley, while Yakama is used to refer to the indigenous peoples and the Yakama Reservation.

Works Cited

Adelman, Bob, and Tess Gallagher. *Carver Country: The World of Raymond Carver.* New York: Macmillan, 1990. Print.

Bethea, Arthur F. *Technique and Sensibility in the Fiction and Poetry of Raymond Carver.* New York: Routledge, 2001. Print.

Carver, Maryann Burk. *What It Used to Be Like: A Portrait of My Marriage to Raymond Carver.* New York: St Martin's, 2006. Print.

Carver, Raymond. *All of Us.* Ed. William L. Stull. New York: Knopf, 1998. Print.

___. *Raymond Carver: Collected Stories.* Eds. William L. Stull and Maureen Carroll. New York: Lib. of Amer., 2009. Print.

Findlay, John M. "Something in the Soil? Literature and Regional Identity in the 20th Century Pacific Northwest." *Pacific Northwest Quarterly* 97.4 (2006): 179–89. Print.

Gallagher, Tess. Foreword. *Call If You Need Me.* Ed. William L. Stull. New York: Vintage Contemporaries, 2001. Print.

Gentry, Marshall B., and William L. Stull, eds. *Conversations with Raymond Carver.* Jackson: U of Mississippi P, 1990. Print.

Neuberger, Richard L. *Our Promised Land.* New York: Macmillan, 1938. Print.

Newlove, Donald. "Fiction Briefs." *Saturday Review* Apr. 1981: 77. Print.

O'Connell, Nicholas. *On Sacred Ground: The Spirit of Place in Pacific Northwest Literature.* Seattle: U of Washington, 2003. Print.

Schwantes, Carlos A. *The Pacific Northwest: An Interpretive History.* Lincoln: U of Nebraska P, 1989. Print.

Sklenicka, Carol. *Raymond Carver: A Writer's Life.* New York: Scribner, 2009. Print.

CRITICAL
CONTEXTS

The Critical Reception of the Works of Raymond Carver

William L. Stull and Maureen P. Carroll

On April 26, 1981, the cover of the *New York Times Book Review* hailed the opening of a new frontier in American literature, a hitherto unexplored territory that would come to be known as "Carver Country." The news of its discovery came in the form of Raymond Carver's so-called minimalist masterpiece, a bone-thin book of stories with a weighty title, *What We Talk About When We Talk About Love*. Accompanying the review by Michael Wood was a full-length photo of the author, whose sealed lips, shadowed eyes, and half-smoked cigarette mirrored the demeanor of his shell-shocked characters. Their stories, recounted impassively, without apology or explanation, chronicled the failure of love to overcome the life-destroying forces of infidelity and alcohol.

In the *Saturday Review* Donald Newlove summed the book up in a sentence: "Seventeen tales of Hopelessville, its marriages and alcoholic wreckage, told in prose as sparingly clear as a fifth of iced Smirnoff" (77). Across the United States (and within a year throughout the English-speaking world, thanks to a British edition) critics marveled at how much Carver said and suggested in so few words. Reviewers searched for terms to describe a mode of writing in which commonplace objects and actions—a forgotten sack of candy, an ill-starred fishing trip, two couples having drinks before going out to dinner—tell tales too painful for words. "In Raymond Carver's stories, it is dangerous even to speak," wrote the Irish critic Denis Donoghue. "Conversation completes the damage people have already done to one another in silence."

The speaking silences in *What We Talk About When We Talk About Love* left other critics equally impressed but at a loss for words. In place of analysis they proffered labels for what they took to be Carver's signature style of writing. Among the tags were "dirty realism"

(Buford), "K-Mart realism," (Wolfe 50), even "yuppie postmodernism" (Kaufmann). As time passed and other writers with styles and subject matters similar to Carver's came to prominence, the label most often affixed to their work was "Minimalist Fiction" (Herzinger). This rubric was loosely defined but unmistakably pejorative. Carver told the *Paris Review* in 1983, "There's something about 'minimalist' that smacks of smallness of vision and execution that I don't like" (*Conversations* 44). At the surface level, what the minimalists shared was an understated mode of storytelling comprised of short declarative sentences, short paragraphs bracketed by space breaks, and fragmented plotlines that end in anticlimax, with major conflicts unresolved. At a deeper and more significant level, however, what Raymond Carver, Mary Robison, Amy Hempel, and other noted minimalists of the early 1980s had in common was an editor.

That editor was Gordon Lish (b. 1934). First in his self-proclaimed role as Captain Fiction at *Esquire* magazine in the 1970s, later as a senior editor at the prestigious New York publishing firm of Alfred A. Knopf in the 1980s and early 1990s, Lish actively solicited, aggressively edited, and tirelessly promoted "new fiction" that launched literary trends. Writers he published in *Esquire* included a number of authors later labeled minimalists. Among these were Frederick Barthelme, Joy Williams, Ann Beattie, Richard Ford, and, early in Lish's tenure, Raymond Carver. Carver's story "Neighbors," its original manuscript now known to have been heavily edited by Lish, appeared in the June 1971 issue of *Esquire* and soon became a fixture in anthologies of "new fiction" (Polsgrove 241–43).

But was Raymond Carver, who rebuffed interviewers when they pinned the label on him, ever in fact a minimalist? And what, precisely, was the role of Gordon Lish in the making, shaping, and marketing of Carver's stories? These questions have been central to the critical reception of his fiction during the quarter century since his death from lung cancer at age fifty on August 2, 1988. In essays and interviews Carver thanked Lish for bringing his stories to a national readership, first in *Esquire* and later in three major-press collections: *Will You Please Be Quiet, Please?* (1976); *What We Talk About When We Talk About Love* (1983); and, with Lish's involvement greatly reduced, *Cathedral* (1983). He praised Lish's "wonderful eye" or cutting needless words and sharpening a story's focus (*Conversations* 181). Above all, he expressed gratitude for Lish's faith in him despite two bankruptcies and a decade lost to alcohol. Never, however, did Carver speak of Lish as the coauthor of his stories.

Innuendos to that effect quietly circulated among a few New York publishing insiders during and after Carver's life but did not become public until years later. Carver's early death in 1988 was mourned throughout the literary world, with the London *Sunday Times* lamenting the loss of "the American Chekhov" and readers who had anticipated future Carver books feeling suddenly bereft of them (Kemp G1). For devotees of Raymond Carver, then, it was a shock when rumors questioning his authenticity became public in a *New York Times Magazine* cover story timed to mark the tenth anniversary of his death. In "The Carver Chronicles," published on August 9, 1998, journalist D. T. Max took a two-pronged approach to demythologizing Raymond Carver. This widely discussed article temporarily destabilized the positive critical reception that Carver's work had garnered since the 1970s. For a time it also called his reputation—indeed, his identity as a writer—into question.

Max's first prong chipped away at Carver's character, which had been the subject of fond recollections by friends and fellow writers in Sam Halpert's . . . *when we talk about Raymond Carver* (1991; revised as *Raymond Carver: An Oral Biography*, 1995) and *Remembering Ray: A Composite Biography* (1993). Max interviewed Gordon Lish, who had participated in neither of these memorial volumes and had left his editorial post at Knopf in 1994. Ten years after Carver's death, his erstwhile friend and mentor described him as an ingrate whose amateurish stories had been saved from "mediocrity" only by Lish's wholesale cuts and brilliant alterations (39). Max also interviewed Carver's first wife, Maryann Burk Carver, who intimated that a number of her former husband's stories drew their subjects from the couple's sometimes violent domestic arguments. Carver's second wife, the poet and short story writer Tess Gallagher, declined to be interviewed for Max's article. She had been Carver's companion during what he celebrated in a posthumously published poem as ten prosperous and productive sober years of "Pure gravy" (*All of Us* 292). Lacking Gallagher's participation, Max quoted passages from her published interviews that recalled how Carver had sometimes drawn on their shared experiences and taken her editorial suggestions in revising his stories. Overall, the impression left by "The Carver Chronicles" was disconcerting and equivocal. Instead of being a singular writer, Raymond Carver was made to seem so indebted to others as to be a composite author.

The second prong of Max's deconstruction was textual and archival. In the 1980s Carver arranged for his literary papers, what few he had salvaged from his alcoholic years and the far more complete files of manuscripts and correspondence dating from after he gave up drinking on June 2, 1977, to be deposited in the William Charvat Collection of American Fiction at the Ohio State University Library. In the 1990s Gordon Lish made a similar arrangement for his papers to be preserved in the Lilly Library of Indiana University. Lish's massive archive encompasses some 80,000 items—letters, marked-up manuscripts, page and galley proofs, publicity materials—related to the myriad writers he had edited and published since the 1960s, including Raymond Carver.

Max's research for "The Carver Chronicles" took him to both libraries. Carver-related materials in the Lish archive spanned the years 1969 to 1983, the period of Carver's near-fatal alcoholism and the early stages of his sobriety. Some 250 letters from Carver to Lish revealed that during Carver's darkest days Lish had been his literary mainstay, printing his stories in *Esquire*, making possible the publication of his first trade book, *Will You Please Be Quiet, Please?*, and promising to publish a future collection of his stories under the respected imprint of Alfred A. Knopf. Up to the early 1980s the Carver manuscripts in the Lilly archive bear abundant evidence of Lish's signature style of editing: strip down the writer's sentences, keep the plotlines short and open-ended, betray no sympathy or judgment. After Carver stopped drinking, however, his fiction moved in new directions. Even as he wrote about the damage he had seen and done in his "Bad Raymond" days, his stories grew longer, denser, more compassionate, and more hopeful. Fiction associated with Gordon Lish was also changing, but in a contrary way. It was shrinking toward a verbal vanishing point in size, scope, and sympathy. Lish was beginning to write stories and novels of his own in which he put his stringent editorial principles into practice, often to exaggerated effect. (A 1997 collection of his stories bears the metafictional title *Self-Imitation of Myself.*) Moreover, as a senior editor at Knopf he was discovering, editing, and publishing a new generation of writers, many of whom would be called minimalists. (The critic Sven Birkerts termed this relatively youthful cadre "The School of Gordon Lish.") In addition, Lish was teaching college courses for aspiring writers, classes he would later offer as much-touted private seminars.

In April 1980, at Lish's invitation, Raymond Carver gave him the manuscript of an as yet untitled new book of short fiction. Although Carver considered the stories to be finished, he told his trusted editor to apply his skills. "If you see ways to put more muscle in the stories, don't hesitate to do so," he wrote Lish (*Collected* 991). What Lish did over the course of two rounds of heavy editing and secretarial retyping was the opposite. In the words of Enrico Monti, who in 2007 published a detailed analysis of the editing of *What We Talk About When We Talk About Love*, what Lish performed was "essentially a subtractive operation" (55). The editor's strikethroughs, always liberal, increased exponentially. The total word count of Carver's manuscript was reduced by 55 percent, with several stories losing more than 70 percent of their content. Lish changed Carver's titles, reduced his paragraphs to sentences, and canceled the closing pages of any story that worked toward resolution, revelation, or forgiveness. Late in the publication process, when Carver read the outcome of Lish's editing, some of his stories were all but unrecognizable to him. Complicating matters was the fact that a number of them had recently appeared in magazines in uncut forms. Friends, fellow writers, and sharp-eyed critics were bound to see the changes and ask questions.

Early on the morning of July 8, 1980, Carver wrote Lish a deeply conflicted letter. He was torn between loyalty to his mentor and insistence on the integrity of his own voice and vision. Carver was scarcely three years into his sobriety, and his confidence was fragile. He flailed for options: postpone publication; better yet, cancel the book. "Now, I'm afraid, mortally afraid," he wrote, "that if the book were to be published as it is in its present edited form, I may never write another story, that's how closely, God Forbid, some of those stories are to my sense of regaining my health and mental well-being" (*Collected* 993). Within days, however, his resistance collapsed. Lish told D. T. Max, "My sense was that there was a letter and I just went ahead" (40).

Going ahead with the editorially "minimalized" book brought Carver to the cover of the *New York Times Book Review* and other major periodicals. With this attention came interviews in which he struggled to explain, without betraying his editor or himself, how his work had gone from long to short. "Pare, pare, and pare some more," he said, invoking Hemingway but leaving out the details (*Conversations* 182). As time went by, he preferred not to talk about *What We Talk About When We Talk About Love* but instead to speak about his upcoming books. These included *Fires* (1983), a small-press miscellany of essays, poetry, and fiction that included three seemingly expanded stories corresponding to shorter counterparts in *What We Talk About When We Talk About Love*: "Distance / Everything Stuck to Him," "Where Is Everyone? / Mr. Coffee and Mr. Fixit," and "So Much Water So Close to Home." *Cathedral*, a major collection slated for publication by Knopf in September 1983, would include eleven of Carver's latest stories, each in his opinion more substantial and more "generous" than anything in his prior book with Knopf (*Conversations* 45). *Cathedral* would also contain "A Small, Good Thing," a long, spiritually inflected story that appeared to be an expanded version of "The Bath," one of the shortest, starkest tales in *What We Talk About When We Talk About Love*. What readers, including book reviewers, did not know was that these "later" versions were not revisions or expansions. They were virtually complete restorations of Carver's stories to their earlier forms in the manuscript he had given Lish in 1980. "*Cathedral* shows a gifted writer struggling for a larger scope of reference, a finer touch of nuance," wrote the eminent critic Irving Howe (43). In truth, the struggle had been going on for years, and Carver had emerged the winner.

With Lish still serving as Carver's editor at Knopf, conflict over the form and content of *Cathedral* was inevitable. This time, the writer was prepared for it. Lish disliked all of the new stories, including the title piece and, most of all, the restored "A Small, Good Thing." (The latter had won the annual O. Henry prize when it appeared, uncut by Lish, in *Ploughshares* magazine in 1982.) Anticipating the editor's proposed changes, the writer stopped him cold. "I don't need to tell you that it's critical for me that there not be any messing around with titles or text," Carver reminded Lish in February 1983 (*Collected Stories* 985). In effect, Raymond Carver had declared his literary independence. Correspondence between writer and editor ceased in the spring of 1983, and by the summer Lish was no longer in charge of *Cathedral*. Nor would he edit any future work by Carver. In interviews and essays Carver had only good things to say about his longtime mentor. But Lish was angry, as his bitter comments about Carver to Max made plain.

The above account of the making and unmaking of *What We Talk About When We Talk About Love* is supported by materials in the second archive D. T. Max consulted, the Carver papers at Ohio State. There, the copies of the stories that Carver retained correspond to the uncut versions he gave to Lish in 1980 or indicate his own subsequent revisions of them. They reflect none of Lish's editing. Nor do Carver's manuscripts for *Cathedral* show signs of Lish's editing beyond minor clerical corrections. Instead, those stories are preserved in sometimes more than a dozen orderly drafts, corrected and polished in Carver's hand, with occasional suggestions jotted in the margins by Gallagher.

The triumphant critical reception of *Cathedral* brought Carver many honors, including nominations for a National Book Critics Circle Award and a Pulitzer Prize. Despite the clamor for more stories, during the middle 1980s he returned to writing poetry. His first book of verse, *Near Klamath*, had appeared in 1968. Several more collections had followed, all issued by small presses. Two books of his poems written in the 1980s, *Where Water Comes Together with Other Water* (1985) and *Ultramarine* (1986), were published by the Knopf affiliate Random House. Both received good reviews, and Carver was awarded the Levinson Prize by the Modern Poetry Association in 1985. Thereafter he resumed writing fiction, producing seven stories that broached new subject matter and explored new modes of storytelling, including the quasi-novelistic long short story form he discusses in his essay "On Longer Stories" (*Call* 227–32). Carver's last-written story was "Errand," a genre-bending tribute to his lifelong "companion soul," the Russian short story master Anton Chekhov (*All of Us* 315). The seven recent stories and thirty others chosen from Carver's previous major-press collections were published in May 1988 by Atlantic Monthly Press under the title *Where I'm Calling From: New and Selected Stories*. Like its antecedents, the book received a glowing front-page notice in the *New York Times Book Review*, this time by award-winning novelist Marilynne Robinson. Accompanying the review was a luminous photograph of Raymond Carver in which he looked the viewer in the eye and smiled. Three months later, he was dead.

Had "The Carver Chronicles" revealed the intricacies of the Carver-Lish relationship without animus or speculation, it could have been a timely tribute to a writer's struggle to overcome addiction and speak for himself in his finest work. Instead, D. T. Max and others, particularly Gordon Lish, raised questions that only Raymond Carver could answer, and he could not speak from the grave. The living had the last word over the dead, and "The Carver Chronicles" ended, much like a Lish-edited story, with the central issues unresolved. What ensued came to be known as the Carver controversy, and it dogged discussion of the writer's work well into the new millennium. Further complicating matters was the fact that during this time new evidence of Carver's literary prowess reached the public. Five previously unpublished stories, none bearing evidence of editing by Lish, were found among his papers. All appeared in magazines, and two of them, "Kindling" and "Call If You Need Me," were selected for inclusion in annual volumes of best and prize American short stories.

Research in any field is built upon a framework of assumptions. In "The Carver Chronicles" the central assumption was that the key figure in the Carver controversy was not the rumpled writer from the Pacific Northwest but the urbane editor in New York City. In our 2006 essay titled "Prolegomena to Any Future Carver Studies" we called for a change of assumptions about the Carver-Lish relationship. The fundamental question was not how Gordon Lish had edited Raymond Carver. The answer to that was readily available in *What We Talk About When We Talk About Love* and, to a lesser degree, in Carver's previous Lish-edited book, *Will You Please Be Quiet, Please?* To settle the Carver controversy and clear the way for reliable future studies, the question had to be recast: "What did Raymond Carver write?" (16).

To answer that question, we spent several years researching the same archives that D. T. Max had visited. Gradually we deciphered, transcribed, and reconstructed Carver's 1980 manuscript that lay beneath the pen-and-ink alterations made by Lish as he edited the book for publication in 1981 under the title *What We Talk About When We Talk About Love*. In Carver's manuscript, "Beginners" was the original name of what became the title story of the book. "But it seems to me we're just rank beginners at love," says the central character. (*Collected* 932). With the approval of Tess Gallagher, we sought to reveal the true arc of Carver's literary development by making public his original versions of the edited stories in *What We Talk About When We Talk About Love*. Readers could then decide for themselves whether, without the mediation of Gordon Lish, Raymond Carver was the hapless figure depicted in "The Carver Chronicles" or the master writer he had long been thought to be.

The decision to publish "Beginners was controversial. Motoko Rich of the *New York Times* interviewed influential figures in the book trade, and some of them vehemently opposed the effort, fearing further damage to the writer's reputation ("The Real Carver"). Others who had read the restored story felt otherwise, including the preeminent American novelist Philip Roth. "Pitch, tone, rhythm, time, mood, proportion, vocabulary, variety, repetitions—everything in the original version of Raymond Carver's story 'Beginners' is perfectly judged and executed," he wrote. "If ever a piece of fiction required no editing, it was this one" (*Principianti*). "Beginners" made its debut in the 2007 Winter Fiction issue of the *New Yorker*, accompanied by an unsigned preface titled "Rough Crossings" and excerpts from the Carver-Lish correspondence. Resources for comparing the unedited and edited versions of the story, the latter 50 percent shorter than the former, were posted on the magazine's website. The restored text of "Beginners" was presented dispassionately, with no case made for the superiority of either version of the story. Ten years after "The Carver Chronicles," people around the world could finally read what Carver wrote.

Scholarship is not the arbiter of taste. In print publications and online postings some readers expressed a preference for Carver's original version of the story, others for Lish's edited version. Beyond preferences, what matters is that a new phase in the critical reception of the works of Raymond Carver has begun. In the ensuing years "Beginners" the story and *Beginners* the book of seventeen stories, subtitled *The Original Version of* What We Talk About When We Talk About Love, have been published in English, Italian, French, Danish, Japanese, and other languages. The restored manuscript of *Beginners* is also included in what is now the most complete and authoritative one-volume edition of Carver's fiction, the Library of America's *Collected Stories* (2009). And, yes, that book received an enthusiastic front-page notice in the *New York Times Book Review*, with a picture of Raymond Carver accompanying it. The reviewer, who well understood the perils of literary stereotyping and the struggle to overcome addiction, was the ceaselessly self-reinventing writer Stephen King.

In the wake of the Carver controversy and the publication of *Beginners*, studies of Carver's work published before the year 2000 require varying degrees of reassessment. Introductory books such as Arthur Saltzman's *Understanding Raymond Carver* (1988), Ewing Campbell's *Raymond Carver: A Study of the Short Fiction* (1992), and Adam Meyer's *Raymond Carver* (1995) are out of date in their coverage of the now expanded body of Carver's work and the genetic relationships among the multiple published versions of many of his stories. Kirk Nesset's *The Stories of Raymond Carver* (1995) remains the most accessible introduction to the major-press books of Carver's fiction published during his lifetime. *Technique and Sensibility in the Fiction and Poetry of Raymond Carver* (2001) by Arthur F. Bethea is more comprehensive, especially when supplemented with Bethea's essay on the five posthumously published stories in *Call If You Need Me* (2001).

At the advanced level, several books examine distinctive features of Carver's work. The earliest specialized study, Randolph Paul Runyon's *Reading Raymond Carver* (1992), discloses "intratextual" lexical and thematic patterns within Carver's books and stories. Runyon, like Bethea, has supplemented his book with a separately published essay on Carver's five "recovered" stories. In *The Carver Chronotope* (2004) G. P. Lainsbury applies the "dialogic" method of discourse analysis inaugurated by Russian literary theorist Mikhail Bakhtin to the "life-world" of Carver's fiction. In his essay "On Writing" (1981), Carver noted "a sense of menace" in his favorite stories (*Call* 92). The Chinese scholar Jingqiong Zhou explores the darkly comic side of this motif in *Raymond Carver's Short Fiction in the History of Black Humor* (2006). In *The Visual Poetics of Raymond Carver* (2010) Israeli scholar Ayala Amir provides a book-length analysis of Carver's fiction in relation to the camera and the visual arts.

The exponential proliferation of periodical articles about Raymond Carver, both in print and online, over the past three decades is a good-news-bad-news story for the student. The good news is that commentary on Carver's fiction, poetry, and biography is readily available, global in its origins, and wide-ranging in its critical approaches. The bad news is that this same body of commentary is massive, repetitious, and uneven in its factual accuracy and intellectual depth. Entering the term *Raymond Carver* in a general-purpose search engine will yield a blinding fusillade of hits, the vast majority of them uncritical and outdated. Better results can be obtained by performing focused searches in proprietary databases.

These resources will reveal that every book, nearly every story, and a great many poems by Carver have been the subjects of scholarly studies. A complete list of works and critics would far exceed the confines of an essay. The widely anthologized story "Cathedral" has received the most commentary, closely followed by the longer but also frequently reprinted tale "A Small, Good Thing." Stories that have been the subject of two or more critical articles include (in alphabetical order, with alternate titles bracketed) "Fat," "Feathers," "Popular Mechanics" ["Little Things"], "Put Yourself in My Shoes," "What We Talk About When We Talk About Love" ["Beginners"], "Where I'm Calling From," and "Will You Please Be Quiet, Please?" Studies of Carver in relation to other writers, both American and international, are also numerous. Either as a matter of influence or affinity, Carver has been paired with Sherwood Anderson (Bruyere); Anton Chekhov (Boddy); Stephen Crane (Banks); Ernest Hemingway (Bethea); James Joyce (McDermott); D. H. Lawrence (Cushman); Haruki Murakami (Seemann); and Flannery O'Connor (Lonnquist).

Scholarly journals that have published multiple articles on Carver's work include *Critique*, the *Explicator*, the *Journal of the Short Story in English, Studies in Short Fiction*, and the eponymous online journal the *Raymond Carver Review* (2007–). These and other periodicals have also devoted special issues exclusively to Carver. In 1993 the pioneering French scholar Claudine Verley edited an issue of *Profils américains* that took stock of Carver studies in the aftermath of the writer's death in 1988. To mark the tenth anniversary of Carver's passing, Patrick Henry, an editor of the international journal *Philosophy and Literature*, included a special section focused on Raymond Carver and Tess Gallagher in the October 1998 issue. In 2006 another prolific European Carver scholar, Vasiliki Fachard, edited a special issue of the *Journal of the Short Story in English* that addressed the Carver controversy and the addition of new stories to the Carver canon. An emerging area of interest for Carver scholars is gender studies. In 2009 an issue of the *Raymond Carver Review* comprised of essays on Carver and feminism was guest-edited by Claire Fabre-Clark and Libe García Zarranz. Complementing these special issues is the book *New Paths to Raymond Carver* (2008), a collection of critical essays compiled and edited by two founders of the International Raymond Carver Society (2005–), Sandra Lee Kleppe and Robert Miltner.

The purpose of this essay has been to tell the story of the making of Raymond Carver's critical reception, the near-unmaking of it by "The Carver Chronicles," and the exciting prospect of remaking it on firmer ground in coming years. For the newcomer to Carver studies, three relatively early articles provide an introduction to abiding issues in discussion of his work. The first scholarly article on Carver, a 1980 study of voyeurism and dissociation in *Will You Please Be Quiet, Please?* by David Boxer and Cassandra Phillips, remains seminal, as evidenced by several essays on voyeurism in *New Paths to Raymond Carver* (2008). The 1985 essay "Beyond Hopelessville: Another Side of Raymond Carver" by William L. Stull (one of the authors of this essay) began an inquiry into the nature of Carver's realism that has been carried forward into the new century by Kerry McSweeney in *The Realist Short Story of the Powerful Glimpse: Chekhov to Carver* (*2007*). Finally, the 1986 essay "Living On/Off the Reserve: Performance, Interrogation, and Negativity in the Works of Raymond Carver" by the French literary theorist Marc Chénetier set the pattern for much European scholarship, including valuable studies by Claudine Verley, Harold Schweizer, and Vasiliki Fachard. Articles by the American short story theorist Charles May consistently shed light on the storytelling structures within Carver's narratives.

In sum, the body of literary criticism devoted to Raymond Carver over the past thirty years has been substantial and illuminating. At the same time, with the waning of the Carver controversy and the availability of *Beginners*, what the *New Republic* observed in 2010 holds true: "we are only at the very beginning of our understanding of this extraordinary storyteller" (Benfey 31).

Works Cited

Amir, Ayala. *The Visual Poetics of Raymond Carver*. Lanham: Lexington, 2010. Print.

Banks, Russell. "Raymond Carver: Our Stephen Crane." *Atlantic* Aug. 1991: 99–103. Print.

Benfey, Christopher. "Mr. Coffee and Mr. Fixit." Rev. of *Collected Stories*, by Raymond Carver, and Raymond Carver: A Writer's Life, by Carol Sklenicka. *New Republic* 25 Mar. 2010: 28–31. Print.

Bethea, Arthur F. "Now This Is Affirmation of Life: Raymond Carver's Posthumously Published Stories." *Journal of the Short Story in English* 46 (2006): 89–106. Print.

___. "Raymond Carver's Inheritance from Ernest Hemingway's Literary Technique." *Hemingway Review* 16.2 (2007): 89–104. Print.

___. *Technique and Sensibility in the Fiction and Poetry of Raymond Carver*. New York: Routledge, 2001. Print.

Birkerts, Sven. "The School of Gordon Lish." *An Artificial Wilderness: Essays on 20th-Century Literature*. New York: Morrow, 1987. 251–63. Print.

Boddy, Kasia. "Companion-Souls of the Short Story: Anton Chekov and Raymond Carver." *Scottish-Slavonic Review* 18 (1992): 105–12. Print.

Boxer, David, and Cassandra Phillips. "Will You Please Be Quiet, Please? Voyeurism, Dissociation, and the Art of Raymond Carver." *Iowa Review* 10.3 (1980): 75–90. Print.

Bruyere, Claire. "Sherwood Anderson and Raymond Carver: Poets of the Losers." *Winesburg Eagle: The Official Publication of the Sherwood Anderson Society* 22:1 (1997): 3–6. Print.

Buford, Bill, ed. *Dirty Realism: New Writing from America*. Spec. issue of *Granta* 8 (1983): 1–249. Print.

Campbell, Ewing. *Raymond Carver: A Study of the Short Fiction*. New York: Twayne, 1992. Print.

Carver, Raymond. *All of Us: The Collected Poems*. Ed. William L. Stull. New York: Vintage, 2000. Print.

___. "Beginners." *New Yorker* 24–31 Dec. 2007: 100–109. Print.

——. *Call If You Need Me: The Uncollected Fiction and Other Prose*. Ed. William L. Stull. New York: Vintage, 2001. Print.

___. *Collected Stories*. Eds. William L. Stull and Maureen P. Carroll. New York: Lib. of Amer., 2009. Print.

___. *Conversations with Raymond Carver*. Eds. Marshall Bruce Gentry and William L. Stull. Jackson: UP of Mississippi, 1990. Print.

Chénetier, Marc. "Living On/Off the Reserve: Performance, Interrogation, and Negativity in the Works of Raymond Carver." *Critical Angles: European Views of Contemporary American Literature*. Ed. Marc Chénetier. Carbondale: Southern Illinois UP, 1986. 164–90. Print.

Cushman, Keith. "Blind Intertextual Love: 'The Blind Man' and Raymond Carver's 'Cathedral.'" *D. H. Lawrence's Literary Inheritors*. Eds. Keith Cushman and Dennis Jackson. New York: St. Martin's, 1991. 155–66. Print.

Donoghue, Denis. Dust jacket. *What We Talk About When We Talk About Love*. By Raymond Carver. New York: Knopf, 1981. Print.

Fabre-Clark, Claire, and Libe García Zarranz, eds. *Carver and Feminism*. Spec. issue of *Raymond Carver Review* 2 (2009): 1–126. Web. 30 July 2012.

Fachard, Vasiliki, ed. *Raymond Carver*. Spec. issue of *Journal of the Short Story in English* 46 (2006): 1–187. Print.

Halpert, Sam. *Raymond Carver: An Oral Biography*. Iowa City: U of Iowa P, 1995. Print.

Henry, Patrick, ed. *Raymond Carver and Tess Gallagher*. Spec. section of *Philosophy and Literature* 22.2 (1998): 413–77. Print.

Herzinger, Kim, ed. "Minimalist Fiction." Spec. section of *Mississippi Review* 40–41 (1985): 7–94. Print.

Howe, Irving. "Stories of Our Loneliness." Rev. of *Cathedral*, by Raymond Carver. *New York Times Book Review* 11 Sep. 1983: 1+. Print.

Kaufmann, David. "Yuppie Postmodernism." *Arizona Quarterly* 47.2 (1991): 93–116. Print.

Kemp, Peter. "The American Chekhov." *Sunday Times* (London) 7 Aug. 1988: G1+. Print.

King, Stephen. "Strong Poison." Rev. of *Collected Stories*, by Raymond Carver, and *Raymond Carver: A Writer's Life*, by Carol Sklenicka. *New York Times Book Review* 22 Nov. 2009: 1+. Print.

Kleppe, Sandra Lee, and Robert Miltner, eds. *New Paths to Raymond Carver: Critical Essays on His Life, Fiction, and Poetry*. U of South Carolina P, 2008. Print.

Lainsbury, G. P. *The Carver Chronotope: Inside the Life-World of Raymond Carver's Fiction*. New York: Routledge, 2004. Print.

Lonnquist, Barbara C. "Narrative Displacement and Literary Faith: Raymond Carver's Inheritance from Flannery O'Connor." *Since Flannery O'Connor: Essays on the Contemporary American Short Story*. Eds. Loren Logsdon and Charles W. Mayer. Macomb: Western Illinois UP, 1987. 142–50. Print.

Max, D. T. "The Carver Chronicles." *New York Times Magazine* 9 Aug. 1998: 34+. Print.

May, Charles E. "'Do You See What I'm Saying?': The Inadequacy of Explanation and the Uses of Story in the Short Fiction of Raymond Carver." *Yearbook of English Studies* 31 (2001): 39–49. Print.

McDermott, John A. "American Epicleti: Using James Joyce to Read Raymond Carver." *Raymond Carver Review* 3 (2011): 37–52. Print.

McSweeney, Kerry. *The Realist Short Story of the Powerful Glimpse: Chekhov to Carver*. Columbia: U of South Carolina P, 2007. Print.

Meyer, Adam. *Raymond Carver*. New York: Twayne, 1995. Print.

Monti, Enrico. "Il Miglior Fabbro? On Gordon Lish's Editing of Carver's *What We Talk About When We Talk About Love*." *Raymond Carver Review* 1 (2007): 53–74. Print.

Nesset, Kirk. *The Stories of Raymond Carver: A Critical Study*. Athens: Ohio UP, 1995. Print.

Newlove, Donald. Rev. of *What We Talk About When We Talk About Love*, by Raymond Carver. *Saturday Review* Apr. 1981: 77. Print.

Polsgrove, Carol. *It Wasn't Pretty, Folks, but Didn't We Have Fun?* Esquire *in the Sixties*. New York: Norton, 1995. Print.

Rich, Motoko. "The Real Carver: Expansive or Minimal?" *New York Times* 17 Oct. 2007: E1+. Print.

Robinson, Marilynne. "Marriage and Other Astonishing Bonds." Rev. of *Where I'm Calling From*, by Raymond Carver. *New York Times Book Review* 15 May 1988: 1+. Print.

Roth, Philip. Dust jacket. *Principianti [Beginners]*. By Raymond Carver. Trans. Riccardo Duranti. Turin: Einaudi, 2009. Print.

Runyon, Randolph Paul. *Reading Raymond Carver*. Syracuse: Syracuse UP, 1992. Print.

___. "Dreams and Other Connections among Carver's Recovered Stories." *Journal of the Short Story in English* 46 (2006): 63–74. Print.

Saltzman, Arthur M. *Understanding Raymond Carver*. Columbia: U of South Carolina P, 1988. Print.

Schweizer, Harold. "Waiting and Hoping: Raymond Carver's 'A Small, Good Thing.'" *On Waiting*. New York: Routledge, 2008. 110–24. Print.

Seemann, Brian. "Existential Connections: The Influence of Raymond Carver on Haruki Murakami." *Raymond Carver Review* 1 (2007): 75–92. Print.

Stull, William L. "Beyond Hopelessville: Another Side of Raymond Carver." *Philological Quarterly* 64.1 (1985): 1–15. Print.

Stull, William L. and Maureen P. Carroll. "Prolegomena to Any Future Carver Studies." *Journal of the Short Story in English* 46 (2006): 13–18. Print.

___, eds. *Remembering Ray: A Composite Biography of Raymond Carver*. Santa Barbara: Capra, 1993. Print.

Verley, Claudine, ed. *Raymond Carver*. Spec. issue of *Profils américains* 4 (1993): 1–147. Print.

Wolfe, Tom. "Stalking the Billion-Footed Beast." *Harper's* Nov. 1989: 45–56. Print.

Wood, Michael. "Stories Full of Edges and Silences." Rev. of *What We Talk About When We Talk About Love*, by Raymond Carver. *New York Times Book Review* 26 Apr. 1981: 1+. Print.

Zhou, Jingqiong. *Raymond Carver's Short Fiction in the History of Black Humor*. New York: Lang, 2006. Print.

Minimalism, Dirty Realism, and Raymond Carver_____

Enrico Monti

From the beginning of his career, Raymond Carver was associated with the literary movement dubbed "minimalism," a term that he always resisted. He was heralded as the literary descendant of Hemingway, writing in a style that reduced language and narrative to the simplest yet most effective structure. Students in creative writing programs across the nation began imitating that style, as they did with Hemingway's a generation before. Yet, a number of critics denigrated minimalism, while others accused Carver of taking it too far. As it turns out, Carver's editor, Gordon Lish, was the one who pushed the bare bones concept beyond what Carver himself could accept. This essay situates Carver in the context of such influences as Hemingway, minimalism, and Gordon Lish.

Minimalism: The "Less Is More" Aesthetics for the 1980s

Raymond Carver has long been considered the father of literary minimalism, but today one may wonder to what extent he was really part of that trend. In retracing the artistic trajectory of the "most influential writer of American short stories in the second half of the 20th century" (King), one can see how he came to epitomize minimalism, what features of that trend can be found in his writing, and why he persistently resisted the minimalist tag that was put upon his name and body of works. To do so, a preliminary definition of literary minimalism is in order, which may bring out the salient features as well as the boundaries of such a movement.

Minimalism started in the United States as an art movement in the late 1960s, and it is based on the much celebrated "less is more" aesthetics, an old concept that had found theorizers and supporters in philosophy and literature throughout history, from the classic era through Edgar Allan Poe, Samuel Beckett, and Ernest Hemingway.

In the 1960s, visual artists such as Frank Stella and Sol LeWitt started to apply and develop that principle to their art; then it was applied to music, with composers such as Steve Reich and Philip Glass designing musical pieces with limited or minimal materials and highly repetitive patterns. In the 1980s, the term was applied to literature, and Raymond Carver, especially after the publication of *What We Talk About When We Talk About Love* (1981), was acclaimed as the father of a new wave of American minimalist writers. Literary minimalism in the 1980s was never a school but rather a tag attached by critics to a group of fiction writers active in the United States (such as Bobbie Ann Mason, Frederick Barthelme, Ann Beattie, Amy Hempel, and Mary Robison) who knew each other and even admired each other's works but who rarely endorsed that tag. However, literary minimalism did become a major, fashionable trend for a short period of time in the 1980s and 1990s, and creative writing programs spread it to a number of apprentice writers.

In the literary scene of those years, minimalism was in many respects a response to and a reaction against some of the metafictional writing that had dominated the scene in the 1960s and 1970s, with influential writers-critics-teachers such as John Barth, Robert Coover, Thomas Pynchon, and William Gass. Barth dubbed such writers, including himself, as "maximalists," and he saw in the minimalists versus maximalists dispute the latter example of a cyclic opposition in American letters and beyond (such as Dickinson versus Whitman, Beckett versus Garcia Márquez). While the metafictional writers explored and expanded the novel form with their long, experimental novels full of intertextual and erudite references, the short story became the preferred ground for the American wave of minimalist writers in the wake of its most celebrated living father, Raymond Carver.

But what are then the trademarks of literary minimalism? An attempt to define the most salient features of such writing identified them in "equanimity of surface, 'ordinary' subjects, recalcitrant narrators and deadpan narratives, slightness of story, and characters who don't think out loud," "spareness and cleanness" (Herzinger 7, 14); or again "terse, oblique, realistic, or hyperrealistic, slightly plotted, extrospective, cool-surfaced fiction," in Barth's words. Minimalism in fiction, as Barth points out in his clear analysis of the 1980s minimalist trend, can be of several ways:

> There are minimalisms of unit, form and scale: short words, short sentences and paragraphs, super-short stories [...]. There are minimalisms of style: a stripped-down vocabulary; a stripped-down syntax that avoids periodic sentences, serial predications and complex subordinating constructions; a stripped-down rhetoric that may eschew figurative language altogether; a stripped-down, non-emotive tone. And there are minimalisms of material: minimal characters, minimal exposition ("all that David Copperfield kind of crap," says J. D. Salinger's *Catcher in the Rye*), minimal mises en scene, minimal action, minimal plot.

If such analysis, as we will see, may be fitting to describe part of Carver's writing, it remains largely inadequate to describe stories such as "Cathedral," "A Small, Good Thing." or "Errand" which could hardly be accounted for as being 'minimalist' in unit, style and material.

Carver always rejected the minimalist tag that was first attached to his works in a review of his *What We Talk About When We Talk About Love* (Gentry and Stull 44, 80, 126, 153, 185, 206). One of the reasons for his rejection is that the term *minimalism* soon took a pejorative and reductive connotation (beside the simplification and generalization involved in any tag as well as its appeal on lower-level, imitative epigones once become fashionable). The result is that minimalist writing soon started being attacked by critics for their gimmickry and a lack of grasp on reality, although such attacks rarely touched Carver's works directly. However, there may well be other reasons for all that resistance on his part to the minimalist label, and those reasons can come clear at a closer look at his own trajectory as a writer.

The Evolution of Carver's Writing: The 1981 Minimalist Turn

Carver had a relatively short literary career, leaving us with some sixty stories (plus his poems and a few essays) gathered into six collections, spanning from 1976 to 1988. Most of his stories dwell in what has been defined as Carver Country: rural or suburban areas inhabited by battered middle-class people, often struggling among alcohol and familiar problems. His trademark style is characterized by the use of a simple, referential vocabulary that devoid of any rhetorical literariness (e.g. metaphors are almost invariably absent); simple syntactic patterns; a massive use of ellipsis and repetition; and very little moral judgment or psychological investigation. While such features can be found in most of his writing, they are present at different degrees in his collections of short stories. More specifically, a turning point has been identified in his career where the minimalist trend gains momentum (in both thematic gloom and stylistic sparseness) only to be put aside or redefined shortly afterwards.

Such veer takes place in Carver's career between 1981 and 1983, namely between the publication of *What We Talk About When We Talk About Love* and *Cathedral*: so stark, despaired, and thin the former collection, so fuller and hopeful the latter. The change is palpable: To savor the difference, one only needs to compare "The Bath" in the former collection with its "extended version" in the latter, "A Small, Good Thing." The stories in *Cathedral* are more articulated, and a glimpse of light often finds its way into the dark lives of the working-class antiheros inhabiting Carver Country. Some critics tried to explain such change in terms of personal events and a different frame of mind: In short, Carver's happier "second life" with poet Tess Gallagher (and without alcohol) produced more articulated, hopeful stories.

In his thorough investigation of Carver's career, Adam Meyer identified a trajectory resembling the curve of an hourglass (239) with the 1981 collection representing the narrowest middle part that followed and preceded richer narratives. The "watershed," as Carver himself acknowledged the book in his introduction to his last collection of stories (Carver, *Collected* 748), is the publication of *What We Talk* in 1981, by far his thinnest and most "minimalist" collection of stories and possibly his most popular, although one "I didn't want to duplicate or write again." It is now clear and widely accepted that such minimalist turn in Carver's writing was instigated by Knopf's editor Gordon Lish, who had a profound impact on Carver's career up to that point.

Carver and Lish: A Controversial Relationship

The professional relationship between Carver and Lish has been the object of a long controversy, with rumors circulating since the mid-1980s about the major role played by Lish in shaping Carver's stories. The theories found a national and international echo in 1998 when D. T. Max published in the *New York Times Magazine* the result of his investigation on the Lish Papers, which he accessed at the Lilly Library of Indiana University. Those archives hold Carver's manuscripts with Lish's editorial remarks scribbled upon them, and they tell an unexpected and upsetting story: Original titles and endings were radically changed, and entire pages from the stories Carver had submitted for *What We Talk About When We Talk About Love* were crossed out by Lish.

More than ten years after those revelations, speculations about the "genuine" Carver were finally put to an end by the Library of America edition of the *Collected Stories* (2009), where the original version of those stories appeared for the first time as Carver had written them and with the initial title Carver had thought for the title story, *Beginners* (subtitle: "The Manuscript Version of *What We Talk About When We Talk About Love*"). Retrieving Carver's typescript drafts before Lish's heavy editing, this edition allowed readers "to trace Carver's true trajectory as a writer," as Tess Gallagher announced.

Controversial relationships between writers and editors are not rare, nor is the publication of restored versions (or original drafts) of classic works: A similar thing happened for example to William S. Burroughs (*Naked Lunch*), T. S Eliot (*The Waste Land: A Facsimile and*

Transcript of the Original Drafts Including the Annotations of Ezra Pound), Thomas Wolfe (*Look Homeward, Angel* published as *O Lost* in its unedited version), Jack Kerouac (*On the Road: The Original Scroll*), and others. Such publications are of interest mostly for scholars and students, although they may raise some interest among general readers who are questioning the romantic conception of the author as the sole creator of his works. This is particularly true in the case of Carver, since the "original version" was not initially published by itself in English but only as an appendix to his collected stories. Such editorial choice has two major consequences: On the one hand, the revised stories may have reached a larger audience, including those readers who bought the book, attracted by the idea of owning Carver's collected stories without being necessarily attracted by those versions; on the other hand, the original versions were not detached from their other, published versions, thus facilitating a comparative analysis. Indeed comparing previously unpublished stories to their 1981 versions—and knowing that most if not all changes are due to Lish's editing—gives a clear sense of how Lish transformed an articulate and compassionate short-story writer into a highly stylized minimalist hero. Before moving on to such analysis, some preliminary information is necessary in order to fully understand the Carver–Lish controversy, as well as the role of the latter in shaping Carver's writing.

Carver and Lish were friends since the mid-1960s: they had been exchanging manuscripts since then and continued doing so while Lish made his way up as a fiction editor (at *Esquire* first, then at McGraw-Hill, and later at Knopf) and Carver his way down into alcoholism. It was Lish who accepted his first story for a major magazine ("Neighbors" in 1971), and it was Lish who gave Carver his first major contract for *Will You Please Be Quiet, Please?* (1976), which appeared during Carver's darkest period. Shortly after that first book of stories, Carver had quit drinking and had met his future second wife (poet Tess Gallagher), and his life took a new turn. When Lish became fiction editor at Knopf, he announced that he would publish new fiction, and part of that project—the biggest part, as it would turn out—was Carver's new collection, which appeared in 1981, with a title that became almost proverbial, *What We Talk About When We Talk About Love.*

The collection made quite an impact at the time and received widespread praise from both critics and the public, gaining recognition on the front pages of most important literary magazines, and becoming quintessential Carver for many American and international readers (indeed, it is his most translated collection), ultimately "[altering] our old notions of style and artistic convention, of realism, of the parameters of the American short story, and of the short story abroad" (Nesset 50). Those spare, elliptical stories, with their threatening and abrupt endings became Carver's renowned signature, and they gained him a place and a name in literary history, as well the much hated minimalist tag.

Carver was quite dissatisfied with the unexpected turn the collection had taken in Lish's hands and, while acknowledging Lish's good work on some of the stories, he objected to the extent of his editing on several others (Carver, "Letters" 95–97). Nonetheless Lish's changes were finally included in the published collection, and Carver's contempt was partially toned down by its great success. However, his professional (and personal) relationship with Lish could not but turn to an end: Lish edited (ever so slightly) Carver's following collection of stories, *Cathedral* (1983), which set a new tone for Carver's works. Now an acclaimed writer, he was no longer willing to undergo the kind of "surgical amputation" Lish had performed in his earlier writings. Moreover, he had taken another direction as opposed to the one Lish had encouraged him to take: "I knew I'd gone as far the other way as I could or wanted to go, cutting everything down to the marrow, not just to the bone. Any farther in that and I'd be at a dead end" he argued in an interview (Gentry and Stull 44). This is the reason why after *Cathedral*, the writer and editor finally parted ways: Carver to become the praised master of the short story and Lish to continue his work as fiction editor, talent scout, and writer with discontinuous success and a slow descent in popularity on the literary scene.

Lish's Aggressive Editing: A Minimalist Was Born

Analyzing Lish's editing of *What We Talk About When We Talk About Love*, one feels the presence of a clear project behind his editorial work on that collection. Lish wanted to shape Carver's stories into a cohesive and groundbreaking collection of innovative fiction, forging a new way for the realist short story. And to do so, he felt he had to give Carver Country an eerie tone and its style a minimalist turn. A clear confirmation of such agenda on the part of Lish is to be found in the fact that he had previously edited some of the stories included in that collection (such as "Tell the Women We're Going"), and yet his new editing transformed them radically.

How did he change the stories so radically? First and foremost by cutting out things: from simple words to whole paragraphs to entire pages. As it turns out, Lish was more fascinated than Carver by the threatening power of what is left unsaid, and therefore his editing is essentially a subtractive work. The result is that all the stories end up shorter than they initially were—with a few of them, such as "The Bath" and the title story, being reduced roughly by a half—and in the end seventeen of them fit a thin and rarefied 150-page book. Several subplots in the stories are either cancelled or seriously shortened. The shortening of the stories is particularly apparent toward the end of several of them, with several paragraphs disappearing from Carver's manuscripts only to be transformed in those laconic, icy endings for which the collection became famous. An exemplary case is provided in the last story, "One More Thing":

L. D. put the shaving bag under his arm and picked up the suitcase.

He said, "I just want to say one more thing."

But then he could not think what it could possibly be. (Carver, Collected 326)

Here is how the same story ends in Carver's earlier version, as it was published in *Beginners*:

> L. D. put the shaving bag under his arm again and once more picked up the suitcase. "I just want to say one more thing, Maxine. Listen to me. Remember this," he said. "I love you. I love you no matter what happens. I love you too, Bea. I love you both." He stood there at the door and felt his lips begin to tingle as he looked at them for what, he believed, might be the last time. "Good-bye," he said.
>
> "You call this love, L. D.?" Maxine said. She let go of Bea's hand. She made a fist. Then she shook her head and jammed her hands into her coat pockets. She stared at him and then dropped her eyes to something on the floor near his shoes.
>
> It came to him with a shock that he would remember this night and her like this. He was terrified to think that in the years ahead she might come to resemble a woman he couldn't place, a mute figure in a long coat, standing in the middle of a lighted room with lowered eyes.
>
> "Maxine!" he cried. "Maxine!"
>
> "Is this what love is, L. D.?" she said, fixing her eyes on him. Her eyes were terrible and deep, and he held them as long as he could. (Carver, *Collected* 952–53)

This particular example tells us much about Lish's penchant for omission and his persuasion that the less you give to the readers, the more you may suggest. In this he was a convinced follower of Hemingway's "iceberg theory," defined in these terms by Hemingway himself:

> If a writer of prose knows enough about what he is writing about he may omit things that he knows and the reader, if the writer is writing truly enough, will have a feeling of those things as strongly as though the writer had stated them. The dignity of movement of the ice-berg is due to only one-eighth of it being above water. The writer who omits things because he does not know them only makes hollow places in his writing. (Hemingway 153–54)

The risk that Hemingway anticipates in such a technique does not apply to this specific case because those things were not only "known," but were written down by Carver in his original versions. However, this is the most patent risk behind most minimalist writing and one of the major critiques moved against it. Lish was a firmer supporter of the iceberg theory than Carver ever was, and not only did Lish strenuously pursue the idea of leaving things out from the surface, but he also embraced the coldness implicit in the metaphor of the iceberg. Indeed, Carver's stories turn out colder in Lish's hands: Fewer feelings are involved and the narration becomes detached, icy at times. L. D. in this passage is left without words and unable to express his feelings or communicate, and as a result, the published book ends on a stark, gloomy note. Lish expunged what he perceived as "Carver's creeping sentimentality" (Max)—Stull would probably call it Carver's "humanist realism" ("Beyond" 6)—as well as most introspection, while at the same time lowering the characters' register and vocabulary and reducing Carver's empathy towards his characters. A striking example of this can be found comparing the collection's title story in its two versions. In "Beginners", one finds a long digression on the exemplary story of the Gates, one of the very few functional couples in Carver Country, bound by a solid love amidst their misfortunes. Very little of their healthy story is left after Lish's editing: The couple even loses its name, substituted by epithets such as "the old couple," "oldsters," or even "old fart," and "fucking woman." Here is how they are quickly disposed of in the edited version after being involved in a serious accident:

"I'm telling you, the man's heart was breaking because he couldn't turn his goddamn head and see his goddamn wife."

Mel looked around the table and shook his head at what he was going to say.

"I mean, it was killing the old fart just because he couldn't look at the fucking woman."

We all looked at Mel.

"Do you see what I'm saying?" (Carver, *Collected* 320)

In reading "Beginners," not only is there no rude language, but Herb McGinnis (later renamed Mel) and his wife Terri tell their story in a deeply affectionate way, lingering for several pages on their recovery and their love (938–43). A similar change in tone in the editorial process can be found in other male characters in the book, whose voice becomes ruder and less sympathetic—almost macho at times, another Hemingwaian feature that Lish enhanced in Carver's stories. Such trivialization of male characters is further pursued by editing out all cultivated, sophisticated references from the stories: In *Beginners* one may find a few literary allusions, ranging from *Ivanhoe* to Italo Svevo, which are absent from *What We Talk About When We Talk About Love*. The impression is that Lish's editorial strategies reinforced his bleaker vision of Carver's characters, making them monodimensional, uncultivated, small-town everymen.

A final editorial touch on the collection was the new titles Lish gave to several stories. Long, intriguing titles such "What We Talk About When We Talk About Love" and "The Third Thing that Killed My Father Off" are Lish's touch, as well as the short but cheeky "Sacks," with its clear, intended echo of the word *sex*.

What is apparent from Lish's editing is that he pursued minimalism in a much more profound way than Carver. He cleverly understood what groundbreaking fiction should be at the time and managed to give Carver's stories what it took to leave a trace in the literary scene by taking to the extremes what Carver was doing at the time. Lish was certainly more avant-garde than Carver, more attracted to "new" things, and definitely more willing to embark on the minimalist trail than Carver ever was.

Carver was mostly dissatisfied by such surgery applied on his writing and felt that it had gone too far in the minimalist direction and the edited stories did not reflect his mood at the time. Besides any personal statement in letters and interviews, the proof of such dissatisfaction is in his decision to restore a few stories from this collection to their "original," longer version in his later years. Such peculiar practice of publishing the same story in different versions (although Carver argues they are indeed different stories) offers us the most striking examples of the trajectory of his writing. Until 1981, revising an early story implies for Carver thinning it out (which is what happened to previously published stories included in *What We Talk About When We Talk About Love*), while after 1981 revised versions of early stories are inevitably longer and fuller than earlier published ones.

Carver never revealed the "behind the curtains" of that collection and explained the longer versions as expansions of stories that felt too pared-down. They were never explained in terms of recovery of previous, longer versions (Gentry and Stull 125, 229–30). Lish never made any public pronouncement about his role in that collection either, although his choice to sell his papers to a research library betrays some resentment and a clear will to make everything available to future scholars and to the world. Carver did acknowledge Lish in his essay "Fires" as one of the major influences in his life as a writer (side by side with former his creative writing teacher John Gardner) and declared owing to Lish especially for publishing and revising his first stories and through his first collection in 1976. No mention is made to their collaboration after that date, although that's exactly when Lish's impact on Carver's writing took its most important veering.

The judgment on which version is better, whether the longer *Beginners* or the minimalist *What We Talk About When We Talk About Love* is up for all readers to decide now that both versions are available. It is undeniable that in several cases Lish's changes were brilliant and managed to sharpen the stories and give the collection a certain unity of tone and style, which is what good editorial work should do. In other cases, though, Lish seems to have gone a little too far in building a certain stereotypical vision of a worn-out, dysfunctional, small-town America, thus flattening out the depth to be found in Carver's original versions.

Commonplace but Precise . . . and Startling: Realism and Precisionism

Aside from *minimalism*, several other tags have been attached to Carver's writing such as *dirty realism*, *K-mart realism*, *post-Vietnam*, *postliterary*, and *postmodernist blue-collar neo-early-Hemingway-ism*." *Dirty realism*, in particular, was coined by Bill Buford for a special issue of the British magazine *Granta*, which was devoted in 1983 to "new generations of American authors [constituting] a new voice in fiction." The tag, which proved particularly successful in Britain, did not focus as much on the minimal aspect of things, but rather stressed its link to the realist tradition in American fiction that was spiked by a new, dirty background of the "dark side of Reagan's America," as Carver once defined it (Gentry and Stull 201).

None of these tags encompasses Carver's whole trajectory as an author, however, although he was certainly a proud member of realism as opposed to the wave of formalist, experimental writers who were so influential in the US literary scene in 1960s and 1970s. He openly declared his skepticism vis-à-vis the "formal innovation" demanded by Barth to young writers, arguing that "too often 'experimentation' is a license to be careless, silly or imitative in the writing" (Carver *Collected* 723).

Carver definitely cherished precision in writing. He cherished endless rewritings as the necessary means to achieve that "accuracy of statement," which he claims to have inherited from John Gardner, the other "fire" of his life as a writer. As Carver's first important writing teacher, Gardner transmitted to young Carver the importance of revisions, of using "common language," being wary of "'literary' words or 'pseudo-poetic' language," and that "absolutely everything was important in a short story" (Carver, *Collected* 743–44). That attention to the detail and to a form of "honest" realism is certainly paramount in "his writing. But in Carver's vision, something else is needed, which he persistently pursued: "[writing] about commonplace things and objects using commonplace but precise language, and to endow those things . . . with immense, even startling power" (730). That startling power is exactly what Lish tried to enhance in Carver's writing by drawing from his more extreme aesthetic vision and his strenuous reliance on verbal economy. Lish certainly had a key role in making Carver an icon of the minimalist wave of the 1980s. Reading *Beginners* one may now better understand why Carver never quite recognized himself under the label of literary minimalism, preferring to be considered a realist, and a precisionist. Nonetheless, beyond any label, Carver's legacy is to be found in his ability to create a fictional world that is so recognizably his own and a style blending verbal economy, precision, and startling power. Through his work he has managed to revitalize the realist short story, and the short story *tout court* as a literary genre, giving it a new, dignified, contemporary form, and therefore leading the way for new generations of writers to come.

Works Cited

Barth, John. "A Few Words about Minimalism." *New York Times Book Review* 28 Dec. 1986, late city final ed., 7: 1. Print.

Carver, Raymond. "'Beginners,' Edited: The Transformation of a Raymond Carver Classic." *New Yorker* 24 Dec. 2007: 97. Print.

___. *Collected Stories*. New York: Lib. of Amer., 2009. Print.

___. "Letters to an Editor." *New Yorker.* 24 Dec 2007: 95–98. Print.

Gentry, Marshall Bruce, and William L. Stull, eds. *Conversations with Raymond Carver*. Jackson: U of Mississippi P, 1990. Print.

Hemingway, Ernest. *Death in the Afternoon*. 1932. New York: Scribner, 1999. Print.

Herzinger, Kim A. "Introduction: On the New Fiction." *Mississippi Review* 14.1/2 (1985): 7–22. Print.

King, Stephen. "Raymond Carver's Life and Stories." *New York Times* 22 Nov. 2009, NY ed.: BR1. Print.

Max, D. T. "The Carver Chronicles." *New York Times Magazine* 9 Aug. 1988. Print.

Meyer, Adam. "Now You See Him, Now You Don't, Now You Do Again: The Evolution of Raymond Carver's Minimalism." *Critique* 30.4 (1989): 239–51. Print.

Nesset, Kirk. *The Stories of Raymond Carver: A Critical Study*. Athens: Ohio UP, 1995. Print.

Stull, William L. "Beyond Hopelessville: Another Side of Raymond Carver." *Philological Quarterly* 64.1 (1985): 1–15. Print.

Stull, William L., and Maureen P. Carroll. "Prolegomena to Any Future Carver Studies." *Journal of the Short Story in English* 46. "Special Issue: Raymond Carver." Ed. Vasiliki Fachard (2006): 13–17. Print.

The Carver Triangle: Lost in an Edward Hopper World_____

James Plath

"Ray and I were aware from What We Talk About on . . . of the simi-larities between Hopper's tonal elements, his use of couples, the stripped down interiors and run-out-of-chances feel to some paintings—and Ray's stories."[1] *Tess Gallagher*

Like the Bermuda Triangle where ships and planes purportedly disap-pear, the often triangular structure of Raymond Carver's fiction creates a restricted area—both temporally and spatially—where characters become or stay lost. Furthermore, the sense of helplessness and defla-tion that the point-of-view characters feel is heightened by Carver's frequent manipulation of another triangle—Freytag'spyramid, which German theorist Gustav Freytag used to explain the structure of drama. At the base of this illustrative pyramid lies background exposition with a rising action that builds via a series of crises to an apex or climax, fol-lowed by a falling action and a leveling off, or denouement.[2] As Carver explained to an interviewer, "Most of my stories start pretty near the end of the arc of the dramatic conflict" (Gentry and Stull 229). As such, Carver's fiction can best be described as fiction of aftermath, since the main complications and rising action—even the climax of many sto-ries—have already occurred before the narrative begins. His narrators are at a loss for words because they can't explain what recently hap-pened to them or fight a malaise they're experiencing—an inescapable feeling of being trapped or down for the count. In that respect, they are the fictional equivalent of the subjects in works of American real-ist painter Edward Hopper (1882–1967). Many of people in Hopper's paintings seem terminally isolated—even (or perhaps *especially*) when others are present. Given the body language of Hopper's characters and their relationship to other objects and people in the paintings, it's easy to infer that, like Carver's characters, they too have stories that are implied but not revealed to viewers and that they too feel powerless to change their lots.

Tess Gallagher, who began a serious relationship with Carver in 1978 and married him on June 17, 1988, wrote that they attended an exhibit titled "Edward Hopper: The Art and the Artist" at New York's Whitney Museum of American Art sometime in October or November of 1980. At the show she purchased a Gail Levin book of Hopper paintings that she and Carver looked at together and noticed not only a shared blue-collar element, but also a common technique. Gallagher said that she pointed out how in "Errand" Carver's "making up a sideline character central to the perspective is similar to what Hopper does in *NY Movie*, with the usherette," in which the real "show" where a film is playing to a sparse audience is the female usher who leans dejectedly against the wall on the other side of the action, looking down and lost in thought (Levin, *Art and Artist* 242). Carver agreed with her.[3]

A number of critics also saw affinities. Cathleen Medwick wrote in *Vogue*, "Like Edward Hopper, whose landscape his characters inhabit, Carver depicts a frozen world, blue-shadowed, where time is the betrayer of lives" (94). In a review published in the *New York Times Book Review*, Irving Howe compared Carver to Hopper but insisted that Carver works "on a smaller emotional scale," with characters that are "plebian loners struggling for speech" (1). Years later, Gordon Burn noted that Carver's stories, "like Edward Hopper paintings, portray disappointed and 'applauseless' lives" (42), while Graham Clarke tried to articulate "why Carver's settings have been so compared to the paintings of Edward Hopper" and concluded that "Hopper's images of solitary figures and couples cast amidst an array of empty rooms and environments seem to speak directly to the world Carver's characters inhabit," one which "evinces a particular kind of American loneliness which borders on pathos" (117).

Hopper, whose paintings of everyday life in the first half of the twentieth century made him one of America's most celebrated artists, was labeled a "realist"—though his architectonic paintings of people and places are meticulously structured and highly stylized. Typically his canvases depict static tableaus, usually with three people or less, and a number of them with a single human as still as the objects in the paintings. As Levin observed, "the central figure is often psychologically remote, existing in a private space" (Levin, *Art and Artist* 145). Often there are shadows and sharp angles to suggest tension, and characters are often downcast. But even characters who appear upbeat are nonetheless weighted down by an implied narrative. In the painting *Summertime* (1943), for example, a well-dressed woman in a stylish hat stands on the stone steps of an apartment building, bathed in sunlight and staring, chin up, across the street. Yet, her aloneness is emphasized by tall stone pillars that frame her against a solid stacked-stone building. Tellingly, the window to her left—open and with a breeze blowing the curtain *inward*—invites viewers to speculate upon what she might be leaving behind—or why she paused on the stairs (151). A metaphorical prison, perhaps? Or a life of solidity that now yields to one of uncertainty and instability?

Hopper uses more than one method to create the feeling of limbo-like stasis and isolation that afflicts the people in his paintings and to convey what Levin termed "their anxiety or dismay" (256). In *Sunday* it's the combination of solitude and body language. This 1926 oil painting shows a man in a vest with a long shirt and armbands sitting on the wooden plank sidewalk in front of a store with large windows. The street is empty, save for him. The name of the store can't be read, and it's not clear whether this man, slumped forward with his arms folded across his chest and resting on his legs, is a shopkeeper who's relieved that it's Sunday or is depressed for lack of customers and human interaction (147). In *Hotel Window* (1955) it's a well-dressed, sophisticated woman in a brightly lit room sitting alone on a couch and looking out into the dark night, waiting . . . for what? That's what Hopper's isolated characters and minimalist interiors invite viewers to guess (220). Viewers are made to feel like voyeurs intruding on private moments, outsiders who nonetheless can't help but speculate what each person's story or inner thoughts might be. In *Eleven A.M.* (1926), though the room is cramped with furnishings to emphasize the tiny apartment and the woman sitting in a chair and leaning forward to look out of a high-rise window is nude but for shoes, the same invitation is extended for viewers to wonder: Why is she looking out the window? Is she thinking of someone, or is she just staring out at the city? Why is she nude? Is there someone else in this shabby apartment that we're unable to see? If so, what is their relationship? Again, body language is a tip-off. She is not in a position of rest, or ease, or satisfaction. She's anxious about something, leaning forward, wringing her hands (274). And in *Room in Brooklyn* (1932), we see the back of a modestly dressed woman sitting in a bay window in a still rocking chair, while across from her at the far end of the window rest flowers in a vase on a plant stand. Their careful placement and the fabric on the plant stand draped to match the woman's dress suggest, of course, that the woman's life is as "still" as the floral arrangement (149).

It's impossible to attain the same degree of static isolation in a fictional narrative, because narration typically involves sequence and chronology. But Carver comes close. In his fictional world, the real time of a story is often limited, and so is the location—often to a single room. Many times a story begins with a Hopperesque scene, as in "The Idea," where the narrator had "been at the kitchen table with the light out for the last hour" watching a neighbor's house (14), or "I Could See the Smallest Things," which begins, "I was in bed when I heard the gate. . . . I tried to wake Cliff but he was passed out. So I got up and went to the window. A big moon was laid over the mountains that went around the city" (240).

In story after story, Carver's narrators recount their tales of woe with painful immediacy. Though time obviously has passed, the depressing or perplexing events are still fresh in their minds, and one can easily picture the narrator sitting, as Hopper's shopkeeper or women in windows, in dejection somewhere and feeling isolated, even when they're with other people. Just as Hopper painted figures sitting on porches in such works as *Sunlight on Brownstones* (1956) or *Seawatchers* (1952), Carver's "Where I'm Calling From" positions the narrator and another character on the front porch at "Frank Martin's drying out facility" for most of the story, and "What We Talk About When We Talk About Love" offers two couples "sitting around" a "kitchen table drinking gin." In the beginning, "Sunlight filled the kitchen from the big window behind the sink" and "was like a presence in this room, the spacious light of ease and generosity" (310, 314). But just as the conversation grows darker as the story progresses, so does the space, with the light "draining out of the room, going back through the window where it had come from. Yet nobody made a move to get up from the table to turn on the overhead light" (320). The characters are fixed, and, for a work of fiction, are so static that they remain at the table even after the conversation and light have exhausted themselves and the narrator says he "could hear the human noise we sat there making, not one of us moving, not even when the room went dark" (322). Often, Carver's stories end so abruptly that one suspects it may even be too painful for the teller to continue the narrative or that he or she has simply grown tired of recounting the details.

In *The Barbershop* (1931), Hopper's focus is a manicurist who sits at her table reading a magazine, while a barber stands at the far right corner of the picture frame, his back to the viewer, working on a customer who's visible only by part of his head and a leg draped under a striped hair-cutting cloth. The manicurist's inactivity is amplified by the barber's action, and the fact that most of the action is off-canvas implies that it's not part of her immediate world. She's marginalized, though depicted at the center of the room. Hopper explored that sense of awkward aloneness in the presence of others in many more paintings, among them *Room in New York* (1932), in which a man in shirt, tie, and vest sits at a parlor table, engrossed in his newspaper, while in the same room, not five feet away, a woman sits sideways at the piano, her face in shadow and turned away from him, looking down, one arm draped on the keyboard and plunking a key with a single finger. Body language reveals her boredom, her sense of isolation from the man in her life, despite such close proximity. Hopper explores this idea of estranged-yet-attached couples in more sensual detail in paintings like *Summer in the City* (1949), where a sparsely furnished apartment is cut into geometric shapes by large blocks of shadow and light. On the lone piece of furniture in the room a man lies face down in a pillow while a woman in a loose-fitting nightgown sits in the middle of the bed, arms folded, head tilted slightly downward. She blocks our view of the man's midsection, but because his back and legs are bare, we assume him to be naked or at least partially so. Naked or clothed, it really doesn't matter—not to the woman lost in thought, as if contemplating what she could possibly do to improve her situation (258).

Carver's short story "Menudo" begins in similar fashion with an insomniac narrator whose wife is in the same room, asleep. He goes to the window and looks out at a light at the neighbor's house and concludes that Amanda, a woman with whom he's had an affair, also could not sleep (569). Almost the entire story is told while the man physically looks out the window. At one point he goes downstairs to heat some milk to help him sleep while his wife is "still sleeping on her side" (571). Later in the narrative we learn that his wife has had an affair, too, but his response, in true Hopperesque fashion, was to stay in bed rather than confront her. "I didn't get up for days, a week maybe— I don't know" (572).

The mood of Hopper's paintings is certainly reflected in all of Carver's fiction. They are kindred spirits, as well. Hopper told one interviewer, "I have a very simple method of painting. It's to paint directly on the canvas without any funny business, as it were" (Levin, *Intimate Biography* 533). For his part, Carver said he'd like to put above his writing desk a three-by-five-inch card that reads "No Cheap Tricks" (Gentry and Stull 58). Like Hopper's paintings, Carver told an interviewer that his stories "have a surface simplicity about them" and cited his teacher, John Gardner—"Don't use twenty-five words to say what you can say in fifteen"—as an influence (209, 181–82). Hopper was similarly inclined. Late in his career he became so fascinated by what Levin termed a "strategy of reduction" (*Art and Artist* 561) that he painted sunlight in an empty room, which "seems to reduce reality to its barest outlines, affirming the ability to see sunlight that he associated with life itself" (561). Hopper said he used minimalism "to make one conscious of the elements beyond the limits of the scene itself" (Goodrich 104) and told one art historian that each of his paintings was "an instant in time, arrested—and acutely realized with the utmost intensity" (O'Doherty 82). Carver, who was reluctantly schooled in minimalism by his editor, Gordon Lish, nonetheless has the same impulse. As Carver told one interviewer, "You're trying to capture and hold a moment" (Gentry and Stull 187).

Philosophically, the two men share the view that great art is tied to an artist's vision. In fact, Carver's pronouncement in "On Writing"— which was first published in the February 15, 1981, *New Yorker* shortly after Carver and Gallagher saw the Hopper exhibition together— echoes Hopper's published statement that "Great art is the outward expression of an inner life in the artist, and this inner life will result in his personal vision of the world" (Levin *Intimate Biography* 9):

> Every great or even every very good writer makes the world over according to his own specifications. . . . It is the writer's particular and unmistakable signature on everything he writes. It is his world and no other. (87)

There are superficial similarities between Hopper and Carver as well. Fame came late in life to both men. Both were modest about their achievements, both had slightly pessimistic views of life, both had excellent teachers who helped but also exerted a powerful influence, both admitted that the work process itself does not come easily, both felt that teaching was more draining than rewarding, and both strove to make their work more complex in later years.

But the greatest point of intersection is, as Gallagher noted, their use of couples and offstage elements that triangulate an implied narrative. Hopper's method of working is clear, given studies we have for some of his best-known paintings. The most provocative example for Carver studies is *Hotel Lobby*, a 1943 oil-on-canvas that depicts an attractive young woman with shapely legs outstretched and crossed at the ankles, her calves sharply defined. She is reading a magazine or book, while in the far left background an older, matronly woman sits looking up at an older gentleman who is most likely her husband. He stands facing not her but the phone booth or elevator that is only partially visible at the far left corner of the painting. His head is tilted so that he could very easily be eying the young blonde out of the periphery of his vision. The implied narrative is obvious, but such was not the case in Hopper's original drawing for the painting, which had the older man in the background looking down at his apparent wife and leaning toward her as if to indicate his undivided attention. Meanwhile, the figure in the foreground is a man about the same age who stares straight ahead, legs tucked neatly against his chair. Missing in the drawing is a tone that is so common to Hopper—a mood that, according to Levin, became possible because "Hopper gradually removed figures from his urban scenes" and "these scenes became empty evocative settings into which he could project a mood" (*Art and Artist* 41). Missing as well from the *Hotel Lobby* study is an implied drama—even if, as in the case of the final painting, it's only the *potential* for drama. In the finished painting, Hopper emphasizes a subtle sexual tension. That is, *Hotel Lobby* derives its interest from Hopper's suggestion that the husband *may* have a wandering eye, while the study offers not even the possibility of a narrative triangle. In Carver's short story "Gazebo," the narrator has already strayed, already had an affair with the maid at the motel he and his "older" wife were managing. In "Gazebo" the maid is kept offstage, and readers find out about this third party only through the narrator's interior monologue and brief exchanges of dialogue. But the effect is the same.

Hopper, likewise, often incorporates offstage elements in his paintings. In *Four Lane Road* (1956), a man sits at the side of his remote gas station next to an empty four-lane highway that's layered in between horizontal strips of asphalt, grass, tree lines, and a wispy cloud-segmented sky. It would be a still life with an entirely different implied narrative had Hopper not inserted one other element: a woman with a harsh hair bun leaning out the window behind the man, her face in a scowl, and her mouth open. It's clear that she's giving him an earful, and the man's heavy shadow behind him on the building while he looks out off-canvas suggests that he'd like to be on that highway *now*. Maybe there's another woman, or maybe the implied third element offstage is another job . . . another life, perhaps like a traveler who gassed up earlier that day whose destination seems exotic. Yet, like Carver's characters, he remains.

Hopper's deliberate manipulation of figures to suggest triangles (and triangulated ambiguity) is evident as well in his most famous painting, *Nighthawks* (1942). This painting, on display at the Art Institute of Chicago, shows an empty street at night and a panoramic look inside an all-night diner through the diner's long and large plate-glass windows. A customer wearing a fedora sits with his back toward viewers and at the front left of a triangle-shaped counter, in the center of which a counter man works wearing a white uniform and hat. On a row of stools along the other side sits a man and a woman. They're dressed up, and we can infer that either the man has found female companionship for the evening, or else the couple was out on a late date and became hungry. The woman holds up her hand, as if studying her nails, while the man leans forward, his arms folded on the countertop, looking at the counter man, who crooks his neck to return the look. However, in a study for the painting, Hopper originally painted this triangle of characters—the isolated man, the couple, and the counter man—in their own worlds, no one looking at or acknowledging the others. The man turns to his woman as if to say something, the counter man keeps his head down, and the isolated man is hidden completely from view, rather than having a portion of his face visible, as in the final painting. It's clear, then, that Hopper was "tweaking" the figures so that they could provide more narrative interest (Levin, *Art and Artist* 270) and invite the reader to speculate on the relationship of the three triangular elements.

Hopper does the same sort of thing but with a third element implied off-canvas in *Office at Night* (1940), which depicts a man—presumably hard-working, since it's dark outside and long past normal work hours—sitting at a desk and looking at a stack of papers. Behind him to the left, by a file cabinet, is his secretary, her tight dress accentuating the shape of her buttocks. She pauses over an open file drawer and looks in the man's direction, but also slightly downward as if something had just occurred to her. To the right of the man's desk is an open window, which suggests something (or someone) out there—a wife, perhaps? Have they already had an affair, and now he's ignoring her at work? Is she hoping to have an affair with him? More ambiguity drives *Excursion into Philosophy* (1959). In it, Hopper paints a small room into which a rectangular frame of light falls on the floor, like a reverse shadow. A fully clothed man sits on the edge of a small bed near an open window. Head tipped slightly downward, he is clearly in thought—perhaps about the open book next to him? Or the woman sprawled sleeping behind him, her back to him and clothed only from the waist up in a silky top with her bare lower half bathed in another rectangle of light? Or maybe, once again, it's something outside that window: another woman or a situation that's somehow better than the one in which he finds himself (Levin, *Art and Artist* 261). In this case, the book suggests an off-canvas element that acts as a wedge between the couple.

Carver also creates triangles that are visually strong, slightly off-center, sometimes ambiguous, and often off-canvas. As a reviewer for the *New York Times* noted of Carver's early stories, "The drama is almost always offstage, beyond the characters" (Broyard), leaving readers to fill in the gaps by speculating on the action left out. Carver's oeuvre is full of examples:

In "Gazebo" it's the maid—the one that the narrator had a fling with—who's offstage as the couple drinking gin in a motel suite ignores customers and tries to shut out the world in order to talk about their problems.

In "Fat," a female waitress tells a friend about a grotesquely fat customer whom she can't get out of her mind—and who, though offstage except for her memory, inspires her to tune out her self-centered and controlling husband when he "begins" (intercourse, that is), remarking, "I suddenly feel I am fat. I feel I am terrifically fat, so fat that Rudy is a tiny thing and hardly there at all" (7).

In "Viewfinder," a man with no hands going door to door and offering to take a photograph of the resident's house bonds with a man who, like him, was left by his wife and children. Collectively, those wives and children offstage suggest what momentarily enables the two men to connect, however tenuously.

In "Will You Please Be Quiet, Please?" the offstage element is an incident that happened at a party four years ago when the narrator's wife was unfaithful, though the narrator isn't sure exactly to what degree.

In "Neighbors" it's the couple whose apartment Bill and Arlene watch in their absence—physically removed but still present in their belongings, which, to Bill and Arlene, feels like a "greener pastures" mockery of their own lackluster lives.

In "They're Not Your Husband" it's two men at a diner who collectively come between Earl Ober and his wife, Doreen, insomuch as their poor assessment of her as a woman to be desired causes Earl to see her differently. Even after they're long gone, the damage they've done remains.

In "A Serious Talk," a man returns the day after he'd behaved badly in order to celebrate Christmas with his wife and children—but her "friend," offstage, keeps them from having a normal holiday.

In "Mr. Coffee and Mr. Fixit" the opening scene presents a triangle with one character slightly offstage as the narrator goes to visit his mother: "But just as I got to the top of the stairs, I looked and she was on the sofa kissing a man." That opening view stops the narrator in his tracks and marginalizes him, just as he's marginalized in the main body of the story as he recalls his wife "was putting out too" those days. But as one of the more generous of Carver's victimized narrators marvels, her old fling Ross "did okay for a little guy who wore a button-up sweater" (231–32).

Sometimes the third element isn't human at all. "After the Denim" begins with a standard displacement as a nameless young couple wearing jeans take elderly Edith and James Packer's parking space and customary seats for bingo night at the community center. James becomes so infuriated that the young couple, in effect, comes between him and his wife. But something larger looms offstage: Edith's cancer.

In Carver's most complex short stories, the triangles tend to shift during the course of the narrative, and, like Hopper's paintings, suggest diverse interpretations. After his wife leaves him, the man in "Why Don't You Dance?" arranges all of his furniture on his front lawn, just the way it was inside—even to the point of plugging everything in. Then a young couple arrives, thinking it a garage sale. While readers first notice that a triangle is formed between the man, his offstage wife, and the young couple, a funny thing happens. The man, who had been drinking, gets the young couple to join him, and after some bargaining—for they do, after all, want to buy some of his things—he plays some records for them and suggests, "Why don't you dance?" When the boy claims he's drunk, the girl wastes no time in asking the man to dance, and "she came to him with her arms wide open." Later, he "felt her breath on his neck" and the girl "pulled the man closer." At that point, the man's wife is long forgotten, for it's the boy who's now marginalized as his girl close-dances with a man presumably old enough to be her father. Later, in a curious postscript, the girl tries to downplay the event for friends. "The guy was about middle-aged. All his things right there in his yard. No lie. We got real pissed and danced. In the driveway. Oh, my God. Don't laugh" (227). Ultimately, it's the boy who's offstage, and even in her retelling the story, readers suspect that because of her impulses and behavior, the young couple might be staring at the same situation as the man and his estranged wife, years from now.

Shifting triangles occur even more deftly in "Cathedral," one of Carver's most anthologized stories. The opening sentence sets the stage: "This blind man, an old friend of my wife's, he was on his way to spend the night" (514). As the narrator continues, readers realize that while he's not as overtly jealous as the bulk of Carver's males, he's still feeling a twinge of it, especially since his wife was moved enough by her encounter with the blind man to write a poem in which "she recalled his fingers and the way they had moved around over her face" and "what she had felt at the time, about what went through her mind when the blind man touched her nose and lips" (514–15). Though the narrator tries to downplay his reaction, it's obvious enough for his wife to insist, "If you love me . . . you can do this for me. If you don't love me, okay. But if you had a friend, any friend, and the friend came to visit, I'd make him feel comfortable" (516).

"Cathedral" is about comfort and discomfort, for the narrator's journey is from being uncomfortable around a blind man to becoming at ease with him. But it's also very much about that shifting relationship triangle. For the first part of the story, the narrator is marginalized as his wife and Robert figuratively stroll down memory lane together. The narrator tries to make jokes to relieve his discomfort—as when he announces at dinner, "Now let us pray" and his wife looked at him, "her mouth agape" (520). "They talked of things that had happened to them—to them!—these past ten years," the narrator complains. "I waited in vain to hear my name on my wife's sweet lips," but only heard more talk with Robert, who would turn from time to time and ask the narrator a polite question that seemed shallower than small talk. Though the narrator is right there in the same room, like some of Hopper's characters he feels so marginalized that he's feeling off-stage. However, the fulcrum of the story comes when the wife goes upstairs to "change into something else" and the narrator asks Robert if he would like to smoke marijuana with him. By the time the wife returns in her "pink robe and her pink slippers" she gives her husband a look but then softens and joins them when Robert cheerfully says, "There's a first time for everything" (522). After the narrator's wife falls asleep, the narrator notices her robe "had slipped away from her legs, exposing a juicy thigh," and "reached to draw her robe back over her, and it was then that I glanced at the blind man. What the hell!" he says, and flips the robe open again. Already he's more comfortable. For the rest of the story it's the narrator, dubbed "Bub" (short for "Bubba," an informal, affectionate variation of "brother") by the blind man, and Robert who bond and talk while the wife, as oblivious in her sleep as some of Hopper's characters, has no idea that her husband will, by story's end, share the same intimacy with the blind man as she once did.

In Carver's "Feathers," three distinct images predominate, all of them associated with Bud, a man the narrator barely knows from work, and Bud's wife, Olla. The triangulation of objects that forms the narrative structure is the couple's peacock, a plaster cast of Olla's hideously misshapen teeth before she got them "fixed," and the ugliest baby the narrator had ever seen.

Carver's narrator is typical in that he's dissatisfied with his lot, as evidenced by what he says when they drive closer to Bud and Olla's place some twenty miles from town: "I wish we had us a place out of here," he says, then quickly adds, "It was just an idle thought, another wish that wouldn't amount to anything." But when he sees their house, greener pastures syndrome returns. "I thought it was a pretty picture, and I said so to Fran" (361). Although momentarily startled by "something as big as a vulture," once the narrator and Fran see it's a peacock and the bird spreads its tail feathers for them and "there was every color in the rainbow shining from that tail," they're awestruck. "'My God,' Fran said quietly," while the narrator adds, "'Goddamn" and concludes, "There was nothing else to say." The shared sight was enough to make Fran place her hand on her husband's knee (362).

Once inside, the couple can't help but notice "an old plaster-of-Paris cast of the most crooked, jaggedy teeth in the world" sitting in plain view atop the television set that Olla keeps around to remind her how much she owed her husband, who insisted on paying for her to get new, "pretty" teeth (366, 368). And then, farther into the evening, Olla brings out their baby and the narrator "drew a breath" because, "Bar none, it was the ugliest baby I'd ever seen. It was so ugly I couldn't say anything" (372). "Fran stared at it too," the narrator says, guessing "she didn't know what to say either" (373). That changes, however, once Bud and Olla ask permission to bring the peacock into the house, because apparently the bird and the baby enjoy each other's company. The bird's entry—that is, the entry of something beautiful into the room—has an immediate effect, and Fran asks if she can hold the baby. She plays "patty-cake with it" and, after the bird stops just a few feet from the couple, brings the baby "up to her neck and whispered something" into his ear. Then, the peacock and baby play on the floor, with the peacock "pushing against the baby, as if it were a game they were playing" (374–75). On the way home, the narrator concludes, "That evening at Bud and Olla's was special," and Fran feels the magical effect of that peacock and how, as it played with the baby, somehow some of its beauty rubbed off on the child . . . or beauty and ugliness blurred together. That evening, the triangulation of those three objects—two of them ugly, and one beautiful enough to overpower the others—changes the couple's life forever as Fran asks the narrator to "fill me up with your seed" as they make love. The important offstage element in the new triangle that forms with the narrator, Fran, and the baby boy that the two of them create that evening, is the boy himself, whom the narrator says "has a conniving streak in him" and adds that he doesn't talk about it. "Not even with his mother. Especially her. She and I talk less and less," he says. The outcome of that evening—when three distinct images created an odd triangulation of forces in their lives and a change so profound that it has driven him and his wife apart—is their son, who remains offstage.

Finally, in "Errand," a story that Carver and Gallagher agreed was similar to what Hopper had done with "New York Movie," what's offstage becomes the focal point. Hopper artfully arranged light and strong lines to draw the viewer's eye to a female usher standing alone in the hall, while the main event—a movie playing in an opulent theater to an audience of which she cannot be a part—is marginalized. Carver indeed does something similar in "Errand" by decentralizing the death of one of his idols, Anton Chekhov, and focusing on a room service waiter and the cork that he intuitively saves from the bottle he opens—Chekhov's last. Carver intended "Errand" as "an homage to Chekhov" (Gentry and Stull 213), but, like so many other stories from his writing life, it's also an homage to Edward Hopper . . . or a kindred spirit at work.

Notes

1. Letter to the author. 6 May 1989.
2. Freytag's pyramid is widely taught and available online. A helpful summary can be found at www2.anglistik.uni-freiburg.de/intranet/englishbasics /DramaStructure02.htm#
3. Tess Gallagher, letters to the author dated 6 May 1989 and 10 July 1991. This and subsequent references to Hopper paintings are from Gail Levin's *Edward Hopper: The Art and the Artist* (New York: Norton, 1980).

Works Cited

Broyard, Anatole. "Book of The Times." Rev. of *Cathedral* by Raymond Carver. *New York Times* 5 September 1983: 27. Print.

Burn, Gordon. Rev. of *Where I'm Calling From*, by Raymond Carver. *Sunday Times Magazine* [London] 17 Apr. 1988: 42. Print.

Carver, Raymond. *Call If You Need Me: The Uncollected Fiction and Other Prose.* Ed. William L. Stull. New York: Vintage, 2001. Print.

Clarke, Graham. "Investing the Glimpse: Raymond Carver and the Syntax of Silence." *The New American Writing: Essays on American Literature Since 1970.* Ed. Graham Clarke. London: Vision, 1990. 99–122. Print.

Gentry, Marshall Bruce, and William L. Stull, eds. *Conversations with Raymond Carver*. Jackson: U of Mississippi P, 1990. Print.

Goodrich, Lloyd. *Edward Hopper*. New York: H. N. Abrams, 1971. Print.

Howe, Irving. Rev. of *Cathedral*, by Raymond Carver. *New York Times Book Review* 11 Sep. 1983: 1. Print.

Levin, Gail. *Edward Hopper: The Art and the Artist*. New York: Norton, 1980. Print.

___. *Edward Hopper: An Intimate Biography*. Berkeley: U of California P, 1995. Print.

Medwick, Cathleen. Rev. of *Cathedral*, by Raymond Carver. *Vogue* 173 (Sep. 1983): 94. Print.

O'Doherty, Brian. *Object and Idea: An Art Critic's Journal, 1961–1967*. New York: Simon and Schuster, 1967. Print.

Intimate Divisions: Raymond Carver and Alcoholism

Kirk Nesset

The days after Christmas, in the taverns, were always splendid in their
timelessness. At heart loomed that perfect irresponsibility, long hours
when it was possible to believe we were invisible and shatterproof, walking on water for at least a little while, and beautiful in our souls.

But those afternoons are gone. Ray took a hard fall on the booze. Drink
became his secret companion in a more profound way than anything, even
love, ever really works for most of us. (Kittredge 189)

Raymond Carver's return from the hell of hard drinking is one of the
most striking stories in twentieth-century American letters, as famously sad as it is eye-opening. Chronicled by Carver in interviews and essays and charted in refracted ways in his fiction and poetry, it is a story
of excess and abuse: Carver's teenage marriage and the early burden
of children, his low-paying jobs and heavy debt load, his thwarted am-
bition, his incarcerations and hospital visits, and his unremitting up-
heaval and struggle with alcoholism all involved alcohol acting both
as a response to and a vehicle for Carver's various afflictions. "We
were in a state of penury," Carver explained in a 1983 interview with
Mona Simpson and Lewis Buzbee, "we had one bankruptcy behind
us, and years of hard work with nothing to show for it except an old
car, a rented house, and new creditors on our backs. It was depressing,
and I felt spiritually obliterated. Alcohol became a problem. I more or
less gave up, threw in the towel, and took to full-time drinking as a
serious pursuit" (*Conversations* 37). However, Carver recovered, survived, and moved past his addiction, writing prolifically and well for a
decade. Not surprisingly, the accounts and facts have accrued since his
early death at age fifty; the tale has grown rich and dense thanks not
only to an outpouring of criticism, but also to the appearance of Stull
and Carroll's book-length reminiscence, *Remembering Ray: A Composite Biography of Raymond Carver* (1993); Gentry and Stull's book

of interviews with the author, *Conversations with Raymond Carver* (1990); Sam Halpert's *Raymond Carver: An Oral Biography* (1995); a memoir by Carver's wife, Maryann Burk Carver, *What It Used to Be Like: A Portrait of My Marriage to Raymond Carver* (2007); a roman à clef about Carver by Chuck Kinder, *Honeymooners: A Cautionary Tale* (2001); and most recently, a full-scale biography by Carol Sklenicka, *Raymond Carver: A Writer's Life* (2009), which occupies itself largely with Carver's drinking and spares no detail in describing the pain and mayhem his alcoholism caused him and his family.

It is no secret that during the tumult, during those "ferocious years of parenting"—distracted by family and responsibility—what Carver wanted most was to develop his craft (*Call* 100). He wanted to publish, work, make a living at writing, and not have to borrow a mentor's office to write or to hide in the car in the driveway with paper and pen in order to find a peaceful place to work and write. Such frustration, Carver insists, drove him to drink in the first place. "All I really wanted to do was write," he said in a 1984 interview with Hansmaarten Tromp. "So that's why drinking took hold. . . . If I couldn't find a goal in life anyway, it just might as well have been the bottle" (Gentry and Stull 74–75). By 1977, a professional alcoholic at that point, drinking had backed Carver into a corner, and his life "had pretty much come to an end"—he was out of control and "almost as good as dead" (69). In the last year before he stopped drinking, he admitted, "I was finished as a writer and as a viable, functioning adult male. It was over for me. That's why I can speak of two lives, that life and this life" (88–89).

Making up "this life," of course, were Carver's happiest, most productive, successful, and lucrative years. In the last ten years of his life, Carver's fiction gained meteoric acclaim, his finances grew sound, he found love and stability, and eventually he remarried. And yet "that life"—the nightmare years of drinking and struggle—did not vanish altogether. The past would continue to furnish the subjects and situations of Carver's stories and poems, infusing the years of "pure gravy," as he would describe his final years in the poem "Gravy" (*All* 292).

Carver visited this chaos and pain again and again, as critic Angela Sorby suggested, particularly in his poetry; thanks to such reflection, Carver found himself nourished and made significant inroads crafting the fiction as well. His later story "Intimacy" illustrates this best, certainly, with its situation and characters. The story presents a writer-character who calls on his ex-wife in the wake of the wreck of their marriage. He understands he is "home" in the post-alcoholic tumult they share, but he is dominated and deflated by his ex-wife. He comes away from the visit shaken but not defeated, standing at a remove from himself and seeing the wreck from a distance—even if in part to exploit it. "Intimacy" gathers and recombines patterns, too. Readers find throughout Carver's oeuvre patterns involving voyeurism, self-division, and loss of control. Identity is slippery territory, especially with regard to stability and what one may or may not call "home."

In Carver's drinking stories, specifically, one can see a trajectory, from the early stories to late. The stories (and in their varying ways, the poems) chart not only the desperation and chaos associated with habitual hard drinking, but also the way Carver navigated an adult life of addiction and disease. In his earlier works, readers encounter characters—male, typically—descending into the hell of alcoholism; in his midcareer stories, readers encounter characters living through that hell, and Carver's later stories feature individuals finding their way out of hell, or at least trying. For example, the frustrated, soggy husbands depicted by Carver in his early stories ("Will You Please Be Quiet, Please?," "What is It?," and "Jerry, Molly and Sam") cloud themselves with booze, making murky circumstances more murky and bad problems worse. In Carver's midcareer stories ("Why Don't You Dance," "Mr. Coffee and Mr. Fixit," "A Serious Talk," "One More Thing," and "Gazebo") Carver introduces characters who are more bitter, more full of ire and outrage and with problems more pronounced, depicting them as alternately dazed, bewildered, uncomprehending, inarticulate, and numb. In later stories ("Chef's House," "Where I'm Calling From," "Menudo," "Elephant," and "Intimacy"), Carver's characters rebuild themselves in the midst of or in the wake of addiction, or they try and fail because they are not fully equipped for the challenge. Some characters have succeeded in part, and they walk a fine line between their former and present selves by repairing damaged relations and seeking nourishment if not recovery. In this continuum, early to late, Carver's characters evolve and move from helplessness or near-helplessness to something like helping oneself, albeit without any sure-fire remedies or easy solutions at hand. These characters are invariably at odds with themselves, deeply divided, hovering, or wavering on unsteady ground. And what they do, as they have as always done in Carver's fiction, is measure themselves against others and come up short. They try to find comfort or change and fail, feeling not at all at home in their houses, their lives, or within their own skins.

Voyeuristic attraction is the subject of "Neighbors," the first of Carver's stories to appear in a large-circulation magazine.[1] It seems to Bill and Arlene Miller, the story's protagonists, that their neighbors live "a fuller and brighter life" than their own (*Collected* 8). The Millers vicariously experience their neighbors' lives while caretaking their apartment—dissociating themselves such that when they find they have locked themselves out, they are caught between homes, in limbo, unable physically to enter their neighbors' apartment and reluctant to return to their own, which they now find lacking. In "The Idea," a story collected in *Will You Please Be Quiet, Please?* (1976), a woman watches her neighbor watching his wife undress; the narrator sees the man at his bedroom window next door and is disturbed to the point of outrage, but she is not quite aware—as the reader is—that the problem is in her own marriage, which lacks spice and vitality. She and her own spouse eat and go to bed, barely speaking, not really connecting, least of all physically. While her neighbor peers at his own home life, she barricades herself in hers. As Alan Davis observes in his essay "The Holiness of the Ordinary," such stories in Carver's first collection "chronicle isolation and breakdown, as well as the ache, often acted out in voyeuristic terms, to connect with another life, however perverse or futile the connection might be. Only strangers are able to talk to one another, and then only sporadically; the more intimate the characters, the less they listen to each other" (655).

The alcohol-steeped tales in Carver's first collection, *Will You Please Be Quiet, Please?*, feature even more desperate, intimate problems. In the collection's title story, Ralph Wyman, drunk and impaired after learning of his wife's infidelity, wanders into a bar, drinks, has a mishap in the bathroom, buys a bottle for the road, and casts himself into the night, out of the house and now out of the bar. He walks past the town pier, thinking "he'd like to see the water with the lights reflected on it," wondering how his elegant, handsome, Southern-educated professor-mentor "Dr. Maxwell would handle a thing like this" (*Collected* 185). Ralph at this point "reached into the sack as he walked, broke the seal on the little bottle and stopped in a doorway to take a long drink," thinking that "Dr. Maxwell would sit handsomely at the water's edge" (185). Dr. Maxwell, in other words—Ralph's measuring figure—would not wet his fingers at the urinal, walk around with open bottles, or find himself beaten up and knocked unconscious, which will happen to Ralph momentarily. Conversely, Carver's less-than-sympathetic protagonist, Al, in "Jerry and Molly and Sam," spends much of the story planning to and then abandoning the family dog. The rest of the story is then spent trying to retrieve it once his children discover the dog is missing. More miserable than many characters in Carver's fiction, Al cannot stand being home. He drives and drives, pausing to drink at bar after bar, dropping in at last on Jill, with whom he is having an affair. Al is "drifting" and "losing control over everything," confused about his affair and betrayal; he does not want it to go on and he does not "want to break it off: you don't throw everything overboard in a storm" (117). Filled with regret after dumping the dog, he sees "his whole life a ruin from here on in. If he lived another fifty years—hardly likely—he felt he'd never get over it, abandoning the dog" (126). And then he adds, in a characteristically Carverian moment of self-distancing, "A man who would get rid of a little dog wasn't worth a damn. That kind of man would do anything, would stop at nothing" (126).

Appearing in the collection *What We Talk about when We Talk about Love* (1981), the story "Gazebo" features a marriage spinning wildly out of control, and for the same reason—infidelity, aided and abetted by booze. The story's narrator, Duane, and his wife, Holly, live in and manage a motel. After Duane's affair with a maid is discovered, Holly and Duane barricade themselves in a motel room to sort matters out, with a good amount of liquor. "There was this funny thing of anything could happen now that we realized everything had," Duane says (*Collected* 238). Not unlike Al, who at his cruelest (as Al imagines) "would do anything," Duane is experiencing anything and everything now after his own infidelity; he is torn between faith and faithlessness. Having chosen to follow desire, he is now drowning in the repercussions, not to mention the scotch. The story begins with drinking and desperation: "That morning she pours Teacher's over my belly and licks it off. That afternoon she tries to jump out the window" (234). At one point, Duane rises to "freshen [their] drinks," a kind of sad reminder, in a phrase, of the civilized and refreshing ritual their drinking might have been at one time (236). The original version of "Gazebo" would not be published until years after a heavily edited version of the story appeared in *What We Talk about When We Talk about Love*. The original version of the story was ultimately published in a book called *Beginners* (2009), and later in *Raymond Carver: Collected Stories*. Not surprisingly, the original, longer version is more detailed about drinking and the role of alcohol in this couple's life: There are multiple trips to the liquor store, Holly gets "wild drunk" upon learning of Duane's betrayal, and she begins "some very serious drinking of her own" (776–77). And "here we are in this awful town," she tells Duane, "a couple of people who drink too much, running a motel with a dirty old swimming pool in front of it. And you in love with someone else" (780).

In the heavily edited version of the story, Holly also recalls a day years before when she and Duane met an elderly couple at an old house in the country and sat talking with them; she recalls "a gazebo there out back. . . . It had a little peaked roof and the paint was gone and there were these weeds growing up over the steps" (239). The gazebo represents everything that Holly and Duane are not or have lost: rural serenity, old-world refinement, nostalgia, respectability, domestic accord, and, sadly, love. As a symbolic structure, further, the gazebo signifies (attached as it is to the "old farmhouse," as noted in the original text) a sort of solidity unrelated to the structure they occupy now: the motel, a rest stop, not a home. It is a tawdry, generic place for wayfarers and others, some of them making illicit connections, and all of them just passing through. Again, one sees characters held up as mirrors or yardsticks for others. In this case, the elderly couple is a foil for Holly and Duane. As Holly thinks, "I looked at that old woman and her husband and I thought, someday we'll be old like that. Old but dignified . . . still loving each other more and more, taking care of one another, grandchildren coming to visit" (780). (The rural couple featured in "Feathers" extends this motif, a figuration of what might have been for the story's central couple—what could have been and bitterly was not.) Granted, the gazebo in is less solid than the structure appearing at the end of "Cathedral"—less luminous, less expansive, offering less possibility—but less possibility is exactly the point. A weathered, weed-invaded gazebo, in contrast, is indeed less substantial and is outdated, outmoded, and for many, merely an ornament, rarely used. Still, it claims weight nonetheless; it is the perfect emblem, evoking the sentimental, defeatist grasping at straws Holly does as her marriage collapses.

Similarly, in Carver's poem "Miracle," a husband and his wife are returning on a one-way flight from a hearing for "their second bankruptcy in seven years," and they are "plastered, as usual." The wife beats the husband with her fists until he bleeds, and finally "stops / hitting him, goes back to her drink" (*All of Us* 242–43). Holding his own drink, the husband looks out the window:

Far below, the small steady lights in houses
up and down some coastal valley. It's
the dinner hour down there. People pushing
up to a full table, grace being said,
hands joined together under roofs so solid
they will never blow off those houses—houses where,
he imagines, decent people live and eat, pray
and pull together. People who, if they left
their tables and looked up from the dining
room windows, could see a harvest moon and,
just below, like a lighted insect, the dim glow
of a jetliner. He strains to see over
the wing and beyond, to the myriad lights
of the city they are rapidly approaching,
the place where they live with others of their kind,
the place they call home. (*All of Us* 242–43)

Like Holly in "Gazebo," yearning for what will never be, and like
Ralph and Al, drunk and distressed and making equally desperate comparisons, the speaker in "Miracle" measures himself and his marriage
against others, compounding problems involving identity. Noticing
lights far below in a "coastal valley," he imagines solidity, community, tenacity, faith, and good will. He imagines people looking up,
further, to see the jet he rides on, likening it to a "lighted insect," an
appropriate agrarian touch in the rural world he envisions. The place
where he lives with his wife, however, is not solid or full; the line
lengths at the end of the first stanza indicate this—a long line followed
by a breathlessly short one ("the place where they live with others of
their kind, / the place they call home"). The ambiguous pronoun "they"
suggests diminishment as well, a deflation of self and of the unhappy
couple. Glancing around the cabin, the speaker anatomizes his fellow
passengers, seeking out similarities but noticing difference above all.
Referring to others as "people not entirely unlike / themselves," too, is

a fairly dead-ended gesture; the husband and wife on the plane would like to be like others, but are not.

Desperate men and desperate couples abound in *What We Talk about When We Talk about Love* (1981). The story "Mr. Coffee and Mr. Fixit" is set up as a comparison between men, the once-married narrator (who stays with his mother, unwelcome at home) and Ross, the new boyfriend of the narrator's estranged wife, "an unemployed aerospace engineer she'd met at AA," an even more spectacularly failing alcoholic than the narrator himself (*Collected* 231). Burt and L. D., from the stories "A Serious Talk" and "One More Thing," also visit homes in which they no longer live, breaking windows and pies, behaving like unruly adolescents, acting drunk and indignant, taking whatever they can in the face of what they perceive to be a precipitous, unfair rejection. And at the end of the extreme, readers find a man selling furniture and household goods on a lawn in "Why Don't You Dance?"—his wife absent, the home turned literally inside out, furniture arranged exhibitionistically on the lawn as it had been inside, including the "bedroom suite" with "his side" and "her side" (223). The man drinks unceasingly, sharing whiskey and beer with a boy and girl who stop to shop; the girl, vaguely disturbed, decides he "must be desperate or something" (227).

The two stories Carver wrote specifically about alcohol and alcoholism appear in *Cathedral* (1983), a book as concerned with the psychology of recovery as it is with loss and despair. The first of these stories, "Chef's House," features a man "on the wagon," living in a furnished house—a kind of sanctuary, a gesture of generosity from a friend, "a recovered alcoholic named Chef" (*Collected* 378). Edna, the story's narrator, spends part of a summer there with her estranged husband, Wes, within view of the ocean, fishing, going to movies, and above all not drinking. She gets flowers from Wes at one point, and puts her "wedding ring back on," although she hasn't "worn the ring in two years" (378). But then the unexpected happens; Chef throws them "a knuckleball" when they are asked to leave to make room for Chef's daughter. Wes takes the news very hard. "This has been a happy house up to now," he tells Edna (380). They speak of their summer together in the past tense. Hoping to throw off his fatalism, she asks him to suppose that "this was for the first time," and that "none of the other ever happened . . . Then what?" she asks. Wes answers: "Then I suppose we'd have to be somebody else if that was the case. Somebody we're not. I don't have that kind of supposing left in me. We're born who we are" (381). When Edna objects, he replies:

> I'm sorry, but I can't talk like somebody I'm not. I'm not somebody else. If I was somebody else, I sure as hell wouldn't be here. If I was somebody else I wouldn't be me. But I'm who I am. Don't you see? (381)

Given the story's optimistic opening and hopeful premise, Wes's disappointment and his abrupt about-face are surprising, even if oddly inevitable. "He said he was on the wagon," Edna explains in the opening sentences. "I know about that wagon" (378). Wes's resignation, his willingness to throw in the towel, to admit defeat in what he considers a determined, circumscribed world, constitutes one of Carver's bleakest outcomes in fiction. Like the bankrupt man on the jet who knows he and his spouse "are not like those others"—the "decent people" in houses in the valley below, Wes has already measured himself and decided he does not count with the others. He is not "somebody else," someone who might be able to start over, though that is precisely what he suggests on the phone early on, insisting that Edna come live with him. "He seemed to have made up his mind," she observes, after he has completely shut down (382). Readers may wonder what exactly he has made his mind up about—assuming that Wes knew from the start that his borrowed house was exactly that: borrowed, a temporary shelter, a brief respite from the nightmare of drinking. Readers may also assume that Wes is not ready to see that change comes from within, not without—not thanks to a house, bordering the ocean or otherwise. Still, ironically, he exerts himself to a degree as the story ends, just enough to seem in control of what he has concluded to be an implacable, un-controllable world. He stares out the window, then gets up, pulls "the drapes and the ocean [is gone] just like that" (382).[2]

"Where I'm Calling From," the other alcohol-focused tale collected in *Cathedral*, presents not a house but a halfway house, "Frank Martin's drying-out facility," a shelter, a sanctuary, or, as Robert Coles writes, a "sanatorium" for people "who have been drinking themselves toward extinction" (77). Frank Martin's facility is in essence a liminal zone, a place between home and the streets, or between the skids and jail. The majority of the story occurs on the front porch between the facility proper and the hills (where even strong men and writers like Jack London are undone by drinking); the inmates gather here and on the front steps to converse and tell stories. The story told on the porch in this case, the tale within the tale, concerns J. P., a chimney sweep, who is younger than most at the facility. The story he tells (or that readers hear in summary delivered by the unnamed narrator-character) details his romance with a strong, straightforward woman named Roxy, whom he marries, and it describes the wreck of his marriage brought on by his ingrained and continuous drinking. In fact, Roxy arrives on the porch late in the tale to suddenly make J. P.'s story a living, dramatic entity.

Obviously, the embedded narrative told my J. P.—summarized, embellished, and dramatized—is weighed against the narrator's narrative, against his rocky life, even if tacitly. The narrator exists in a limbo caught between girlfriend and wife, not terribly committed to either (and not altogether committed to his own recovery). J. P.'s story and life, by contrast, accrue as a sort of ideal despite J. P.'s defeats, as a case in which love prevails over weak will and disease, mainly because its characters, J. P. and Roxy, are portrayed as sincere, good-hearted, and earnest. "I see them hug each other," the narrator says. "I look away. Then I look back. J. P. takes her by the arm and they come up the stairs. This woman broke a man's nose once. She has two kids, and much trouble, but she loves this man who has her by the arm" (463). Jaded and pessimistic as he seems at times, the narrator does find himself moved by what he has heard and seen, and moved perhaps by the kiss he receives from Roxy (a kiss for "good luck," mimicking the first moments of the younger man's courtship, which may or may not signal a new beginning for the narrator).

The tendency on the part of characters in Carver's fiction to open up, talk, and tell stories has stirred critics to remark on the optimistic aspects of "Where I'm Calling From" and of *Cathedral* in general. Critic Alan Davis has noted that Carver's stories "bring together characters who have been damaged my alcohol, bad behavior, loss and inconsolable emptiness, circumstances both social and psychological," pointing out that "counterpointing such incessant psychic isolation in later stories is the attempt 'to get it talked out,' to connect authentically in a damaged world" (655). Connecting the act of storytelling with the work of Alcoholics Anonymous, literary scholar Cochrane Hamilton has suggested that while Carver's "experience with AA may not have provided him with specific details, with content for the stories, it must certainly have underscored the restorative power of narrative. Both AA's program of recovery and Carver's *Cathedral* are informed by a belief that telling one's story initiates the healing process" (80). Like other critics, Hamilton sees the tale as redemptive in the broadest terms possible: "Carver depicts alcoholism and its attendant spiritual ills—self-absorption, isolation, the inability to make sense of one's experience—but he also depicts a recovery process, the healing of broken lives, and, metaphorically, a spiritual rebirth based on the principles of community, service, and the telling of one's story—principles just as capable of redeeming modern man as curing an alcoholic" (85).[3]

Indeed, while the stories and characters in *Cathedral* reflect recovery and healing—"A Small, Good Thing," most strikingly—there are others, such as "Where I'm Calling From," with its less than outgoing narrator, that reflect these themes somewhat less. Despite the story's emphasis on community, on helping oneself through connection with others, "Where I'm Calling From" points the way to recovery, although its final emphasis and the tone of the ending indicate that hope and fulfillment in situations such as these is often tentative at best. Granted, the narrator is stirred by J. P.'s tale to recall a morning he spent with his wife in a house he and she lived in and a morning they were awakened by a "weird old fellow," the landlord, outside on a ladder. In this case Carver reverses the usual voyeur-pattern; his narrator says, "a wave of happiness comes over me that I'm not him—that I'm me and that I'm inside this bedroom with my wife" (*Collected* 465). This is a step forward, for sure, for our low-affect speaker. But the story's ending is both final and open-ended, hopeful and yet not promising. The narrator considers Jack London's story "To Build a Fire"; he does not mention its final sentences but mentions enough to suggest the frozen death the story's doomed character suffers. Even more importantly, Carver's narrator remains indecisive. He cannot decide who to call (girlfriend or wife) or what he might say to either because he is torn between sobriety and relapse, hope and despair, between the safe haven he knows and the imminent danger beyond.

The narrating character in "Intimacy," one of Carver's final seven tales (first published in *Where I'm Calling From*) is also caught between worlds, even if he is farther along the trajectory of helping oneself and finding recovery. He is a writer of stories who surprises his former wife by visiting unannounced and hears her out regarding their shared past; it is Carver's most metafictional tale, with its emphasis on writing itself—what writers might or might not use for material. The story is comprised mainly of dialogue—of statements, mostly embittered, coming from the ex-wife who dominates and breaks down her former husband, who narrates and laments that he remembers the "wrong things" in his fiction: the "low, shameful things" from the past (*Collected* 563). "Why don't you wipe the blackboard clean and see what you have left after that?" she asks. "Why don't you start with a clean slate?" (562–63). One may assume, as the former wife assumes, that he will not do so, since "that old business," as she recalls it, is at the heart of his writerly enterprise. And though he does not know what he is going to find at her house, he does know, once she begins to transmit her anguish and humiliation, where he is. "Make no mistake," he confides, "I feel I'm home" (561).

Home in this case is a profoundly interior state, at once psychological and aesthetic, and it is rife with division. The husband feels contrite and abashed, even as he plays opportunist, "hunting for *material*," as the ex-wife surmises (*Collected* 563). Even as he knows he is "home" in the tumult of the shared past, he is divided: He still loves her, but dedicated as he is to forward momentum, he must avoid the codependent, presumably alcoholic mess they became. He cares for her sincerely, but operates as a mercenary and uses memory and grief and despair for material. He is home again, that is, in a home that is not his, rehearsing betrayal and shame even while seeking placation. And placate he does, kneeling, holding the "hem of her dress," until she insists he get up, forgives him, tells him to "tell it like [he has] to," and asks him to leave (567). She is at once angel and muse, the woman he wronged and a ghost of the past, a partner in his nightmare. Amazingly, there is no mention of alcohol anywhere—not one reference to drinks or drinking at all in the story. But their drinking past is present, and all the more present, given its conspicuous exclusion. "That life" is alive in "this life"; it constitutes in large part the damaged heart of the story. It is his "private hobby horse," a "tragedy and then some," as he says she says (561). Given what one talks about when one talks about Carver, alcohol lingers here not only as a source of grief but as a problem too awful to name.

Drinking divided this couple, the reader infers and, in a palpable way, it still divides the recovered but visibly suffering ex-husband. "You have yourself confused with somebody else," the former wife says, as if handing a verdict to him—a dizzying assessment, to say the least (*Collected* 565). Confused with whom, one wants to ask. Whoever he is, the ex-wife tries to rob him of his remaining identity—of what he has left in the wake of divorce and what he has rebuilt alone. But Carver's writer remains intact, shaken and torn as he is. Noting as he departs that the front door is still open—he is not welcome here, at home, he feels as he steps out, observing the mess of leaves in the yard. Unlike tormented, hard-drinking Hughes in "Menudo," the writer/ex-husband will not rake the lawn or the neighbors' lawn but will go after the mess of his life and the past, not with a rake but a pen, arranging it in tidy piles of paragraphs and sentences.[4] Accordingly, he is "somebody else" or an array of somebodies. Beyond the hell of alcoholism, he will divide himself into the separate selves of characters, characters yearning for greener pastures, as well as those too bitter or tired to yearn: Wes behind his closed curtain, the bleeding man on the plane.

As "Intimacy" suggests, one can gain perspective on the past by engaging with that past, and in the case of this story, the examination is aesthetic and emotional. Like the speaker in Carver's poem "Alcohol," as Angela Sorby observes, he "defines himself through alcohol and yet abstains from it; he displays, but does not practice, a loss of control; he is a productive artist whose art requires open access to a chaotic former self" (27). The "productive tension" in Carver's stories and poems in these terms involves "the need to practice restraint" versus "the impulse to embrace chaos" (Sorby 30). Paradoxically, the thing that kept Carver from writing, ruined his health, and fractured his family was also the thing that made him the distinctive—if opportunist—writer he was. This is not exactly surprising, given that Carver's practice of such—as an artist, a man, a husband—began early. In a very real way the chaos was created, promoted, incited, consciously or unconsciously, at least in the eyes of one witness. "Alcohol acted as a sort of fuel for him," Chuck Kinder recalls of Carver, adding:

> It was interesting that so many of the things they did that make up all the Ray and Maryann stories and anecdotes, I could see them being created— not consciously, I'm sure—but as though they were trying to create a story to tell later. An accident would happen that would lead to another, and he would trust the accidents and sort of follow where they led, each moment having its own fan-shaped destiny. . . . We'd have situations when there'd be a shattering of glass and yells and screams and howls in the night, and

the next minute they'd be ordering pizza. And then Maryann would say, 'Did you see what Ray just did?' and then tell the story as if it were all some kind of amazing game whose rules they were trying to discover after the fact. There was a hilarity to it, but that ultimately feeds on itself. The fiction devours itself. (Halpert 123–24)

American playwright Edward Albee's 1962 play *Who's Afraid of Virginia Woolf* presents a married couple playing similar games, if more straightforwardly (which Carol Skelenicka notes in her much-lauded biography of Carver). In Albee's play, George and Martha's meltdown is more grandiose, but it is not unlike what occurred with the Carvers. William Kittredge differs somewhat from Kinder, however, describing the Carvers' routine as something a bit more deliberate: "They took risks constantly—risks with their emotional security. They lived on the edge all the time. They stayed out there, and I really think it was a conscious decision on their part to live on those edges, to court experiences" (Halpert 31). Whatever the case, the "material" arose, bidden or unbidden, and Carver found ways to shape it, bend it, distill it, although such endeavors—alcohol-borne, erratic to the point of violent at times—came at a cost. "The people he dealt with and lived with," Leonard Michaels observes, "were all participants in a way in his writing. I imagine Maryann lived through a hell of a lot of that material with him, and I suspect that she *and* Ray paid for those stories with their lives" (Halpert 18).

And yet, as the stories attest, difficult times—imagined or lived—are often interesting times. They make for provocative fiction if one can frame them and tilt them and not end up dead in the process. And if *not* writing prompted Carver to take up hard drinking, it is fitting that writing helped to end it, helped him shake off that noose and keep it at bay and him alive while the gravy days lasted. "Carver's luck was to have this gift of storytelling," Riccardo Duranti noted in an interview (Muldoon 16). The tensions that arose in Carver's life needed expression, and "these tensions could have had much more violent outlets. The gift

of telling with such power is what eventually saved his life, his sanity"
(16). Carver had "spiraled all the way down," James Houston wrote;
he had "drunk himself into the final coma, which he described as being
at the dark bottom of a very deep well" (Stull and Carroll 19). Unlike
his character J. P., however, who climbs out of a well when handed a
lifeline, Carver's own climb, as recollected by Houston, seems as if he
rose unassisted: "I saw this pinpoint of light, so far up there it seemed
an impossible distance. . . . Somehow I had to climb up toward that
last tiny glimmer. And by God, I managed to do that. What do you call
it? The survival instinct? I climbed out of that hole and I realized how
close I had come, and that was it" (20). And a close call it was. Carver
said repeatedly that he was more proud of having stopped drinking
than anything he had done, calling it his "greatest achievement" (Gentry and Stull 69). He "saved himself," Gary Fisketjon noted, "never
forgetting what it's like to have no prospects whatever" (Stull and Carroll 235). "This is the moment of truth," said Fisketjon, "and it's where
[Carver's] work puts us. He didn't flinch, and his characters stare without blinking. The challenge, then, is what to make of diminished things
and intolerable events" (235–36).

Unflinching, unblinking, Carver renders a world that often seems
cold and sharp as iced vodka, with "stories about people," as Douglas
Unger remarks, "for whom the worst has already happened," in which
readers witness the "dark death of love, and hope, and faith, and youth.
. . . It's as though the stories prove, in a way, that love and hope and
charity and the finer human emotions must still exist, if only because
of their striking absence for his characters after what they have lived
through" (Halpert 66–67). In these ways and others, and in his struggle against alcohol, Carver created a new tenor, a new landscape, a
new movement, a new way of seeing. He was called the "godfather of
minimalism" and the rejuvenator of the American short story, mainly
through updating and cleaning out its cupboards, as Ernest Hemingway had done fifty years earlier. There are no heroics here, Carver

insists—in the stories and poems and off the page in Carver's habitually volatile life. Jay McInerney, a former student of Carver, has said:

> Encountering Carver's fiction early in the 1970s was a transforming experience for many writers of my generation, an experience perhaps comparable to discovering Hemingway's sentences in the twenties. In fact, Carver's language was unmistakably like Hemingway's—the simplicity and clarity, the repetitions, the nearly conversational rhythms, the precision of physical description. But Carver completely dispensed with the romantic egoism that made the Hemingway idiom such an awkward model for other writers in the late twentieth century. The cafes and *pensiones* and battlefields of Europe were replaced by trailer parks and apartment complexes, the glamorous occupations by dead-end jobs. The trout in Carver's streams were apt to be pollution-deformed mutants. The good *vin du pays* was replaced by cheap gin, the romance of drinking by the dull grind of full-time alcoholism. (Stull and Carroll 120)

The worst that can happen has happened, most often, in Carver's fictions, and even then the worst is not done. A young man kills a girl with a rock, a fellow drowns himself in a fishpond; menacing unidentifiable eyes continue to peer in from the hall. Distraught and shattered, characters nevertheless find release here and there, and miraculously they open themselves to change, or at least to something new, if only by degrees. Consider Ralph in bed after his nightmarish journey, or the grieving couple in the bakery in "A Small, Good Thing," finding solace in other lives, other stories. Or consider the writer-husband in "Intimacy" who finds release, if not salvation, in art and in penance. "Certainly there's no more intimate construction of an alcoholic world in contemporary fiction," Gail Caldwell points out of Carver's work. "Carver's drinkers inhabit a boozy, interior space invaded only by the shrill persistence of the telephone or the need for more liquor. But the real region his fiction inhabits, whiskey-sick or otherwise, is a territory of the heart" (Gentry and Stull 247). At the center of Carver's intimate constructions, dark and bare as they seem, readers find compassion and human connection, however muted. One understands that universally "we need a new story," a story "in which we value intimacy," as Kittredge argued in "Bulletproof" (195). "Ray's best work continually suggests the need for attempting to keep decent toward one another while deep in our own consternations."

Notes

1. "Neighbors" was printed in *Esquire* in June 1971. The following retraction can be found in an article by Buddy Kite on the magazine's website: "Due to a printer's error, 948 words were accidentally omitted from "Neighbors," Raymond Carver's first short story published in *Esquire*, in the June 1971 issue. Credit for Carver's influential spare style, once attributed to a former editor at the magazine, should now be directed to a retired print manager in New Jersey."

2. Actually, the house in McKinleyville, California, which figures as "Chef's House," was not revoked, and Carver himself made serious progress in his recovery there. But years of hard drinking were not easy to shake, sober or otherwise. When Kittredge asked if he was writing, Ray told him no—saying he could not convince himself it was worth doing. Kittredge was surprised and unsettled. Ray's statement, he says, "implied a kind of consequence I had never anticipated. We had seen a lot of things by then, but it had never seemed possible to me that even the fractured marriages and falling-down, bite-your-tongue convulsions in the streets could lead to this kind of seriousness. Ray must have witnessed some things I had not imagined" (191).

3. Jung considered alcohol a "misdirected spiritual craving" (Hamilton 79), Hamilton further observes. "According to the historian Ernest Kurtz, an underlying insight of Alcoholics Anonymous is that the alcoholic's 'thirst for transcendence had been perverted into a thirst for alcohol'—a confusion of spirit and spirits" (87).

4. In Carver's story "Menudo," Hughes rakes his own leaves, then rakes his neighbors' yard, working obsessively in an alcohol-battered, compensatory way. At one point, he drops his rake, and thinks, "Mr. Baxter is a decent, ordinary guy—a guy you wouldn't mistake for anyone special. But he is special. In my book, he is. For one thing he has a full night's sleep behind him, and he's just embraced his wife before leaving for work" (*Collected* 582).

Works Cited

Carver, Maryann Burk. *What It Used to be Like: A Portrait of My Marriage to Raymond Carver*. New York: St. Martin's, 2007. Print.

Carver, Raymond. *All of Us: Collected Poems*. Ed. William L. Stull. London: Vintage, 2000. Print.

___. *Call If You Need Me.* Ed. William L. Stull. London: Vintage, 2001. Print.

___. *Collected Stories.* Ed. William L. Stull and Maureen Carroll. New York: Lib. of America, 2009. Print.

Coles, Robert. "Really Something." *Handing One Another Along.* Ed. Trevor Hall and Vicki Kennedy. New York: Random House, 2010. Print.

Davis, Alan. "The Holiness of the Ordinary." *Hudson Review.* 45:4 (1993): 653–58. Print.

Donaldson, Scott. "Writers and Drinking in America." *Sewanee Review* 98:2 (1990): 312–24. Print.

Gentry, Marshall Bruce, and William L. Stull. *Conversations with Raymond Carver.* Jackson: UP of Mississippi, 1990. Print.

Halpert, Sam. *Raymond Carver: An Oral Biography.* Iowa City: U of Iowa P, 1995.

___, ed. *When We Talk about Raymond Carver.* Layton: Gibbs Smith, 1991. Print.

Hamilton, Cochrane E. "'Taking the Cure': Alcoholism and Recovery in the Fiction of Raymond Carver." *University of Dayton Review* 20:1 (1989). 79–88. Print.

Kinder, Chuck. *Honeymooners: A Cautionary Tale.* New York: Farrar, 2001. Print.

Kite, Buddy. "Seventy Five Years of *Esquire* Corrections." *Esquire.* Hearst Communications, 25 Sept. 2008. Web. 24 Aug. 2012.

Kittredge, William. "Bulletproof." *New Paths to Raymond Carver: Critical Essays on His Life, Fiction and Poetry.* Ed. Sandra Lee Kleppe and Robert Miltner. Columbia: U of South Carolina P, 2008. Print.

Muldoon, David. "Carver's Domestic Adaptations: An Interview with Riccardo Duranti, Carver's Italian Translator." *Raymond Carver Review* 3.1 (2011): 6–16. Web. 25 Sept. 2012.

Sklenicka, Carol. *Raymond Carver: A Writer's Life.* New York: Scribner, 2009. Print.

Sorby, Angela. "Raymond Carver's Poetry and the Temperance Tradition." *Raymond Carver Review.* 1:1 (2008): 16–32. Web. 25 Aug. 2012.

Stull, William L., and Maureen Carroll, eds. *Remembering Ray: A Composite Biography of Raymond Carver.* Santa Barbara: Capra, 1993. Print.

Middle-Age Crazy: Men Behaving Badly in the Fiction of Raymond Carver and John Updike_____

Matthew Shipe

So this is adultery, he thought: this homely, friendly socketing. An experience he would have missed, but for marriage. A sacred experience, like not honoring your father and mother. (John Updike, "Bech Wed," *Bech Is Back*, 1982)

I suppose I began to drink heavily after I'd realized that the things I'd wanted most for myself and my writing, and my wife and children, were simply not going to happen. It's strange. You never start out in life with the intention of becoming a bankrupt or an alcoholic or a cheat and a thief. Or a liar. (Raymond Carver, "The Art of Fiction LXXVI," *Paris Review*, 1983)

In "White on White," the concluding story in *Bech Is Back* (1982), the second of three books that John Updike devoted to the misadventures of the Jewish writer Henry Bech, the famously unproductive novelist attends a party celebrating the publication of *White on White*, a high priced collection of photographs by an artist whom Bech had briefly known in the mid-1950s. Fresh off the success of his comeback novel, *Think Big*, and newly separated from his wife, Bech feels somewhat depressed as he circulates among the literati, cultural elites, and mud wrestlers/hookers who are attending the party. As he fights his away to the bar, he encounters "the shapeless face of Vernon Klegg, the American Kafka, whose austere minimalist renderings of kitchen spats and disheveled mobile homes were the rage of writers' conferences and federal and state arts councils" (190).[1] Seemingly modeled on Raymond Carver, whose second story collection, *What We Talk About When We Talk About Love* (1981), had been published to great acclaim the year before, Klegg offers a tantalizing glimpse of Updike's take on his contemporary whose career at the time was in rapid ascent. Updike writes of his contemporary's success:

The enigma [behind his fiction] gave Klegg's portrayal of the human situation a hollowness hailed as quintessentially American; he was published with great faithfulness in the Soviet Union, as yet another illustrator of the West's sure doom, and was a pet of the Left intelligentsia everywhere. Yet one did not have to be a very close friend to know that the riddling texture of his work sprang from a humble personal cause: except for that dawn each day when, pained by hangover and recommending thirst, Klegg composed with sharpened pencil and yellow-paper pad his few hundred beautifully minimal words—nouns, verbs, nouns—he was drunk. He was a helpless alcoholic from whom wives, households, faculty positions, and entire neighborhoods of baffled order slid with ease. Typically in a Klegg *conte* the hero would blandly discover himself to have in his hands a butcher knife, or the broken top fronds of a rubber plant, or the buttocks of pubescent babysitter. (190–91)

The meeting between Bech and his counterpart proves to be humorously anticlimactic as Klegg asks Bech about the mud wrestlers ("Who are all these cunts standing around like cops?") and then abruptly departs to get another drink (192). This brief encounter, however, remains the story's most memorable moment, allowing Updike an opportunity to riff on Carver's ascent in the literary world. The caricature of the Carver-like Klegg is wonderfully amusing—and offers evidence of what a fantastic vehicle Henry Bech was for Updike—as it mimics the bleak subject matter and the minimalist style that had distinguished Carver's first two story collections, *Will You Please Be Quiet, Please?* (1976) and the aforementioned *What We Talk About When We Talk About Love*. These collections had not only established Carver's career, but they also had helped introduce a new wave of short story writers whose careers came to reshape American fiction. As Mark McGurl observes, "one could say that the citizens of Carver Country included not only the downbeat people who populate Carver's own stories but the large group of short story writers—Tobias Wolff, Ann Beattie, Jayne Anne Phillips, Frederick Barthelme, Amy

Hempel, Mary Robinson, and others—who rose to collective and individual prominence in the late 1970s and 1980s under the banner of the ordinary, the modest, the minimal, and the real" (279–80).

Three decades later, it is almost impossible to overstate the impact that Carver's fiction had on the trajectory of American fiction during the early 1980s, and "White on White" offers a revealing, if somewhat askew, snapshot of the moment when Carver's influence was beginning to be felt fully. The emergence of Carver's career resonates throughout the story; Bech appears unmoored as he struggles with his separation from his wife and the renewed celebrity that his new novel has generated. His description of Klegg is not so much a product of writerly jealousy; instead, Bech finds in his colleague yet another variation of himself: a man uncertain of his motive or direction whose words have elevated him to the strange sphere of celebrity. The story concludes with Bech basking in the admiration of his colleagues, yet still desiring to go home with one of the mud wrestlers whom he had talked to earlier in the evening. "Radiant America; where else but here? Still, Bech, sifting the gathering with his inspired gaze, was not quite satisfied," Updike writes in the story's concluding lines. "Another word occurred to him. Treyf, he thought. Unclean" (195). The story's final lines are wonderfully rendered with Bech returning to the Jewish term for unclean, a sentiment that could apply to himself as well as to the cultural spectacle that he is witnessing.

Nevertheless, Bech's diagnosis of Klegg's fiction—that the younger writer's elliptical style is a symptom of his all-consuming alcoholism—points toward the tenuous relationship that exists between Updike and Carver's work, a tension that has prevented critics from reading these two writers, perhaps the two most acclaimed and influential American short story writers of the past sixty years, together. Born only six years apart (Updike in 1932, Carver in 1938), Updike and Carver have been typically and somewhat mistakenly viewed as having belonged to different generations: Critics have tended to align Updike with writers who were a decade or so older than him (John Cheever,

Saul Bellow, J. D. Salinger), whereas Carver's career has been usually read alongside the younger writers (Richard Ford, Tobias Wolff, Fredrick Barthelme, Bobbie Ann Mason) whose fiction had been shaped by his early work. Part of the problem for this misconception is that Updike was so firmly established when *Will You Please Be Quiet, Please?* was published in 1976; Updike's first book of poetry, *The Carpented Hen, and Other Tame Creatures* was released in 1958 when he was only twenty-six, and by the mid-1970s he had long been recognized as one of the premier writers of his generation. While Updike maintained a much longer and consistently productive career, both men came from rural backgrounds—Updike grew up in the small town of Shillington, Pennsylvania, while Carver's childhood was spent in the town of Yakima, Washington—and their fiction was largely shaped by the experience of having grown up in towns that were, in many ways, isolated from the rest of the world. More broadly, both grew up in the shadow of the Depression and their formative adult years were shaped by the economic and political expansion that United States experienced in the wake of the World War II.

For his part, Carver tended to cite Updike as an influence of sorts and, in interviews he would typically include him in the list of contemporary writers who he most admired; in his essay "On Writing" (1981), Carver mentions Updike—alongside John Cheever, Anne Beattie, Cynthia Ozick, Donald Barthelme, and Barry Hannah—as a writer who possessed "a unique and exact way of looking at things, and finding the right context for expressing that way of looking" (728). Moreover, in the interviews collected in *Conversations with Raymond Carver* (1990), Carver frequently expresses his admiration for Updike's work, and in his *Paris Review* interview he singles out *Too Far to Go* (1979), a collection of short stories tracing the marriage of Richard and Joan Maple, as being a particular favorite (Simpson and Buzbee 46). This is not to say that Carver's view of Updike was purely referential; in an amusing episode recounted in Carol Sklenicka's biography when Carver was teaching at Syracuse he assigned Updike's

1965 novel *Of the Farm*, a selection that baffled the class. One of his former students, C. J. Hribal recalls Carver opening class by saying, "Jeez, I read this years ago and I hadn't read it again till last week. You know, it's not very good, is it?" (380).

Updike also wrote warmly of Carver and his work, but his comments tend to echo the reservations that Bech voices in "White on White." In an interview from 1987, Updike noted that when he "[reads] somebody like Carver—who of course is no young writer, he's about my age, but in a way he belongs much more to the younger writers now than I do—and his work, in spirit and prose texture and even in feeling, is sort of exquisite: his stories are like highly polished porcelain pieces. Every word is worked over. Under the seeming colloquial casualness there is this wonderful craft. But you often wonder, 'Why is he telling me this?'" (McNally and Stover 199). Beyond just suggesting an anxiety that he is no longer being read as seriously by younger writers, Updike's comments point to the large differences in prose style and plotting that most clearly distinguishes the writers' work. The wonderfully rendered epiphanies that emerge in Updike's finest short stories—"A&P" (1960) and "Separating" (1974) to name two of the more prominent examples—are models of the post-Joyce short story. Speaking of the latter story, in which the long-suffering marriage of Richard and Joan Maple is brought to a breaking point, James Schiff remarks that "[f]ew stories are more perfect than 'Separating,' perfect in the sense that it appears free of artifice, as if the author is simply and naturally telling the story of a family's breakup, and yet it is in actuality artfully constructed, with recurring motifs, salient metaphors, and a stunning epiphany" (122).

In contrast to Updike's finely wrought stories, Carver's narratives are stripped down, rejecting the stylistic fireworks and neat symmetry that characterize a story like "Separating." At its most radical, as seen in the elliptical tales that constitute *What We Talk About When We Talk About Love,* Carver's style punctures the sense of wholeness that a story like "Separating' strives to achieve—an approach that owes as much (if not more) to the aggressive editing of Gordon Lish than Carver's own artistic aims. Despite these differences in style and approach, Updike and Carver ultimately have a great deal in common and there is much to be gained by reading their depictions of men in crisis alongside one another. Taken together, their work provides a rich social history of the postwar nation, chronicling the lives of married (or once-married) men attempting to negotiate the uncertainties of American life in the latter part of the twentieth century. Frequently separated by class, their male protagonists nevertheless behave similarly, betraying the ones that love them and moving to fulfill their most immediate desires regardless of the damage it might inflict on their family or themselves.

Updike's most famous character, Harry "Rabbit" Angstrom, the ex-high school basketball star turned Toyota salesman whom Updike chronicled over the course of four novels, offers a wonderfully comprehensive case study in male selfishness. Throughout the tetralogy, Rabbit commits numerous transgressions against his family: At various points in the series, he leaves his pregnant wife only to impregnate another woman; carries on an affair with a former teammate's wife; and, in the series' final book, *Rabbit at Rest* (1990), he has sex with his daughter-in-law. Yet, Rabbit remains something of an exception among Updike's unfaithful husbands, possessing a callousness and obtuseness that is largely lacking from his other male protagonists. The more typical Updike husband—Piet Hanema in *Couples* (1968), Richard Maple in *Too Far to Go* (1979), and Owen Mackenzie in *Villages* (2004)—struggles with his own guilt as he decides on whether or not to leave the confines of marriage. Throughout his fiction, Updike plays out the various results that adultery might have, relishing in considering the innumerable consequences that these illicit unions might yield: In *Couples*, Piet marries his lover, Foxy Whitman, and the new couple is exiled from the community; in *Marry Me* (1976) and *Memories of the Ford Administration* (1992) the husband remains in the marriage; in *Villages*, the first wife is surprisingly killed off in a car crash.

In meticulously chronicling the possible outcomes that adultery might have, Updike depicts his men as deeply flawed and, at times, astonishingly selfish creatures, while his female characters—Joan Maple, Janice Angstrom, and Angela Hanema—are not only the more sympathetic figures but also the more dynamic characters. The impetus behind his fiction is not so much to explain or justify his characters' behavior—despite his professed Christianity, little judging occurs in Updike's fiction—but instead it is to describe, to transform lived experience through the prism of art and language. This proclivity for presenting his male protagonists' shortcomings and their narcissism is particularly evident in "Marching through Boston" (1965), one of the early Maple stories; in the tale, Joan convinces her husband Richard to participate in a civil rights march, even though Richard is suffering from a cold. "*How* could you crucify me that way?" Richard whines near the end of the story. "*How* could you make this miserable sick husband stand in the icy rain for hours listening to boring stupid speeches that you'd heard before anyway?" (*Early Stories* 387). The story culminates with Richard unleashing a highly unflattering and offensive parody of black speech—"Shecks, doan min'me, chilluns. Ef Ah could jes' res' hyah foh a spell in de shade o'de watuhmelon patch, res dese ol' bones . . . Lawzy, dat do feel good!"—as his worried children watch and Joan attempts to put him to bed (388). The performance remains shocking and in its own way horrifically funny, but is also characteristic of how far Updike is willing to go to convey his protagonists' failings. In the closing lines of the story, Richard is described as "almost crying; a weird tenderness had crept over him in bed, as if he had indeed given birth, birth to his voice, a voice crying for attention from the depths of oppression" (388). Although much more could be said about Richard's identifying himself as an oppressed female sufferer, as one who is giving birth, the ending captures his nearly binding self-absorption without celebrating or mocking it. It is a delicate balance that Updike manages to hold, and it is one that typifies his treatment of his characters' poor behavior.

Similarly, Carver's stories trace the various offenses that men are capable of committing—whether it's the unemployed husband who coerces his waitress wife into losing weight in "They're Not Your Husband" (1973), the father who gives away the beloved family dog in "Jerry and Molly and Sam" (published as "A Dog Story," 1972), or the men who discover the body of a murdered young woman yet continue their fishing trip in "So Much Water So Close to Home" (1975). "He saw his whole life a ruin from here on in," Carver writes of Al, the unfaithful and unemployed husband who gets rid of the family dog in "Jerry and Molly and Sam." "If he lived another fifty years—hardly likely—he felt he'd never get over it, abandoning the dog. He felt he was finished if he didn't find the dog. A man who would get rid of a little dog wasn't worth a damn. That kind of man would do anything, would stop at nothing" (126). Suzy, the "goddamned" dog (and not surprisingly the discarded dog is female), momentarily becomes the object through which Al views his failures as a husband and a man. However, when he finds the dog near where he had dropped her, Al recoils from his possible shot at redemption, deciding once again to leave the dog behind: "[Al] sat there. He thought he didn't feel so bad, all things considered. The world was full of dogs. There were dogs and there were dogs. Some dogs you just couldn't do anything with" (128). The moral gymnastics that Al performs here, blaming the dog for her own abandonment, are typical of Carver's men as they attempt to account for their own bad behavior. Much like Updike, Carver does not celebrate his characters' bad behavior nor does he condescend or condemn a character like Al for his failings. While the conclusion does little to explain Al's unjustifiable act, the story's concluding lines serve as a useful epigraph for both Carver and Updike's unfaithful husbands: Their fiction makes a strong case for the view that some "dogs" just can't be changed.

Beyond just depicting the various crimes and misdemeanors that men are capable of, Updike and Carver's fiction hinges on the experience of guilt, in particular the guilt of leaving a marriage. Perhaps no other American writers have provided such complex accounts of married life in the middle decades of the twentieth century, a period that not only saw the average marrying age drop, but also the advent of the birth control pill and the loosening of divorce laws. As Elaine Tyler May has observed, the generation who came of age in the early years of the Cold War "were part of a cohort of Americans who lowered the age at marriage for both men and women and quickly brought the birthrate to a twentieth-century high after more than a hundred years of steady decline, producing the 'baby boom'" (1). Both Updike and Carver's first marriages were in many ways typical of their generation as both married young and started a family soon thereafter. Updike married his first wife, Mary Pennington, in 1953 after his junior year at Harvard (she had just graduated from Radcliffe) and had four children by the end of 1960. The couple separated in 1974 and was granted a no-fault divorce two years later; Updike would marry Martha Bernhard the following year, a union that survived until his death in 2009. Similarly, Carver married Maryann Burk when he was nineteen and she was sixteen, and Maryann would give birth to their first child, a girl they named Christine, six months after their wedding, and their second child, Vance, would be born the following year. Much like Updike's first union, Carver's marriage would survive until the late 1970s; he would meet the poet Tess Gallagher in 1977, and they would remain a couple and eventually marry shortly before his death in 1988. Moreover, both men quickly fell into long-term relationships after separating from their first wives and their second marriages somewhat overlapped with their first unions as Updike had initiated his relationship with Bernhard before the divorce from Pennington was granted in 1976 while Carver lived with Gallagher for nearly three years before the divorce with Burk had been made final on October 18, 1982. Despite the largely domestic focus of much their work and the fact that both became fathers at relatively young ages, Updike and Carver seemed to have had little to say about children and, with few exceptions, children play a largely peripheral role in their work. Instead, their stories tend to center on the experiences of the relationship itself as both writers chronicle the slow dissolution of their early marriages.

Not surprisingly, the experiences of Updike's and Carver's first marriages would be the implicit subject of much of their most memorable fiction—terrain that both frequently returned to in their later work. Indeed, the memory of Carver's first marriage pervades his post–*Please Be Quiet* collections and the early days of the marriage—the young husband and wife striving to achieve their wildest ambitions while also raising small children—often appears like a mythical past; the divorced narrator of "Everything Stuck to Him" (also published as "Distance," 1975) recalls to his grown daughter that he and her mother had once been "two kids [who] . . . were very much in love. On top of this they had great ambitions. They were always talking about the places they were going to go" (305). The romanticism of this recollection, however, is dampened by the distant language the father employs: As he attempts to explain the past to his daughter, he cannot tell the story in first person but instead describes himself and his wife as if they were characters in some long-forgotten fairy tale.

A similar nostalgia permeates Updike's postdivorce fiction as his aging narrators attempt to account for and momentarily re-experience the pleasures and the guilt of their former union. "In memory's telephoto lens, far objects are magnified. First wives grow in power and size, just as the children we have had by them do," Updike writes in "First Wives and Trolley Cars" (1982), a short story that was published, strangely enough, in the opening section of his essay collection *Odd Jobs* (1991):

They knew you when, and never let that knowledge go. Their very ability to survive the divorce makes them huge, as judges and public monuments are huge. Tall and silent, they turn at the head of the stairs, carrying a basket of first-family laundry, and their face is that of Vermeer's girl with the pearl earring, of Ingres's Grande Odalisque, of all the women who look at us over their shoulders in endless thoughtful farewell. (21)

The passage is in many ways characteristic of the ambivalence with which Updike's divorced and remarried husbands treat the end of their marriages. These characters rarely express remorse for the separation—and most appear comfortably remarried—yet they exhibit an almost compulsive desire to revisit that now bygone past, the days when they were newly married and erotic possibilities seemed to linger in the air. In "Atlantises" (1978), the concluding story in *Problems* (1979), the divorced and remarried protagonist—this time his name is Farnham—sees his former life as a lost paradise that he no longer has access to: "Rather suddenly, it seemed, all was sunk beneath the water; temples, gardens—all was lost, though an occasional Christmas card floated to the surface, and the gaze of some vanished child, wanting to be taken home, would well up from the sparkle of a flat sidewalk and break Farnham's expatriate heart" (257). A comparable nostalgia pervades Updike's subsequent fiction; as his protagonists age, the present moment appears of less interest and the desire to ruminate on the past—to evoke the pleasures of a more substantial seeming period—increase. "The parties had been vehicles for flirtation and exploration, a train of linked weekends carrying them all along in a giddy den; he and his friends were in the prime of their lives and expected that, as amusing and wonderful as things were, things even more wonderful were bound to happen" (21), Craig Martin recalls of the suburban parties that had dominated his social life in his twenties and thirties in "Personal Archeology" (2000), one of the stories collected in Updike's posthumous collection *My Father's Tears* (2009).

In the aftermath of their divorces, Updike's male protagonists relish (and at times fetishize) their guilt, their guilt-laden memories becoming the mechanism through which they can revisit the past. Indeed, Updike's fiction tends to cling to moments of guilt; in the aforementioned "Separating," Richard Maple savors the moment that he announces to three of his children (his eldest son is at a rock concert) that he and their mother are separating for the summer, a trial separation that will eventually become permanent. Having agreed to tell the children individually, Richard breaks down at the dinner table, but the moment itself—the thin border separating the past from an uncertain domestic future—is delicately preserved: "They became, his tears, a shield for himself against these others—their faces, the fact of their assembly, a last time as innocents, at a table where he sat the last time as head. Tears dropped from his nose as he broke his lobster's back; salt flavored his champagne as he sipped it; the raw clench at the back of his throat was delicious. He could not help himself" (*Early Stories* 791). By so carefully preserving such moments, Updike transforms them, giving them an aesthetically pleasing shape and resonance that enables his protagonists a means through which they can momentarily re-experience the past. "A guilt-gem is a piece of the world that has volunteered for compression," Updike writes in "Guilt-Gems" (1977), the penultimate story in *Problems*. "Those souls around us, living our lives with us, are gaseous clouds of being awaiting a condensation and preservation—faces, lights that glimmer out, somehow not seized, save in this gesture of remorse" (251). Oddly enough, guilt manifests itself as a pleasurable psychological experience for Updike's divorced protagonists. By separating individual moments (the mixture of champagne and tears in "Separating," the memory of his daughter's crestfallen face as he tags her out in a softball game in "Guilt-Gems"), Updike's protagonists reduce a much larger and ambiguous past into a beautiful object that they can recall and appreciate when the mood strikes them.

Guilt plays an equally large role in Carver's stories of marital distress, but his characters experience guilt in a fundamentally different way that begins to illuminate a key difference between the two writers and their craft. Carver's fiction frequently obscures the key moments—the moment of separating from one's wife, of breaking the news to the children—that Updike's work so carefully preserves. If Updike uses language to transform his amorphous guilt into something new and useable, Carver's seemingly haphazard narratives point toward the enormous guilt that his characters are unwilling to articulate, a guilt that underlies most of his short stories. The troubled husbands in his work can rarely identify the moment when things went wrong for them in their marriages, and the stories they voice often appear as distractions from the more difficult narratives that they are unwilling to share or acknowledge. In "Feathers" (1982), the opening story of *Cathedral* (1983), a character named Jack tells of a night that he and his wife, Fran, went to go visit another couple, Bud and Olla, who have recently had a baby but who also keep a pet peacock. The narrative ostensibly centers on Jack and Fran's reactions to this strange pet, but it's not until the end of the story that Jack confesses that his marriage had failed in some fundamental, yet indefinable way after the encounter with bird: "Later, after things had changed for us, and the kid had come along, all of that, Fran would look back on that evening at Bud's place as the beginning of the change. But she's wrong. The change came later and when it came, it was something that happened to other people, not something that could have happened to us" (376). Moments such as this not only radically alter our reading the story—within a single paragraph the story morphs from being a bizarrely humorous character study of a couple who keep a peacock to being a portrait of a marriage unraveling—but it is also striking for how little it tells us about what actually happened to Jack and Fran's relationship. The implication is that such stories simply cannot be told, not necessarily because the narrator is unwilling, but because he has somehow lost access to the material—as if the separation had occurred to "someone else."

Jack's inability to diagnose what happened to his relationship with his wife repeats itself throughout Carver's later fiction as his characters attempt to account for what went wrong with their first marriages. An enormous sense of guilt pervades these later pieces—"Chef's House" (1981), "Careful" (1983), "Intimacy" (1986), "Blackbird Pie" (1986), "Menudo" (1987)—yet Carver's husbands and wives remain unable to define what actually derailed their marriages. While his male protagonists typically avoid recounting the details of the betrayals that had led to their divorces, they remain acutely aware of that past as it continues to reverberate in their current life in the form of disgruntled ex-wives, financially dependent grown children, and aging parents. Nevertheless, Carver's characters' failure to recount what actually happened to destroy their marriages results both in a profound sense of disconnect from that past and the contradictory desire to return to their fragmented memories of that time in hopes of piecing together an even incomplete narrative of that time. This sense of disconnection from the past is perhaps most readily apparent and fruitfully presented in "Blackbird Pie," arguably Carver's finest story. Taking its title from the nursery rhyme "Sing a Song of Sixpence," the story is narrated by a middle-aged man, an amateur historian of sorts, who attempts to recount the night his wife left him. The story hinges on a letter that the narrator's wife "purportedly" dropped under his door on the night in question, a letter that he claims his wife could have never written because the handwriting was not hers (598). As critic Ewing Campbell has noted, "Blackbird Pie" appears to be Carver's nod to the surrealism of Kafka and Barthelme as no explanation is ever given for the mysterious letter and the story emanates "a strange, dreamlike indefiniteness, which gives the narrative an uncanny effect" (79). Adding to the confusion is the fact that the narrator has lost the letter his wife gave him that night, and while he reassures his audience that he has a "good memory," his attempt to reconstruct the letter's contents suggests that he has little insight on his marriage. Midway through the story, the narrator presents random fragments of the charges that his wife had made against him in the letter:

> withdrawing farther into . . . a small enough thing, but . . . talcum powder sprayed over the bathroom, including walls and baseboards . . . a shell . . . not to mention the insane asylum . . . until finally . . . a balanced view . . . the grave. Your "work" . . . .Please! Give me a break. . . . . Not one, not even. . . . Not another word on the subject! . . . The children . . . but the real issue . . . not to mention the loneliness. . . . Jesus H. Christ! Really! I mean (605–6)

The list of charges brilliantly recalls snippets from Carver's earlier stories, but the narrator's refusal to recreate this portion of the letter suggests his complete unwillingness to confront the problems that had plagued his marriage. The implication is that the elided material might tell the real story, but our narrator, despite his excellent memory, does not have the power, or perhaps the desire, to tell that story. Such stories can only be alluded to; they cannot be fully told.

The failure, however, to tell this story gives it more power and furnishes the past with an almost mythic splendor. "I'd like to say it was at this moment, as I stood in the fog watching her drive off, that I remembered a black-and-white photograph of my wife holding her wedding bouquet," the narrator admits toward the end of the story. "She was eighteen years old—a mere girl, her mother had shouted at me only a month before the wedding. A few minutes before the photo, she'd got married. She's smiling. She's just finished, or is just about to begin, laughing. She is three months pregnant, but the camera doesn't show that, of course" (612). The memory here, a recollection preserved through the photograph, points to a now remote-seeming past, one that almost seems incredible with the passage of time. A similar sense of mystery characterizes Updike's treatment of his characters' youthful marriages, unions that had begun during the relative innocence of the 1950s and that had slowly dissolved during the social and political upheavals of the following two decades. "Now: our babies drive cars, push pot, shave, menstruate, riot for peace, eat macrobiotic," the narrator of Updike's "When Everyone was Pregnant" (1971) laments near the end of the story. "Wonderful in many ways, but not ours, never ours, we see now. Now: we go to a party and see only enemies. All the years have made us wary, survival-conscious" (*Early Stories* 450). While Updike frequently appears more unabashed in his nostalgia for the past than Carver, both writers in their post-divorce fiction eulogize the innocence and hopefulness that seem, with the passage of time, to now characterize their early married days, an innocence that appears increasingly appealing in the aftermath of the personal and cultural changes that occurred in subsequent decades.

Despite their vast differences—differences in class, education, prose style, and temperament—both Carver and Updike were ultimately haunted by their memories of their first marriages, and much of their most successful fiction centers on the enormous guilt that was the irreducible byproduct of their divorces. "He was not certain, but he thought he thought that he had proved something. He hoped he had made something clear," Carver writes of the estranged husband who has just severed his wife's telephone line in "A Serious Talk" (1980). "The thing was, they had to have a serious talk soon. There were things that needed talking about, important things that had to be discussed" (296). Such conversations, of course, never occur in Carver's fiction as his protagonists seem unable to take ownership of the destructive behavior that destroyed their relationships. Although Carver's characters appear unable to articulate their remorse for their poor behavior while Updike's characters compulsively revisit their guilty memories, the results are largely the same: Their characters can never adequately account for the dissolution of their youthful marriages nor absolve their lingering guilt for the pain that their actions have caused; the "Why?" that Richard Maple's oldest son asks of his father at the conclusion of "Separating" remains painfully unanswered in both writers' work (798). Such questions are, in the end, probably unanswerable; narrative can capture such moments—or transform them into something more usable and beautiful—but it cannot fully resolve them.

Note

1. I was reminded of Updike's caricature of Carver in "White on White" by Raymond Jacobs's column "Klegg the Drunk: John Updike on Raymond Carver," which appeared on the website *PopMatters*. The bulk of the essay is devoted to a reminiscence of having seen Updike speak during his promotion tour for his 2006 novel *Terrorist*, but at the end of the post Jacobs cites this particular passage while considering Updike and Carver's relationship. "It was more than cheap literary gossip that compelled Updike to paint his brief, stark portrait

of Carver as Klegg the drunk," Jacobs declares at the end of his post. "The two writers had more in common than the common reader may suspect, and, briefly, Updike, the moralist and aesthete to Carver's gruff alcoholic Everyman, acknowledged their bond and kinship."

Works Cited

Campbell, Ewing. *Raymond Carver: A Study of the Short Fiction*. New York: Twayne, 1992. Print.

Carver, Raymond. *Collected Stories*. Eds. William L. Stull and Maureen P. Carol. New York: Lib. of Amer., 2009. Print.

Jacob, Raymond. "Klegg the Drunk: John Updike on Raymond Carver." *PopMatters*. PopMatters Media, 8 March 2012. Web. 1 June 2012.

May, Elaine Tyler. *Homeward Bound: American Families in the Cold War*. 20th Anniversary Ed. New York: Basic, 2008. Print.

McGurl, Mark. *The Program Era: Postwar Fiction and the Rise of Creative Writing*. Cambridge: Harvard UP, 2009. Print.

McNally, T. M. and Dean Stover. "An Interview with John Updike." *Conversations with John Updike*. Ed. James Plath. Jackson: UP of Mississippi, 1994: 192–206. Print.

Schiff, James A. *John Updike Revisited*. New York: Twayne, 1998. Print.

Simpson, Mona, and Lewis Buzbee. "Raymond Carver." *Conversations with Raymond Carver*. Ed. Marshall Bruce Gentry and William L. Stull. Jackson: UP of Mississippi, 1990: 31–52. Print.

Sklenicka, Carol. *Raymond Carver: A Writer's Life*. New York: Scribner, 2009. Print.

Updike, John. *Bech Is Back*. New York: Knopf, 1982. Print.

___. *The Early Stories, 1953–1975*. New York: Knopf, 2003. Print.

___. *My Father's Tears and Other Stories*. New York: Knopf, 2009. Print.

___. *Odd Jobs: Essays and Criticism*. New York: Knopf, 1991. Print.

___. *Problems and Other Stories*. New York: Knopf, 1979. Print.

Feminist Perspectives on the Works of Raymond Carver

Claire Fabre

The two decades spanned by Carver's writing career, from the late 1960s through the 1980s, coincided with the years during which feminism, both as a political force and a critical discourse, was in full bloom in the United States, Canada, and Europe. It is currently considered that feminist criticism has entered its third generation, an age of "postfeminism," in which feminist assumptions no longer rely on the postulate of intrinsic feminine or masculine "essence," according to French critic Frédéric Regard (8). The overt political stance that "protofeminist" works bore in the eighteenth and nineteenth centuries has gradually shifted to a more complex approach, according to which femininity and masculinity are considered as phenomena to be read in their "social, cultural and discursive dimension(s)" (Regard 8). In effect, femininity and masculinity do not exist per se, yet the belief that they do exist still informs cultural stereotypes, which are considered by many to be cultural invariants. In other words, studying fiction from a postfeminist point of view consists partly in analyzing the discourses that construct and deconstruct both female and male identities and, most important, in showing that the literary text is a privileged locus for the disruption of gender dividing lines.

The latest developments in the field of gender studies have thus offered new perspectives both on Carver's treatment of male and female identity in his stories and on the presence of feminist discourse in their undercurrents. Such was the challenge of the second issue of the *Raymond Carver Review*, published online in 2010. These essays proposed groundbreaking ideas that will be used here as guidelines for an overall reading of gender issues in Carver's *Collected Stories*, ranging from the variety of female figures who appear in the stories, the necessity to redefine masculinity and the variably successful attempts at doing so (Zarranz 30),[1] the underlying critique of male-dominated social discourse, the crossing of gender boundaries, and the appropriation of language as an empowering tool by women (Fachard 10).

This essay intends to show that, despite the superficial impression that Carver's short stories fit the social stereotypes generally attached to "male" culture, they can be read as avant-garde instead, even more than two decades after their author's death. The following study is based on a selection of short stories that will hopefully shed light on Carver's whole body of work. Fishing and hunting stories such as "Distance," "Nobody Said Anything," and "The Calm" put the codified values of masculinity to the test through the evocation of these traditionally male activities and provide both the literal and metaphorical material for the expression of the protagonists' desires. Then readers will see that stories such as "Tell the Women We're Going" and "So Much Water So Close to Home" adopt a critical angle to address the underlying violence of the gender dividing line. Finally, it might be relevant to focus more specifically on stories that are either narrated by women or whose point of view is that of a woman, such as "Why Don't You Dance?" and "The Bridle," which offer valuable metafictional insights.

Feminist Discourse

Though Carver's prose does not overtly promote feminist positions, traces of feminism can nevertheless be found in his work. Clearly the stories in which women are represented are far from being univocal or dogmatic, and Carver's feminism is of a rich and subtle form, which deconstructs social stereotypes rather than reinforces them.

For instance, as critic Vasiliki Fachard has shown, the story "Fever" offers a multiplicity of feminine figures that can all be interpreted as successive embodiments of the emancipation women were experiencing in the late 1970s. According to Fachard's reading of the story, Debbie, the adolescent babysitter, stands for the immature girl who has not yet grappled with her own feminine identity, a confused character who cannot relate to the world of men other than through temporary loss of identity (with her boyfriend) or confrontation (with the narrator). Her inaptitude at taking care of the children and the house exemplifies the still nascent state of her awareness. Opposite Debbie stands the wife Eileen, who has abandoned the house and her children in favor of accomplishing herself both artistically and personally. Carol, the narrator's girlfriend, who only has occasional sexual relationships with the narrator, also represents one of the multiple facets of womanhood. Lastly, the governess, Mrs. Webster, appears as a fully developed woman who is able to take care of the household (children and domestic chores), the narrator (she cures him when he has a fever), and her own husband (Fachard 16).[2] In other words, she is the ephemeral figure who can restore order to the narrator's chaotic intimate life, but who ultimately leaves him to face reality. Her providential intervention is quite unique in Carver's world, whose stories generally preclude this kind of positively endowed character. In spite of her definitely positive and transcending powers—or because of them—the governess is consistently reminiscent of the disquieting character of the governess in Henry James's 1898 novel *The Turn of the Screw*.[3] Although the story never veers into the fantastic, the "perfection" of the character is tinged with a sense of improbability and uncanniness that never leaves the narrator's consciousness—or that of the reader. This fundamental ambiguity of the character prevents the story from veering into a theoretical stance in favor of a "feminist" approach, leaving indirectness to prevail.

"He and She Stories"

Rather than through open discourse, male and female stereotypes are indirectly undermined by the antiheroic posture of the protagonists and by the crises they undergo. In several stories, activities such as hunting and fishing, which might have been expected to stage all the values of traditional male heroism, reveal the characters' weaknesses and doubts instead of asserting their power.

In "Distance," the narrator is having a conversation with his daughter who asks him about the past: In the episode he recounts to her the contradictions he first refuses to confront about hunting—"But there are all kinds of contradictions in life. You can't think about all the contradictions" (*Collected Stories* 920)—ironically backlash on him as he has to face the personal dilemma of either staying close to his wife and distressed baby or remaining loyal to his male friend who has offered to take him out goose hunting. The demands of domesticity are clearly at odds with the understated values of male loyalty, as the wife and the baby are the obstacles he needs to overcome in order to remain faithful to his word. The whole story thus stages the character's inner conflict and the plot is seemingly resolved by the "decision" not to go hunting after all.[4] The enthusiasm about the outing had been indirectly expressed by the care with which he prepared his gear, a paragraph in which the word "hunting" was repeated no less than four times:

> He was happy about going hunting the next morning. He was happy about going hunting, and he laid out his things a few minutes later: hunting coat and shell bag, boots woolen socks, brown canvas hunting cap with fur earmuffs, 12-gauge pump shotgun, long john woolen underwear. (*Collected Stories* 919)

After his failed attempt, he spills his breakfast on the very clothes that had been the locus of his jubilatory anticipation:

> He spread butter and poured syrup over the waffle, but as he started to cut into the waffle he turned the plate into his lap.
>
> I don't believe it he said, jumping up from the table.
>
> The girl looked at him, then at the expression on his face, and she began to laugh.
>
> If you could see yourself in the mirror, she said and kept laughing.
>
> He looked down at the syrup that covered the front of his woolen underwear, at the pieces of waffle, bacon, and egg that clung to the syrup. He began to laugh. (*Collected Stories* 925)

Naturally, this situation is quite typical of the frequent domestic catastrophes and the more or less tragic consequences the characters have to face in Carver's other stories. Prosaic details, and especially food items, can usually be interpreted as the focus onto which emotions are displaced (Nesset 21).[5] In the case of "Distance," one is tempted to read this episode as the victory of the triviality of the everyday over heroic action and the triumph of a miniature instance of domestic happiness over the overall difficulties of life. The picture of this young man dirtying his underwear definitively undermines the virile stereotype of the hunter. This is confirmed by the end of the story, which sums up the failure of the couple: "After that morning there would be those hard times ahead, other women for him and another man for her, but that morning, that particular morning, they had danced" (*Collected Stories* 926). Not only does the hunting expedition never take place, but the narrator's efforts are met by Carl's dismissal, who verbally "shoots" him: "'You should have stepped to the phone and called me, boy,' Carl said. 'It's okay. Shoot, you know you didn't have to come over here to tell me. What the hell, this hunting business you can take it or leave it. It's not that important'" (*Collected Stories* 924).

"The Calm" is another hunting story that has recently been reconsidered by critics as a text in which typical "male culture" is both shown and questioned. Following the scholarship of literary critics Josef Benson and Libe Garcia Zarranz, one can assert that the story stages traditional male stereotypes and debunks them simultaneously. The social signs and symbols of masculinity are strongly exhibited at the beginning of the story. The scene takes place at a barbershop where the customers all seem to fit the stereotypes of virility:

I was getting a haircut. I was in the chair and three men were sitting along the wall across from me. Two of the men waiting I'd never seen before. But one of them I recognized, though I couldn't exactly place him. I kept looking at him as the barber worked on my hair. The man was moving a toothpick around in his mouth, a heavyset man, short wavy hair. And then

I saw him in a cap and uniform, little eyes watchful in the lobby of a bank. (*Collected Stories* 297)

Beyond the presence of phallic symbols in the story, such as tooth-picks, cigarettes, and boots, the coarse language used by Charles, who tells the story of the hunt, promises to reinforce the masculine atmosphere. However, when one compares the story told by Charles and the framing story told by the narrator, most of the narrative undercuts those assumptions, a movement that is initiated by the discrepancy between Charles's physical appearance and his voice, as the narrator notices: "I didn't like the man's voice. For a guard, the voice didn't fit. It wasn't the voice you'd expect" (*Collected Stories* 297). Under the sign of such discordance, the whole story shows the failure of stereotypical male behavior: The deer hunt is bungled by the hungover son who shoots the deer but only wounds him, leaving the place covered in blood: "Drinking beer and chasing all night, then saying he can't hunt deer. He knows better now, by God. But sure, we trailed him. A good trail, too. Blood on the ground and blood on the leaves. Blood everywhere. Never seen a buck with so much blood. I don't know how the sucker kept going" (*Collected Stories* 299). After such a description, the old customer implicitly accuses Charles of not respecting the hunting codes and of indulging in feminine passivity: "You ought to be out there right now looking for that deer instead of in here getting a haircut" (*Collected Stories* 299). Significantly, Charles has to be content with a "spike," in other words, a deer that has not yet reached maturity and that he did not even shoot himself. After all of the customers have left the barbershop one by one, the narrator is left alone with the barber and experiences a moment of shared sensuality, which can be read as an opening toward homoeroticism:[6] "He ran his fingers through my hair. He did it slowly, as if thinking about something else. He ran his fingers through my hair. He did it tenderly, as a lover would" (*Collected Stories* 301). The story can thus be read as an interesting shift from the failure of stereotyped masculinity to a reinvention of male relationships, based on complicity and tenderness rather than on competition and violence. The change that the narrator's epiphany expresses at the end of the story remains unspecified but it is undoubtedly anchored in a remodeling of traditional gender assumptions (Bullock 347).[7]

"His Side, Her Side"—Crossing Lines?

Couples in Carver's stories are rarely happy. They can be on the verge of breaking up, or trying to reconcile, or simply dealing with the aftermath of adultery or divorce. Instead of drawing a typology of all these situations, readers may look closely at the short story "Why Don't You Dance?"—which almost reads like a fable summing up the various ages and crises of ordinary couples. As is sometimes the case in Carver's stories, none of the characters have a proper name but each is designated through their generic identity: "the man," "the boy," and "the girl." This sense of economy is further conveyed by the opening paragraph in which readers see all the furniture that has been taken out by the man onto his front lawn:

> In the kitchen he poured another drink and looked at the bedroom suite in his front yard. The mattress was stripped and the candy-striped sheets lay beside two pillows on the chiffonier. Except for that, things looked much the way they had in the bedroom—nightstand and reading lamp on her side. *His* side, *her* side. He considered this as he sipped the whiskey. (*Collected Stories* 751)

Although the description is factual, the whole couple's history is presented in a single nominal phrase: "*His* side, *her* side," and the comma reads like what French philosophers Gilles Deleuze and Félix Guattari would call a "rigid line of segmentarity" (Deleuze and Guattari 216), one of those lines that divide the world binarily, originally for political reasons. The dichotomy expressed in this one sentence suffices to evoke the whole past history of a married couple, their habits, their

comforts, and their routines but also because of the warlike conno-
tations attached to the word *side*, their multiple crises and conflicts.
Although the man faithfully reproduces the pattern of his home to the
public view, his turning his house "inside out" disrupts the normal order of things and induces a series of other transgressions. The young
couple that visits the place, initially thinking it is a yard sale, may represent the return for the man of his now-defunct relationship. By inviting the young couple to dance in his living room, to his records,
he is creating a stage where he becomes a voyeur of his own past.
But transgression becomes particularly dangerous and disquieting for
the girl when the man wants her to dance with him, inviting her to
cross both the temporal and generational lines, not to mention the implicit adultery line. What she experiences on that day is unnamable, as
obscure and mysterious to her as desire itself: "She kept talking. She
told everyone. There was more, she knew that, but she couldn't get it
into words. After a time, she quit talking about it" (*Collected Stories*
755–56). Even though the stage created by the man is made up of his
props, the girl is the one who wants to make love with her boyfriend
in the bed. As the narrative moves from an external point of view to
the girl's point of view at the end of the story, readers may reread the
whole story as an appropriation of feminine desire.

From "He and She Stories" to "Her Stories"

While there are relatively fewer stories narrated by women than by
men in Carver's work, they all crucially address the question of feminine desire, and storytelling is often viewed as an empowerment tool
for women who otherwise feel trapped in stifling lives. "So Much Water So Close to Home" is a story in which the central focus is the appropriation of feminine desire under the cover of an ostensibly "masculine" story. There are two versions of this story,[8] the longer one of
which Carver himself had selected for his last collection *Where I'm
Calling From* (1988). As many critics have already shown, the narrator's role is much more active and ambiguous in the longer version, to

the extent that she can be viewed as a manipulative or even unreliable narrator. Indeed, although the material of her story can be summed up in very few words (during a fishing expedition her husband and his friends find the dead body of a young girl in the river but they decide to keep on fishing, stay overnight, and go to the police the next day), all the narrative choices she makes show that the real focus of the story is on the crisis this event has triggered in her relationship and in her own identity. In the opening dialogue between the narrator Claire and her husband, the reader is left with the suspicion that someone has committed murder and possibly rape, but Claire's husband refuses to cut short his trip to report the crime: "Goddamn it, why can't people mind their own business? Tell me what I did wrong and I'll listen! It's not fair. She was dead, wasn't she? We talked it over and we all decided. We'd only just got there" (*Collected Stories* 864). Several strata of discourse are superimposed in Claire's narrative: the *doxa* of respectability, "They are decent men, family men, responsible at their jobs" (*Collected Stories* 865); the men's desires as she indirectly re-creates them through her language, "all the while the flashlights of the other men played over the girl's body" (*Collected Stories* 866); and finally, her own identification with the young girl, "I look at the creek. I float toward the pond, eyes open, face down, staring at the rocks and moss on the creek bottom until I am carried into the lake where I am pushed by the breeze" (*Collected Stories* 870). The fact that Carver preferred the longer version of the story confirms that its interest lies in the critical interpretation of the facts and the implicit denunciation of violence, even though Claire's vision is muddled by her unconscious desire to identify with the victim.

A comparison of the two versions of the story "Tell the Women We're Going,"[9] which considers violence against women from the men's point of view, corroborates the latent repudiation of male violence against women.[10] Indeed, a detailed analysis would show that Bill's point of view is much more fully developed in the longer version, and that his reluctance to follow Jerry on his drunken spree offers a critical, if weak, counterpoint to his friend's brutality.

Telling stories empowers both men and women in Carver's fiction in a paradoxical way: It does not give them answers or definitive opinions—on the contrary, it enables them to question the rigid lines of readymade categories. Gender issues in Carver's work are tied to his treatment of stereotypes in general and his constant wish to avoid any form of oversimplification. The close reading of these stories from the angle of gender confirms that significant subversion of clichés springs from minor displacements, syntactical games, and subtle changes in viewpoints. If readers can dub Carver a "postfeminist," it is precisely because the displacement (or remodeling) of gender lines takes place within a more global questioning of identity, types, and codes.

Her Voice, His Voice

The main Carver stories told by women are "Fat," "The Idea," "Why, Honey?," "I Could See the Smallest Things," "So Much Water So Close to Home," and "The Bridle," as well as "Preservation," "The Student's Wife," and "Why Don't You Dance." In each of these stories, the woman's voice is eager to achieve self-assertion and self-definition, and to simultaneously acknowledge her limitations. Just as the young woman of "Why Don't You Dance?" was confronted with the difficulty of passing on her story, so is the narrator of "Fat," who gives up trying to share her experience: "That's a funny story, Rita says, but I can see she doesn't know what to make of it. I feel depressed. But I won't go into it with her. I've already told her too much" (*Collected Stories* 7). Although Carver never explored the territory of metafiction per se, it is possible to suggest that these brief comments on the difficult task of storytelling somehow resound with questions on authorship in general. In this perspective, "The Bridle" can be read both as a story and as a commentary on the fictional process, as readers follow Marge's struggle to record and make sense of the minutest events she witnesses. Her lodge-apartment is the vantage point from which she observes all the tenants of the condominium she and her husband, Harley, look after for a living. The Holits family, and especially Betty Holits, is the focus of her attention, as is evident in this passage of the beginning of the story when Marge is showing the apartment to the Holits for the first time:

> "I guess we won't waste any more time. I guess we'll take it." Holits looks at her as she says it. This time she meets his eyes. She nods. He lets out breath through his teeth. Then she does something. She begins snapping her fingers. One hand is still holding the edge of the drainboard, but with the other hand she begins snapping her fingers. Snap, snap, snap, like she was calling her dog, or else trying to get somebody's attention. Then she stops and runs her nails across the counter. I don't know what to make of it. Holits doesn't either. He moves his feet. (*Collected Stories* 499–500)

As the story moves on, we understand that Marge gradually merges her own identity with that of Betty Holits and that the destiny of this ungraspable character enables her to follow a redemptory line of flight, at least in her imagination. One could say that Marge is almost a fictional version—if metaphorical and stylized—of the author himself: she pays attention to the smallest details,[11] and she tells about other people's lives without really taking part in them. Like all of Carver's narrators, her questions as to the meaning of things and gestures remain suspended in indeterminacy, which tends to drill metaphysical holes in the midst of the narrative. What is more, she signs her name on the fifty-dollar notes the Holits paid her for rent, and she imagines the bills traveling across the country: "I think about one of those bills changing hands during Mardi Gras. They could go anyplace, and anything could happen because of them. I write my name in ink across Grant's broad old forehead: MARGE. I print it. I do it on every one. Right over his thick brows. People will stop in the midst of their spending and wonder. Who's this Marge? That's what they'll ask themselves, Who's this Marge?" (*Collected Stories* 500). Just like an author of fiction, Marge is eager to leave her imprint on the "margins" of papers that will circulate among strangers and trigger their imaginations. The words she uses to describe herself thus resonate with metafictional accents: "I call myself a *stylist*. That's what my cards say. I don't like the word *beautician*. It's an old-time word" (*Collected Stories* 497). Such a statement reminds us that Carver's aesthetics is indeed about "style" and its capacity to embrace detail, rather than about a grandiloquent and outdated conception of "beauty."

The most recent wave of gender criticism has thus enabled a (re) reading of Carver's work as one that disrupts formulaic representations of gender dividing lines. Although Carver rarely espoused feminist stances overtly, his treatment of marital tragedies and the constraints imposed on women within a patriarchal world suggest his awareness of most of the issues addressed by feminist criticism. There is no denying that "many of Carver's women . . . are trapped in the monotony of unsatisfying routines [and] their inability to liberate themselves from these routines is linked by many feminist critics to the plight of women within patriarchy", as has been argued by literary critic Aoileann Ní Éigeartaigh (43); however, this author has also shown that domesticity was not the exclusive domain of women in Carver's work, as all characters seemed equally trapped in the constraints of the everyday. The rejection of codified male heroism, together with a form of empowerment achieved by a few female characters (namely through language and storytelling) shape Carver's own brand of feminism, in which one can recognize his inimitable voice: both critical and tender, slightly ironic, and poignantly insightful.

Notes

1. As Libe García Zarranz put it at the end of her essay "Passionate Fictions": "As some Carverian critics like Robert Miltner or Vickie Fachard have anticipated, a third wave of Carver scholarship is beginning to show its face. In fact, many hidden regions in Carver Country are longing for revision if we consider those feminist voices and spaces that are still unheard and the queer homoerotic desire that pervades some of his most well-known collections. It is high time now to

blow the dust off Carver's pages and unveil the hidden desires that are still in the closet of this male icon of American literature" (30).

2. Fachard notes that "Mrs. Webster's voice, steady and reassuring as opposed to the febrility in Eileen's, is the only one that soothes and heals him from the 'fever' he has succumbed to at the closing of the story. Significantly, her feminine voice is the one the story ends with, investing her with the role of representing the maturity needed to integrate feminism's principles without severing herself from others. With her, feminism has come to fruition, its message assimilated so as to become productive, caring, healing and, above all, capable of reconciling the two sexes to each other" (Fachard 16–17).

3. James's novel *The Turn of the Screw* is told from the point of view of the governess who is a highly ambivalent and disquieting character, and she is often cited as the paragon of unreliable narrators.

4. However, the text never mentions any decision on the character's part but rather a form of passive acceptance of his wife's arguments and of his friend Carl's advice.

5. Hence the fish cut in half in "Nobody Said Anything" can be interpreted as a metaphor for the splitting up of the narrator's family as critic Kirk Nesset has shown, arguing that, "in 'Nobody Said Anything' a sickly green steelhead—nebulously tied to family disintegration, a chief concern in the story—is cut in half Solomonwise with a knife by the narrator and brought home, and while the fish tends to glow with tentative meaning, Carver the author chooses not to spell it out" (Nesset 21–22).

6. As Libe García Zarranz puts it, "Playing with male identification by employing mirrors and metaphors of the double, Carver manages to transform a masculinist scenario where men use toothpicks and discuss violent stories into a place of homoerotic possibility between the barber and the protagonist" (29).

7. Chris Bullock comes to a similar conclusion in his study of "Cathedral," writing, "How attainable is the new masculinity imaged in the cathedral? Treating masculinity as architecture emphasizes the importance of socialization, of that which is built rather than simply given. In both Easthope and Foucault, the constraining aspect of the metaphor predominates; there seems little chance of breaching the modern fortress-prison. Carver offers a more optimistic vision. His narrator, initially presented as firmly under the constraint of castle and Panopticon, receives the help of a mentor and is able to take one of the mechanisms of constraint—the television—as the source of an image of alternatives. Carver's point seems to be that what is built can be differently built, however constrained the conditions. Thus 'Cathedral' offers an encouraging lesson for modern men struggling themselves with the architecture of masculinity" (Bullock 347).

8. The longer one was originally published in 1975 and the shorter one in 1976. Both versions appear in the *Collected Stories*, respectively on pages 273–79 and 864–83. This study will exclusively focus on the longer version, which Carver himself had selected for *Where I'm Calling From* (1988).

9. The short version is to be found page 258 and the longer version page 831 of the *Collected Stories*.

10. On this subject, see Sandra Kleppe's enlightening essay "Women and Violence in the Stories of Raymond Carver," in the *Journal of the Short Story in English* 46 (2006): 107–27.

11. Just like the narrator of "I Could See the Smallest Things", who is also a woman.

Works Cited

Benson, Josef. "Masculinity as Homosocial Enactment in Three Stories by Raymond Carver." *Carver and Feminism.* Spec. issue of *Raymond Carver Review* 2 (2009): 81–95. Web. 25 Sept. 2013.

Bullock, Chris. "From Castle to Cathedral: The Architecture of Masculinity in Raymond Carver's 'Cathedral.'" *Journal of Men's Studies* 2.4 (1994): 343–51. Print.

Carver, Raymond. *Collected Stories.* Ed. William L. Stull and Maureen P. Carroll. New York: Lib. of Amer., 2009. Print.

___. *Where I'm Calling From: New and Selected Stories.* New York: Vintage Contemporaries, 1988. Print.

Chiland, Colette. *Changer de sexe* [*Changing sex*]. Paris: Odile Jacob, 1997. Print.

Deleuze, Gille, and Félix Guattari. *A Thousand Plateaus.* Trans. Brian Massumi. London: Continuum, 2004. Print. Trans. of *Mille Plateaux.* Paris: Editions de Minuit, 1980. Print.

Fachard, Vasiliki. "Four Female Voices in 'Fever': Introduction to Feminism and Carver." *Carver and Feminism.* Spec. issue of *Raymond Carver Review* 2 (2009): 10–19. Web. 25 Sep. 2012.

Kleppe, Sandra Lee. "Women and Violence in the Stories of Raymond Carver." *Journal of the Short Story in English* 46 (2006): 107–27. Print.

Nesset, Kirk. "The Final Stitch: Raymond Carver and Metaphor." *Profils Américains 4: Raymond Carver.* Ed. Claudine Verley. Montpelier, Université Paul-Valéry, 1993. Print.

Ní Éigeartaigh, Aoileann. "Space, Domesticity and the Everyday: Re-reading Raymond Carver's Women." *Carver and Feminism.* Spec. issue of *Raymond Carver Review* 2 (2009): 34–53. Web. 25 Sep. 2012.

Regard, Frédéric. *L'écriture féminine en Angleterre, perspectives postféministes* [*Women's writing in England, postfeminist perspectives*]. Paris: Presses Universitaires de France, 2002. Print.

Zarranz, Libe García. "Passionate Fictions: Raymond Carver and Feminist Theory." *Carver and Feminism.* Spec. issue of *Raymond Carver Review* 2 (2009): 20–32. Web. 25 Sep. 2012.

CRITICAL READINGS

First Inclinations: The Poetry of Raymond Carver_____
Robert Miltner

Most readers of Raymond Carver's stories can tell you that his 1976 fiction collection *Will You Please Be Quiet, Please?* was his first book from a trade press. Many however are unaware that in 1974, Carver published *Put Yourself in My Shoes*, a limited edition, single-story chapbook in the Capra Chapbook series that included authors Anaïs Nin and Henry Miller. Perhaps even less well-known is that among Carver's earliest publications were three collections of poetry: the chapbook *Near Klamath* (1968) and two full-length collections, *Winter Insomnia* (1970) from Kayak Press and *At Night the Salmon Move* (1976), also from Capra Press. Clearly, from the beginning of his writing career, Raymond Carver's poetry was interlaced and concurrent with his fiction. He repeatedly told interviewers a seemingly apocryphal anecdote about how, when he was an undergraduate at Humboldt State University in California, he received, on the same day, acceptance letters for his first poem and his first off-campus story (Simpson and Buzbee 36).[1] The linking of poetry and fiction as two concurrent tracks of writing are supported by his statement that "there's more of a similarity between writing a short story and writing a poem than there is between writing a short story and writing a novel" (Pope and McElhinny 13). Moreover, in an interview with William Stull, he qualified the similarities by first acknowledging an overlapping of narrative and imagery, then adding the commonality of "economy and unity," and "capturing and holding a moment," as well as a similarity of process: "I write my stories and poems in the same way, building from one word to the next, one line or sentence to the next" ("Matters" 187).

A study of Raymond Carver's poetry shows three phases to the body of his poetic work. The "early poems"—as seen in *Near Klamath, Winter Insomnia, At Night the Salmon Move*, and the uncollected poems gathered in the posthumous 1991 collection *No Heroics, Please*—show a young man discovering his craft. The "late poems"—*Where*

Water Comes Together with Other Water (1985) and *Ultramarine* (1986)—introduce a mature man in his "second life" of sobriety. The "last poems"—*A New Path to the Waterfall* (1989)—present a man facing his own mortality. Furthermore, a relatively common trajectory can be seen between Carver's poetry and the fiction for which he is better known.

The Early Poems

Readers of Raymond Carver's early poems encounter the stereotypical masculine persona evident in American culture during his formative years in the 1950s. The speaker in many of these poems is a close fit to the profile of what writer Norman Mailer labeled in 1963 as the "desperado mandate," a man who could

> fight well . . . love well and love many, be cool, be daring, be dashing, be wild, be wily, be resourceful, be a brave gun. . . . And this myth, that each of us was born to be free, to wander, to have adventure and to grow on the waves of . . . the unexpected, had a force which could not be tamed. (qtd. in Faludi 37)

This coming-of-age code shaped Carver's adolescence into what he would call the "bozo days" of his high school years in Yakima, Washington, "stealing hubcaps [and] hanging out with his pals" (Gallagher, *Carver Country* 9), and it continued into his early adult years, as his friend Richard Ford recalls in his memoir *Good Raymond*: "There was . . . a whole job set of 'Bad Raymond' stories . . . tales from drinking days . . . Cars towed away, rows with everyone, unpaid debts, stolen checks, stolen kisses, stolen time" (np). That Carver "enjoyed telling [the 'Bad Raymond' stories] on himself" (Ford np) suggests a "desperado" persona, ripe with source material for the storyteller in him both to hold forth with among friends and to select from and turn into either poems or stories about hard-drinking desperados, wild-loving 1950s males, imitations of literary models, and voyeuristic mirrored figures.

"Drinking While Driving"(3)[2] follows two restless young brothers who "do not have any place in mind to go, / [they] are just driving" and drinking from "a pint of Old Crow." The car functions as a vehicle for escape from "a sense of loss and faint desperation" ("On 'Drinking While Driving'" 179) by acting out his "removing himself from society . . . by driving ever faster on an empty road" (Faludi 15), as if in imitation of Jack Kerouac's *On the Road*. Here are the desperado and his sidekick seeking the unexpected, the thrill of the road with its seemingly infinite possibilities where "any minute now, something will happen," ("Drinking" 3) be it the excitement of engaging something new and unknown, or the menacing potential for a car accident.

Menace is also below the surface of "The Man Outside" (304), which introduces the reflected figure so characteristic of Carver's work. The window and the mirror are where the couple discover the voyeur, the "someone—/something, [that] breathes, shuffles" outside the bedroom window. The couple's acquiescence to the voyeur is discovered below the surface as they transform into exhibitionists: "But then I begin to demand more / and more of my wife. In shame she / parades up and down the bedroom floor," leading to what Sandra Lee Kleppe calls the "end weight" (69) of the poem as the first person narrator states:

> I touch my wife lightly
> and she springs awake anxious
> and ready. Lights on, nude, we sit
> at the vanity table and stare frantically
> into the glass. Behind us, two lips,
> the reflection of a glowing cigarette.

Believing that this poem "contains the most explicit treatment of voyeurism in Carver's poetry" (65), Kleppe holds that

> the voyeuristic project has become a joint effort in which the roles of the
> passive viewer and the active viewed overlap. The fusing of the images of

the 'glass' in front of the vanity table and the window becomes the focal point and physical location of the characters' intersecting contact. (70)

Here, the voyeur and viewed become paired, linked, connected in the moment of the poem, yet this poem is representative of Carver's signature use of paired characters whose lives mirror each other, as the Stones and the Millers in his short story "Neighbors" (8–13),[3] or the young couple and the older man in "Why Don't You Dance?" (223–27).

In "For Semra, with Martial Vigor" (11–13) the male narrator, in pursuit of the thrill of sexual conquest of a Turkish woman, views her as an exotic other, an idea reinforced by the references to the love poems of Lebanese American Kahlil Gibran and Afghani Omar Khayyam. Semra makes it clear to the narrator-writer that "in her country" where "Istanbul is the loveliest city," those with college educations "would never sweep floors," though the narrator-writer explains writers also pick fruit and work in mills—emphasizing the lived experiences that a writer channels into his work—and he is fully capable of offering to write her a love poem, since "all poems are love poems." But, all things being fair in love and war, Semra asks if he has served in the military; his drunken fumbling for a saber he can use to pose as an officer ends with "the teapot flying across the table" and Semra wondering why she let him "pick [her] up." Readers note here the influence of Charles Bukowski, a writer whose work is recognized for its conversational bar banter, distinctive voice with a forced machismo tone, sexist attitudes, and, as poet and critic Hayden Carruth notes, "stock figures from American Romanticism: noble drunks [and] downtrodden artists" (4). Carver claimed that Bukowski was "a kind of hero to me" in the early 1960s when his first poems were being published (Simpson and Buzbee 36), though where Bukowski's humor is expressed through irony and sarcasm, Carver's humor is more akin to situational comedy, as in the narrator-writer attempting a love poem on a napkin with a pencil, and to parody, as in the faux saber disturbing a teapot.

These poems show Carver looking for his poetic voice as he crafts, without intention, the early exhibition of the dominant lyric-narrative poem that would become the signature style of his later poems. Some of these same tendencies can be observed in his early fiction as well. Carver used the short stories of American writer Ernest Hemingway as models for his fiction, evidenced by the underlying menace in "Big Two-hearted River, Part II" (171–78) when Nick Adams is reluctant to wade into the deep water while fishing; readers see this in the fishing stories Carver wrote, such as "Pastoral" (193–204), which leads G. P. Lainsbury to claim that it is "a corrupted version of Nick Adam's experiences in 'Big Two-Hearted River'" (37), for "the Hemingway influence, such as it is, is more evident in Carver's early stories than in his later ones" (36). Moreover, as Kerry McSweeney argues, "Despite their differences, Hemingway remained a crucial point of reference for Carver in terms of both technique and stance" (97), yet his influence was so strong in Carver's early writing that a line from Hemingway's "Hills Like White Elephants" is "echoed in the title of Carver's story 'Will You Please Be Quiet, Please?'" (97–98); as Lainsbury has noted, "[f]rom the earliest reviews" of "Will You Please Be Quiet, Please?" "his debt to the fiction of Ernest Hemingway has been noted" (36). The same voyeurism seen in "The Man Outside" is central to the story "Neighbors" (8–13) as Bill and Arlene Miller "try on" the lifestyle of their friends, Jim and Harriet Stone, while apartment sitting. Readers observe Bill, after dressing in Jim's clothes, seeing himself as he "sat on a chair, crossed his legs, and smiled, observing himself in the mirror" (11), a scene that mimics the situation of "The Man Outside." Furthermore, in "Bicycles, Muscles, Cigarettes" (147–56), Evan Hamilton, agitated as he is trying to quit smoking, becomes angry with a neighbor's comment and turns suddenly violent as he

> lunged at the man where he stood on the porch. They fell heavily onto the lawn. They rolled on the lawn, Hamilton wrestling Berman onto his back

and coming down hard with his knees on the man's biceps. He had Berman by the collar now and began to pound his head against the lawn. (153)

Hamilton is the "wild" desperado, the "brave gun" who is able to "fight well," offering readers a more extended view of 1950s male whose persona is central to Carver's early fiction and poetry.

The Late Poems

During the period from 1975 to 1977 in which Carver published a chapbook of fiction and two full-length collections of stories, his alcoholism had become so debilitating that he was experiencing blackouts that led to hospitalization and finally treatment at a residential detox center, after which he commenced a "second life" of sobriety. At the age of thirty-nine, he moved beyond the "desperado" phase of his young adult life, operating in his post-alcoholic life like a man who has completed a midlife transition. He became a university professor, began and maintained a relationship with a new partner, poet Tess Gallagher; and his poetry—as well as his fiction—grew fuller, dealing with more middle-aged issues. When he received a Strauss Living Award that required he quit teaching and write full time for five years, he returned his attention to poetry, producing *Where Water Comes Together with Other Water* in 1985 and *Ultramarine* in 1986. These two books, which constitute the body of the late poems written during some of the last years of his life, are characteristically different from the early poems, both in style and content.

Most noticeable about the style of the late poems is Carver's shift to writing "lyric-narrative" poetry that characterizes his late poetry. Through the fusion of the lyrical (interior) and the narrative (exterior)—what Tess Gallagher calls "an interior (emotional progression) and an exterior (plot) narrative structure"—the "poet's imagination" is the hero, occurring "by virtue of the intimacy of the speaker's voice as it confides its fears and resolutions" ("Again" 74). For Carver, this meant that he was able to fuse the poetic/lyrical dimension with the prosaic/narrative dimension of his writing, writing perhaps more holistically than he had ever done before. After receiving the Strauss Award for his short stories, he moved to Port Angeles, Washington, returning to the Pacific Northwest of his childhood. The fusion of past and present, of poetry and prose, produced a rich period for Carver who told William Stull that "they gave me an award on the basis of my fiction, and the first thing I did was write two books of poems" ("Matters" 178). Furthermore, the content of the late work was different from the early work: fuller, more thoughtful, more confident and mature, poems that celebrated sobriety, memory, creativity, new relationships, and identity.

Occurring when it did in his life, Carver's transition to a recovering alcoholic operated in much the same way as a midlife transition did for other men in their early middle age. Because sobriety became his "second life," many of the poems in his late poetry focus on his life during and after alcoholism. Tess Gallagher has written, for example, that "when he finished a book, Ray asked me to choose a title and give the poems an order," including the poems in *Ultramarine* in which she "tried to emphasize the back and forth movement between his old alcoholic life and his life of sobriety and productive work" ("False Sky" 5).

"Next Year" (68), from *Where Water Comes Together With Other Water*, tells the sad tale of a codependent alcoholic couple in denial. They go out dancing then they "[pass] out / on the table." After they get pulled over and arrested on the way home, he "bailed her out [of jail] when he got out of Detox. / They drove home in ruins" to discover their daughter had run away from home, from their life style, from them. Throughout the poem, Carver using an incremental refrain to show the escalating denial: "wasn't the worst thing," "not the worst either," "not the worst," "still not the worst," because the worst is how

> They went on
> thinking they were the people they said they were.
> . . . . .

> Telling themselves that this time next year,
> this time next year
> things were going to be different.

Loss, ruin, destruction, devastation: this is the effect of alcoholism on a family. Carver turns his attention to the sober life with its recovery and rediscovery and creativity, however, in poems like "Hope" (159–60). Here, the wife and her boyfriend throw the husband out—it could almost be the same couple in "Next Year"—and she believes he will continue on his destructive path. Yet the situation changes, for the speaker in the poem relates how

> when I did show
> my face at that house again,
> months, or years, later, driving
> a different car, she wept
> when she saw me at the door.
> Sober. Dressed in a clean shirt,
> pants, and boots.

Whether the wife's joy is just for his recovery, or the implied possibility that they are meeting at this later time when each of them has recovered, the moment is one of forgiveness and tenderness. When paired, these two poems illustrate Carver's memories of his alcoholic "Bad Raymond" days and the sober "Good Raymond" days he was living as he wrote these poems.

Another emergent theme in the late poems is memory, evident from the opening lines of the first poem from *Where Water Comes Together With Other Water*, "Woolworth's, 1954" (3–5), as Carver states, "Where this floated up from, or why, / I don't know," remembering his first job at sixteen, his mid-adolescence and a mere two years before his early marriage to his wife Maryann Burk. Among these poems are those that consider his relationship with Maryann. "Where They'd Lived" (150) opens with a recognizable trope of "kicking through piles / of memories" of how he and Maryann had "lived by their wills, / determined to be invincible." But later, in the temporal space of a motel, he leans against a window and feels how the "cold air passed / through and put its hand over his heart." The coldness is, of course, from the emotional loss, but it also suggests his regret over the painful actions of his alcoholic past.

Other poems from this period consider the loss of his father, a typical midlife consideration as Carver considered his relationship, as a father, with his own children, set against his being a grown man and his father's death. This latter is seen in the poem "My Dad's Wallet" (89–90) as the speaker and his mother visit the undertaker to make final arrangements. When his mother takes the father's wallet from her purse, it is "old and rent and soiled. / But it was my dad's wallet," and from it they extract "a handful of money that would go / toward this last, most astounding trip." This poem is contrasted with the idea of loss as well as a positive memory in the penultimate poem in *Where Water Comes Together With Other Water*, "The Trestle" (136–37), another poem about his father. The poem opens with Carver confessing his self-disappointment, chastising himself for "wasting [his] time this morning," and is "deeply ashamed" for not getting up to go fishing in his father's memory, even though he thought of his father the night before. The missed opportunity prompts a memory of being "a kid sitting on a timber trestle, looking down. / Watching my dad drink from his cupped hands." To salvage the loss, he turns to his art, to creativity and writing to restore him, as he imagines himself turning

> From bed to desk back to childhood.
> From there it's not so far to the trestle.
> And from the trestle I could look down
> and see my dad when I needed to see him.

Carver completes the transition from destruction to creativity as he recognizes that:

> I know it's time I changed my life.
> This life – the one with its complications
> and phone calls – is unbecoming

These changes in his relationship with his father mirror the changes in his own personal life. His children had grown and were living their own lives, and Carver began making recompense for the past, as in the case of his son Vance who moved to Syracuse to attend college when Carver taught there, so that, "Able to offer his son something, Ray had become, at forty-two, a proud father" (Sklenicka 363).

Transition is clearly central to the late poems, evidenced by the title poem (63–64) of *Where Water Comes Together With Other Water*, an occasional piece Carver wrote for his forty-fifth birthday. As he inventories the kinds of water that excite him—creeks, rills, springs, streams, rivers, the sea—he considers the growth, the flow, ultimately to the sea, then connects his observation of the natural world to his own life:

> I'm 45 years old today.
> Would anyone believe it if I said
> I was once 35?
> My heart empty and sere at 35!
> Five more years had to pass
> before it began to flow again.

This poem demonstrates Carver's acknowledgement that in the years between alcoholism and sobriety: his heart, like the water, has begun "to flow again."

Offsetting the loss of his father and the end of his marriage was his new relationship with poet Tess Gallagher. *Where Water Comes Together* opens with the memory of "Woolworth's, 1954," which ends with the word "dead" as Carver remembers how some of the girls he used to date when he was young have aged or died. Yet the poem that ends the book, "For Tess," in which he considers his own mortality—"until it really sank in: Dead"—is ultimately a celebration and appreciation of her positive impact on his sober life, as he tells Tess how "I thought of you. /I opened my eyes then and got right up / and went back to being happy again. / I'm grateful to you, you see. I wanted to tell you."

While the poem expresses gratitude to Tess Gallagher directly, it also is a poem about gratitude for his new life as shown through the poems with their mature themes, observing that "the wind in the tops of the trees. The same wind / that blows out on the Strait [of Juan de Fuca], but a different wind, too." But it may also offer comment on how Carver's identity was changing in his sober period. In the same poem, "For Tess," he not only accepts his mortality, but the way he views his own life. Despite the water being "rough" and "whitecapping" while he is fishing—he is "fine" with not catching any fish; in fact, he "felt so happy [he] had to quit / fishing." An avid fisherman and occasional hunter—still proving himself in some vestige of the desperado—he has discovered a contentment through his new identity.

"If this sounds / like the story of life, okay," he says at the conclusion of the first stanza of "Locking Yourself Out, Then Trying to Get Back In" (73–74), a seminal poem regarding his changed identity. Discovering he has "shut the door without thinking," Carver tries the ground floor windows, but to no avail, so, from the outside, he looks inside at "the sofa, plants, the table / and chairs, the stereo set-up. / My coffee cup and ashtray," then climbs up to the second floor where he still has no access, as he looked in at his "desk, some papers, and my chair." But the poem shifts when Carver reflects on what the totality of the experience is like:

> This is not like downstairs, I thought.
> This is something else.
> And it was something to look in like that, unseen,
> from the deck. To be there, inside, and not be there.

Carver is conscious that this is a different life he is living, and by gaining objectivity on his life he is able to conclude "I brought my face close to the glass /and imagined myself inside, / sitting at the desk. Looking up /from my work. " Like the early voyeurism in "The Man Outside," Carver is both mirroring himself and acting as a self-voyeur, looking from the outside into his new life. So he stands in the rain that symbolically washes away the past, and thinks for a moment that this situation is comical, that there are worse things than being locked out, for he describes how

> Even though a wave of grief passed through me.
> Even though I felt violently ashamed
> of the injury I'd done back then.

These are the thoughts of a mature man accepting responsibility for his past actions, owning his feelings without denial. He addresses relationships ("people I had loved then), memory ("injury I'd done back then), mirroring/self-voyeurism ("that beautiful window"), creation (going back in, writing the poem), and the sad necessity of destruction sometimes to make space for that creativity as, at the end, he tells how "I bashed that beautiful window. / And stepped back in." This final action represents the intersection of the narrative—"bashing" and "stepping"—and the lyrical, as it operates symbolically, emblematically of his interior need to return to the new life he saw inside the house, and not outside looking in on it. In a sense, this poem encapsulates the late lyric-narrative poetry; located in Port Angeles, in the Pacific Northwest where he grew up, he not only steps back into his new life, but returns home, literally and symbolically.

Carver's fiction during this period, the stories published as "New Stories" in *Where I'm Calling From* and published as a separate book, *Elephant*, in the United Kingdom, represent new directions for him as well. "Boxes" (533–45), the story of a man who helps his mother move back to California, and "Elephant" (583–97), about a man who works incessantly to support his family members, show characters with the same tendency toward responsibility that Carver showed toward his own life in the poems. "Intimacy" (561–68) is primarily a story of memory—of reclaiming memories—as a writer visits his ex-wife looking for material for new stories, as is "Blackbird Pie" (598–613), though in the latter story the nature of the memories are suspect, especially regarding identity of the letter writer and the full reason why it was delivered. Yet "Intimacy" and "Menudo" (569–82) are also about men who act responsibly regarding their relationships with women in their lives and are linked through the common image of the men cleaning up after themselves; the narrator in "Intimacy" says there are "piles of leaves everywhere I look. . . . I can't take a step without putting my shoe into leaves. . . . Somebody ought to get a rake and take care of this" (568), while at the end of "Menudo," Mr. Hughes rakes leaves out of his yard and a neighbors' yard:

> I rake our yard, every inch of it. It's important it be done right, too. . . .
> There are other yards, more important yards for that matter. I kneel, and,
> taking a grip low down on the rake handle, I pull the last of the leaves into
> my bag and tie off the top. (581–82)

The late poems of Raymond Carver, as well as the stories written during that time, are relatively consistent thematically in their treatment of responsible, middle aged narrators and characters who are recovering their lives.

The Last Poems

In late 1987, Raymond Carver experienced pulmonary hemorrhages; like Chekov, about whose death from tuberculosis he had written just a year previously in "Errand" (614–25), Carver's lungs were diseased. Diagnosed with lung cancer, he died in his sleep on August 2, 1988. Though the period of his last poems was brief, his final book, *A New*

Path to the Waterfall (published posthumously, in 1989), was different from the late poems in style and content.

The book was not only comprised of new work, but also brought older poems forward. The most significant change in style was one influenced by the Polish Nobel laureate Czeslaw Milosz, whose book *Unattainable Earth* (1986) Carver had read, and that "began to affect his idea of the form and latitude his own book might have" (Gallagher, *New Path* xix). Milosz had experimented with what he referred to as "a more spacious form," one in which process and product—by showing the poet's context for the poems—would merge in "one book, along with my poems, poems by others, notes in prose, quotation from various sources and even fragments of letters from friends" (xiii). By using a spacious form himself in *A New Path to the Waterfall*, Carver was also able to blend art and life, so that readers encounter a mixed-genre collection that includes new and old poems, poems and excerpts from other writers (especially Chekhov), a prose memoir, and quotations.

Regarding content, poems in *A New Path to the Waterfall* added new themes, such as childhood innocence, "traps and violences of the real," and "stages of awareness . . . as he moved toward death" (Gallagher *New Path* xxiii–xxvii), and of these themes, the most dominant is the latter, evidenced in the number of obvious time-related titles: "Sunday Night" (257), "Nearly" (2802), "Wake Up" (287–9), "Afterglow" (293), and "Late Fragment" (294). Two of the more pronounced poems about Carver's "awareness" of his impending death are "What the Doctor Said" (289) and "Another Mystery" (255).

"What the Doctor Said" is a monologue, by the speaker in the poem, of the dialogue he had with his doctor on the day he was informed of his lung cancer. Unpunctuated and conversational, it moves quickly, almost a blur that emulates the shock of the moment recollected in the aftermath:

> He said it doesn't look good
> he said it looks bad in fact real bad

The repetition of the phrase *he said* evokes the micro fiction/minimalist trope of the "he said—she said" dialogue model, suggesting the dramatic effect of the moment, and adds the anaphora common to poetry. The central passage of the poem is critical:

> he said are you a religious man do you kneel down
> in forest groves and let yourself ask for help
> when you come to a waterfall
>
> . . . .
>
> do you stop and ask for understanding at those moments
> I said not yet but I intend to start today.

The waterfall acts as a symbol here, as a zone of important contact, as the place where transitions are evident. The appearance of the waterfall also refers to the poem "Looking for Work" (237–38), one of the poems brought forward from *Winter Insomnia* (1970), in which the speaker finds "a new path / to the waterfall," symbolic in that instance for a place of miracles and dreams, as the place he would catch the brook trout that he "always wanted . . . for breakfast."

The other poem that comments on his "awareness" of death is "Another Mystery." The speaker recalls going with his father to pick up the suit his grandfather would be buried in, followed by the memory of his own father "dressed . . . gruesomely / in a cheap sports coat and tie, / for the occasion." Using the theme of memory threads through the late poems, the speaker states how "today I reeled this clutter up from the depths," recalling the opening line of "Woolworth's, 1954," then the speaker recalls picking up his own suit, the one he will be buried in. Standing in the sunlight, he "tore a hole through to the other side" of the plastic bag, literally, but the linking of the lyric and the narrative here configures the "other side" as that place he imagines on the other side of life, referring back to the first stanza in which he recalls how, as a boy, "Those days, [death] was just another mystery."

In the finely honed, lyric-narrative style that he had discovered in his late poems, Carver wrote the poems of his own impending death. His legacy as a fiction writer, as the American Chekhov, is certain, though his legacy as a poet continues to grow. First and last, his work was as a poet, though readers can see the similarities at any given period of his writing running close to the topics and themes of his fiction. In the final poem of his life, "Late Fragment" (294), he stated what he had hoped he had gotten from his life: "To call myself beloved, to feel myself / beloved on the earth." That poem is inscribed on his grave marker in Port Angeles, Washington, where he is buried. Listed on his grave, at his request, is how he wished to be remembered: poet first, followed by short story writer, then essayist. In time, we may agree with him.

Notes

1. The poem was "The Brass Ring," published in *Targets* 11:35 (September 1962), and the story was "Pastoral," published in *Western Humanities Review* 17:1 (Winter 1963).
2. All poems cited are from *All of Us: The Collected Poems by Raymond Carver* (New York: Knopf, 1996).
3. All stories cited are from *Collected Stories* by Raymond Carver (New York: The Library of America, 2009).

Works Cited

Carver, Raymond. *All of Us: The Collected Poems*. Ed. William Stull. New York: Vintage, 2000. Print.

___. "Bicycles, Muscles, Cigarettes." *Collected Stories* 147–56. Print.

___. "Blackbird Pie." *Collected Stories* 598–613. Print.

___. "Boxes." *Collected Stories* 533–45. Print.

___. *Collected Stories*. Eds. William Stull and Maureen Carroll. New York: Lib. of Amer., 2009. Print.

___. "Drinking While Driving." *All of Us* 3. Print.

___. "Elephant." *Collected Stories* 583–97. Print.

___. "Errand." *Collected Stories* 614–25. Print.

___. "For Semra, with Martial Vigor." *All of Us* 11–13. Print.

___. "Hope." *All of Us* 159–60. Print.

___. "Intimacy." *Collected Stories* 561–68. Print.

___. "Locking Yourself Out, Then Trying to Get Back In." *All of Us* 73–74. Print.

___. "The Man Outside." *All of Us* 304. Print.

___. "Matters of Life and Death." Interview by William L. Stull. Gentry and Stull, 177–91. Print.

___. "Menudo." *Collected Stories* 569–82. Print.

___. "My Dad's Wallet." *All of Us* 89–90. Print.

___. "Neighbors." *Collected Stories* 8–13. Print.

___. "Next Year." *All of Us* 68–69. Print.

___. "On 'Drinking While Driving.'" *No Heroics, Please: Uncollected Writings*. New York: Vintage, 1992. Print.

___. "Pastoral." *Collected Stories* 193–204. Print.

___. "Raymond Carver." Interview by Mona Simpson and Lewis Buzbee. Gentry and Stull 31–52. Print.

___. "Raymond Carver Speaking." Interview by Robert Pope and Lisa McElhinny. Gentry and Stull 11–23. Print.

___. "The Trestle." *All of Us* 136–37. Print.

___. "Where Water Comes Together With Other Water." *All of Us* 63–64. Print.

___. "Why Don't You Dance?" *Collected Stories* 223–27. Print.

___. "Where They'd Lived." *All of Us* 150. Print.

___. "Will You Please Be Quiet, Please?" *Collected Stories* 171–89. Print.

___. "Woolworth's, 1954." *All of Us* 53–55. Print.

Carruth, Hayden. "Images." *Bookletter* 31 March 1975: 4. Print.

Faludi, Susan. *Stiffed*. New York: Perennial, 2000. Print.

Ford, Richard. *Good Raymond*. London: Harvill, 1998. E-book.

Gallagher, Tess. "Again: Some Thoughts on the Narrative Impulse in Contemporary Poetry." *A Concert of Tenses: Essays on Poetry*. Ann Arbor: U of Michigan P, 1986. 67–82. Print.

___. "Carver Country." *Carver Country: The World of Raymond Carver. Raymond Carver*. Photographs by Bob Adelman. Introduction by Tess Gallagher. New York: Scribner's, 1990. 8–19. Print.

___. "False Sky." *New Paths to Raymond Carver: Critical Essays on His Life, Fiction, and Poetry*. Sandra Lee Kleppe and Robert Miltner, eds. Columbia: U of South Carolina P, 2008. 1–7. Print.

Gentry, Marshall Bruce and William L. Stull, eds. *Conversations with Raymond Carver*. Jackson: UP of Mississippi, 1990. Print.

___. Introduction. *New Path to the Waterfall: Poems*. By Raymond Carver. New York: Atlantic Monthly P, 1989. Print.

Hemingway, Ernest. "Big Two-hearted River, Part II." *The Complete Short Stories of Ernest Hemingway*. The Finca Vigia Edition. New York: Scribner's, 1987. 171–80. Print.

___. "Hills Like White Elephants." *The Complete Short Stories of Ernest Hemingway*. The Finca Vigia Edition. New York: Scribner's, 1987. 211–14. Print.

Kleppe, Sandra Lee. "Raymond Carver's Poet-Voyeur as Involved Spectator." *New*

Paths to Raymond Carver: Critical Essays on His Life, Fiction, and Poetry. Sandra Lee Kleppe and Robert Miltner, eds. Columbia: U of South Carolina P, 2008. 62–74. Print.

Lainsbury, G. P. The *Carver Chronotope: Inside the Life-World of Raymond Carver's Fiction*. New York: Routledge, 2004. Print.

McSweeney, Kerry. *The Realist Short Story of the Powerful Glimpse: Chekhov to Carver*. Columbia: U of South Carolina P, 2007. Print.

Milosz, Czeslaw. *Unattainable Earth*. New York: Ecco, 1986. Print.

Sklenicka, Carol. *Raymond Carver: A Writer's Life*. New York: Scribner, 2009. Print.

Cycling Fiction: On the Structure of Raymond Carver's Three Major Story Collections

Randolph Runyon

Textual evidence suggests that Gordon Lish edited Carver's collections *Will You Please Be Quiet, Please?* and *What We Talk About When We Talk About Love* with two aims in mind. One was to make Carver into what came to be called a "minimalist," a term Carver himself rejected, by cutting the stories to their bare bones and giving them a harder edge. The other aim was to create unified collections by arranging the stories so that they would appear to relate and even sometimes refer to each other, and by making slight changes and adding small details that would increase these internal connections. In other words, Lish's editing was both subtractive and additive. Lish also edited *Cathedral*, but bowing to Carver's insistence he made only minimal changes to its stories. Consequently that collection was welcomed by readers as evidence of a new and more generous Carver. But it was actually what Carver would have been all along had Lish not intervened. A famous instance of this is the *Cathedral* story "A Small, Good Thing," which Lish had deprived of its feel-good ending when it appeared as "The Bath" in *What We Talk About*.

This essay will show how several of the stories in these three major collections were arranged and in many instances altered from their original separate publication so that together they would create a unified esthetic whole. Taking note of the effect of this arrangement and of the alterations allows us to see aspects of the stories that were not apparent before. Yet to some extent those aspects were not there when the stories were separately published, particularly when some of the words are changed when they appear together in a collection. The alterations undoubtedly enhance the esthetic qualities of the collection but at the possible expense of reducing the emotional charge of the individual stories. It is clearly a trade-off. One way to account for this, perhaps to have one's cake and eat it too, is simply to admit that we are talking about different texts: one is the individual story, the other is the collection.

There is a basic similarity of plot between the first two stories in *Will You Please Be Quiet, Please?* The mere fact that the stories have been arranged in this way brings out the similarity. In "Fat" a waitress fantasizes about becoming fat like the obese man she served in the restaurant; in "Neighbors" the Millers fantasize about becoming their next-door neighbors, putting on their clothes, lying on their bed. A couple of small details create additional connections: the waitress' husband remembers two fat men he knew, one of whom was his next-door neighbor, and he wishes he had their pictures so that he could show them to his wife. Mrs. Miller finds some pictures in their neighbors' apartment that she invites her husband to see, but then she suddenly realizes she's inadvertently locked herself out of the neighbors' apartment, with the result that she won't be able to show her husband the pictures. The pictures become as inaccessible as the ones the waitress' husband never had in the first place.

Fascination with sexually exciting neighbors returns in the third story, "The Idea." Vern and his wife spy from their window at the couple next door, watching as the husband peers through his own bedroom window at his wife undressing. In Carver's original version of this story the last words were "the house shook against the wind" ("The Idea" 84), providing an echo to the last words of "Neighbors": "They leaned into the door as if against a wind, and braced themselves" (*Collected* 13). Carver gave his editor Gordon Lish free rein in preparing the stories in this collection for publication, and Lish deleted the last sentence, with the result that the story ends with an almost brutal abruptness: "I used even worse language, things I can't repeat" (17). Carver allowed Lish to arrange the stories in *Will You Please* and *What We Talk About* as he wished, yet in the processing of writing and revising them he may have had ideas of his own about how they might be arranged. The original echo linking the last sentences of "Neighbors" and "The Idea" could have worked across the pages of a collection even if the stories were not contiguous there. Yet the fact that both stories are about neighbors (and about one set of neighbors aware of what the other set is doing while the latter are unaware that they are doing so) has a potentially self-reflexive resonance if the two stories are themselves neighbors in the collection.

We may never know how Carver might have arranged the stories had he had free rein to do so, but apart from the fact that "Neighbors" and "The Idea" work so well together, when we read the fourth story, "They're Not Your Husband," we might well wonder why it was not placed immediately after "Fat," as it is almost its mirror-reversed image. In "Fat" a waitress dreams of becoming as obese as one of her customers so that she can dominate her husband. When he starts making love to her, she tells us, "I suddenly feel I am fat. I feel I am terrifically fat, so fat that Rudy is a tiny thing and hardly there at all" (7). In "They're Not Your Husband" a husband exerts his dominance over his waitress wife by making her lose weight. Sitting at the counter of the restaurant, he had felt ashamed to hear two male customers who were observing his wife bend over to scoop up some ice cream comment on how fat she was. But this story at the same time parallels "The Idea," in which a husband spies on his wife, who has her back turned to him, as if he were not her husband but a total stranger. In "They're Not Your Husband" the husband returns to the restaurant after his wife has lost nearly ten pounds, so much that her waitress uniform no longer fits, and pretends to be a total stranger to his wife as he tries to get another customer to notice how good she looks from behind (23).

Nevertheless, an intriguing connection links "They're Not Your Husband" with the story that follows it, "Are You a Doctor?" In browbeating his wife to lose weight, the husband made her weigh herself each morning on the bathroom scales and kept a record (20), consulting it each time she was weighed. "The paper was covered with dates, days of the week, numbers. He read the number on the scale, consulted the paper, and either nodded his head or pursed his lips" (22). A different kind of number on another piece of paper is the necessary but puzzling hinge on which the plot of the next story turns. Arnold Breit has an unlisted phone number; nevertheless, he received a call from a woman with whom he is not acquainted who had found it "written down on a piece of paper" (25), left for her by the baby sitter. The sitter had evidently written it incorrectly. The woman talks Breit into coming over to her apartment, even though he explains that it is a wrong number and that there is no reason for him to come. She uses the error in transcription as an opportunity to try to establish a relationship with him, and she almost succeeds when she does manage to get him to kiss her.

For her the wrong number turns out to be the right number, or almost. But for the reader of Carver's stories who is intrigued by the ways they seem to refer to each other, the wrong number is an allegory of itself, an allegory of a textual misreading that leaves the reader wondering if it is right or wrong. It could truly be a wrong number. This is because a reader who pays attention to how the stories fit together and who by this point in the book has seen connections among the first four is likely to pick up on the repetition between the fourth and fifth of the motif of "a piece of paper" with numbers on it. But when it appears in the fifth story it is clearly an instance of error. Could that be Carver's little joke on the reader, with the implication that to read the repetition of this motif in two sequential stories as itself part of the book is also an error? But who is responsible for this sequential repetition? Is it Carver or his editor, Lish? We just don't know. But we do know that the result, whatever the cause, is that the book itself is far from being merely a realistic depiction of a certain reality (the world of the working poor, the unemployed, the alcoholic). It is a kind of short- story cycle in which the whole is more, and in some ways more interesting, than the sum of its parts. The second and third stories, as we have seen, are both about neighbors, but they are themselves neighbors. Like the wrong number, this is an instance of stories referring not just to themselves as stories but as pieces in a larger picture that the reader is invited to put together.

"Collectors" and "What Do You Do in San Francisco?" are another pair of neighboring stories in this collection and offer a particularly striking list of mirroring connections. In "Collectors" a Mr. Slater is waiting for the mail: "Now and then I . . . look through the curtain for the mailman" (79). In the other story, a Mr. Marston is waiting for the mail, but we see it from the point of view of the mailman, who is the narrator: "I'd catch a glimpse of him . . . each day, waiting for me . . . looking out at me through the curtain" (92).

Before the mail can arrive, Slater must put up with an annoying vacuum-cleaner salesman who demonstrates the power of his machine on his carpets, but, what is more serious, the salesman intercepts a letter that had dropped through the slot in the door while he was there. He may have been peeved that Slater would never reply when he asked if Slater was his name. He keeps blocking Slater's way to the letter and finally picks it up before he can get to it. "It's for a Mr. Slater, he said. I'll see to it" (83). Marston in the other story likewise resists declaring his name: Although the mailman was well aware of his identity, Marston's never complied with the mailman's repeated requests that he declare it in an official way by painting over on the mailbox the name of the previous occupant and writing his own.

Most striking perhaps is the echo between the following two passages. When he intercepted Slater's letter, the salesman "folded the letter in half" (83). On one occasion when Marston was particularly distressed after his wife left him he gave the mailman an angry look that "froze the words in my mouth. I stopped in my tracks with his article of mail. . . . He stared at it as if dumbfounded. 'Occupant,' he said. It was a circular. . . . He folded it in two and went back to the house" (91). Like the wrong number in "Are You a Doctor?" these two half-folded pieces of mail name themselves as doubles of each other and as allegories of the relationship between their two stories, for each story seems to be the other's half. Or, to put it in a different way, the two stories invite us to fold one over the other. They not only complement each other, but each is almost the other's mirror-reversed image. One is told from the point of view of the receiver of mail, the other from that of the one who brings it. These two stories also halve the collection, being the eleventh and twelfth of the book's twenty-two stories.

These kinds of contiguous connections continue in Carver's second collection, *What We Talk About When We Talk About Love*. The recent publication of the original versions of those stories under the title *Beginners* in the Library of America edition of Carver's works offers an invaluable opportunity to see how stories can be revised to become a short-story cycle. Gordon Lish gave the stories the order they have in the book. Some of his word substitutions and insertions appear to have been made to allow contiguous stories to echo each other in some of their details.

In the original version of the first story ("Why Don't You Dance?") the man who put his furniture and appliances on the lawn in front of his house "turned the record over and the girl came up to him. They began to dance" (755). In the revised version, the young woman invited him to dance with her "and when the man stood up, *she came to him with her arms wide open*" (*Collected* 227; emphasis added). This new focus on arms will find an echo in "Viewfinder," the second story in which a man with no hands, the photographer of houses, takes up half the action.

The third story originally bore the title "Where Is Everyone?" This was changed to "Mr. Coffee and Mr. Fixit." In the original version, the narrator said of Ross, his wife's lover, "I wish him well now. But it was different then. More than once in those days I mentioned weapons. I'd say to my wife, I'd shout it, "I'm going to kill him!" But nothing ever happened" (761). In the revised version two new elements are introduced (indicated here and in subsequent quotations by italics): "I wish him well now. *Ross. What a name!* But it was different then. In those days I mentioned weapons. I'd say to my wife, '*I think I'll get a Smith and Wesson.*' But I never did it." (231). The expression "Smith and Wesson" will resonate with another pair of men's names added to the revised version to justify the story's new title. Originally, in a description of the company where Ross (to whom the narrator in both versions gives the nickname "Mr. Fixit," because of his mechanical ability) worked: "It's a modern operation out there . . . Mr. Coffees in every office" (767). The revised version includes two insertions: "It's a modern operation out there, *the aerospace place where Mr. Fixit used to work. I've seen it.* Cafeteria lines, executive dining rooms, and the like. Mr. Coffees in every office. *Mr. Coffee and Mr. Fixit*" (233). The addition of "Smith and Wesson" resonates within the story with the insertion of the other pair of surnames "Mr. Coffee and Mr. Fixit" (itself resonating with the story's new title). But it also resonates with an addition to the next story, "Gazebo." A passage in that story originally read: "You weren't my first boyfriend, my first boyfriend was named Wyatt and my folks didn't think much of him, but you were my first lover. You were my first lover then, and you've been my only lover since. Imagine" (778). This was revised to become: "You weren't my first, you know. My first was Wyatt. Imagine. *Wyatt. And your name's Duane. Wyatt and Duane*" (238). This addition creates two connections to the preceding story, in fact two *additions* to that story. One is that while the narrator in "Mr. Coffee and Mr. Fixit" calls attention to Ross's name and seems to make fun of it ("Ross. What a name!"), the speaker in "Gazebo" calls attention to the names Wyatt and Duane, and seems to make fun of them too—or least to make fun of their combination. The second connection is that the addition of "Wyatt and Duane" to "Gazebo" echoes the two pairs of names added to the preceding story: "Smith and Wesson" and "Mr. Coffee and Mr. Fixit."

In "The Third Thing That Killed My Father Off," after a flood the narrator and a friend find "a cow *wedged* in up against the wire. She was bloated . . . . It was the first dead thing of any size I'd ever seen" (288). This encounter with death and a dead floating female (note that Carver writes "She" when he could have written "It") parallels the discovery of the dead young woman floating in the water in "So Much Water So Close to Home," which immediately precedes this story in *What We Talk About.* In the original version: "Mel Dorn found the girl floating face down in the river, nude, *lodged* near the shore against some branches" (865). In the revised version "lodged" becomes "wedged," to match the passage in "The Third Thing" about the floating cow: "She was *wedged* into some branches that stuck out over the water" (274).

In "The Calm" the hunter who was taken to task for not finding the deer he had wounded in order to put the deer out of its misery said, "But, sure, we *trailed* him. A good *trail*, too. Blood on the ground and blood on the leaves. Blood everywhere" (299). In the immediately preceding story "A Serious Talk" Carver had written "the fireplace had black smoke stains reaching up the bricks toward the mantel" (903). That was revised to "A *trail* of smoke stains rose up the bricks to the mantel, where the wood that stopped them was scorched black" (292). Thanks to this alteration, the trail in "The Calm" leads back to the trail in "A Serious Talk." As a result, the emotional charge for the reader of a trail of smoke from a potentially disastrous house fire and that of a trail of blood from a mortally wounded animal have the potential to be transformed into a trail of words. The emotional charge is replaced by an aesthetic one, but only for the reader willing and able to read the stories as a collection.

In "What We Talk About When We Talk About Love," which gives the collection its title, a doctor describes the power of love by telling the story of an elderly married couple who were grievously injured in a car accident. During their hospitalization they were immobilized in body casts from head to foot with little holes for their eyes, nose, and mouth. In the original version they were in separate rooms, and the doctor recounts that what was most depressing to the husband, "after he was assured his wife was going to be all right . . . was the fact they couldn't be physically together. That he couldn't see her and be with her every day." (939–40). But in the book version they are in the same room and "the man's heart was breaking because he couldn't turn his . . . head and see his . . . wife" (320). So near yet so far, as we say.

This alteration in the story for its publication as part of a short story cycle seems to speak to the fact that it is now in that cycle, for like the husband in the doctor's story, the stories at times seem to show that they "know" (were such a thing possible) that they are right next to another story with which they have some important things in common. It's almost as if they would like to be able to turn in the direction of that story and see it. A revision to "One More Thing," the story that follows in the collection, adds an echo to the eye-holes in the body casts that would have allowed the couple to see each other. A character in "One More Thing" picks up a jar of pickles and throws it though a window. Subsequently, in the original version, "He could feel the draft of air from the window on his face" (950). In the book, this was changed to "He could feel air from the hole in the window on his face" (324). The added hole is, like the wrong number in "Are You a Doctor?" and the pieces of mail folded in half in "Collectors" and "What Do You Do in San Francisco?" which becomes an allegory of the relation that arises between neighboring stories in a collection whether by virtue of their being placed together at all or because of revisions made to one or both when they are placed together. Like the trail added to "A Serious Talk" that a perceptive reader can follow (as one follows a trail) to the trail in "The Calm," this hole leads to the holes in the other story. In fact, additional "holes" were given to that neighboring story, with the effect of increasing the resonance of the word. In the original version the couple's body casts "had eye holes and a place for their mouths and noses" (939). In the revised version they had "Little eye-holes and nose-holes and mouth-holes" (320). Those "places" became "holes."

Neighboring stories continue to feature parallels to each other in *Cathedral*, Carver's third and final major collection, and apparently to do so without Lish's altering the text of the stories. Here are a few.

In both "Feathers" and "Chef's House," the first and second stories, a husband and wife visit someone else's house (in one they are invited to dinner; in the other they rent the house), and the husband reports having experienced a sense of happiness that he will always remember.

In "Feathers": "That evening I felt *good* about almost everything in my life. . . . What I wished for was that I'd never *forget* or otherwise let go of that evening" (*Collected* 376). In "Chef's House": "This house has been a *good* house for us. This house has *good memories* to it" (380); he tells his wife he's glad she consented to join him there: "I won't *forget*" (381). In both stories the child of the house's owners is "fat": in "Feathers" the baby "had three or four fat chins. . . . Fat hung over its wrists. Its arms and fingers were fat" (372); in "Chef's House" Wes and Edna are displaced from the house where they had been so happy because of the unexpected return of Chef's daughter, Linda, consistently called "Fat Linda" (379, 380, 382) throughout the story. This parallel between two fat children is undergirded by the similarity of the stories' sad endings. The fat baby together with the good feelings they enjoyed at Bud and Olla's house inspire Fran and Jack to have a child, but after they do their marriage goes sour, which Fran blames on "those people and their ugly baby" (376); Jack is unhappy with their child, who "has a conniving streak" (377). The parallel is that the other fat child, Fat Linda, destroys by her unexpected return what happiness Wes and Edna had been able to achieve in the brief time they spent at the house. "This has been a happy house up to now, [Wes] said. We'll get another house, [Edna] said. Not like this one, Wes said. It wouldn't be the same, anyway" (380). In both stories the married couples were happier before the child arrived.

Wes was so depressed at the news of their being displaced by Fat Linda that he fell into a state of lethargy on the sofa. "He leaned back on the sofa, folded his hands in his lap, and closed his eyes" (382). "Preservation," the next story, begins where this one ends, with a man who has just received bad news falling into lethargy on a sofa: "Sandy's husband had been on the sofa ever since he'd been terminated three months ago" (383). "Chef's House" ended with Edna cleaning out the refrigerator: "I went in to start supper. We still had some fish in the icebox. There wasn't much else. We'll clean it up tonight, I thought, and that will be the end of it" (382). In "Preservation" it likewise becomes necessary to clean out a refrigerator, in this case because it stops working. "I'll have to cook everything tonight" (387), Sandy announces. The loss of the refrigerator's ability to preserve is the central event of this story and is an event that almost seems to find its origin in those last sentences of the story that comes just before.

Sandy, who plans to go to an auction to buy a new refrigerator they can afford, thinks back to the auctions she enjoyed going to with her father, and then on a more somber note to his death from carbon monoxide that leaked from a car he bought at one of those auctions. It had "caused him to pass out behind the wheel. . . . The motor went on running until there was no more gas in the tank. He stayed in the car until somebody found him a few days later" (390). This leaking gas parallels the leaking Freon gas that, according to Sandy's husband, is the reason the refrigerator stopped working, as the car found at an auction parallels the replacement refrigerator she hopes to find at another such auction. We can see in this the care with which Carver creates echoing stories within a single story.

But in it we can also see the care with which he sets up echoes between neighboring stories, for in "The Compartment," the next story, a father who has traveled by train to meet his son decides to stay in his train compartment and not get out at his destination to meet his son. In this way "The Compartment" refers back to both the refrigerator, whose "freezer *compartment*" (a word that probably appears nowhere else in *Cathedral*) shows the worst effects of the breakdown: "An awful smell puffed out at her that made her want to gag" (386), and to the father who was planning to go somewhere but never got out of the car.

The father on the train had bought an expensive wristwatch to give his son, and his losing it on the train to theft precipitates his decision not to meet his son after all. But in addition, he had a deep-seated anger against his son and had once threatened, in the heat of an argument, to kill him (393). A father's antipathy to his child is a recurring theme in Carver; we saw a milder version of it in "Chef's House" in Jack's attitude toward his "conniving" offspring. The father in the immediately following story, "A Small, Good Thing," has no such hostility towards his son (indeed, he loves him unconditionally), yet events there form a sad reverse parallel to the situation in "The Compartment." This son is about to receive a gift and is thinking about it just at the moment he receives the injury that will cause his death: he "was trying to find out what his friend intended to give him for his birthday that afternoon. Without looking, the birthday boy stepped off the curb at an intersection and was immediately knocked down by a car" (403).

Other connections link the stories in *Cathedral* one by one from beginning to end, such as the preserved ear of a Viet Cong soldier proudly displayed in "Vitamins" that seems to morph into the blocked right ear on which the protagonist is fixated throughout "Careful." There is not enough room to present them all here, but the last two stories provide insight into what is at stake in a Carver collection.

"Cathedral," the collection's concluding story, invites us to reflect on artistic collaboration. The protagonist and his guest, a blind friend of his wife's, are taking in a television program about cathedrals. The host tries to explain what a cathedral is but finds he cannot. The blind man asks him to get some heavy paper and a pen, and he places his hand on his host's as the latter draws a cathedral's walls, towers, and flying buttresses. The blind man had learned from the television program that a cathedral is a collaborative effort among generations, and said he knew that "The men who began their life's work on them, they never lived to see the completion of their work" (525). In a question-and-answer session with a class at the University of Akron in 1982, probably not long after he completed this story, Carver spoke of artistic collaboration between a writer and his editor, citing the famous cases of Maxwell Perkins editing Thomas Wolfe and Ezra Pound editing T. S. Eliot; in both instances the editor greatly reduced the length of the original, which Carver's own editor Lish also did in his case, especially the stories in *What We Talk About When We Talk About Love*. Carver then says of that kind of collaboration "it's in a way like building a fantastic cathedral. The main thing is to get the work of art together. You don't know who built those cathedrals, but they're there" (*Conversations* 23). At first the blind man's hand rides his host's as it traces the form of a cathedral, and the host is in charge. But at a certain moment the blind man tells him to close his eyes and continue drawing. "So we kept on with it. His fingers rode my fingers as my hand went over the paper. It was like nothing else in my life up to now" (*Collected* 528). In yielding control he learns what it is like to be blind. In addition, their joint effort becomes something more like a true collaboration, the kind of collaboration that made cathedrals possible.

But at the same time the similarity to what happens at the conclusion of the immediately preceding story is brought to completion. The narrator of "The Bridle" finds a horse's bridle left behind by a guest at her motel, and muses: "Reins go over the head and up to where they're held on the neck between the *fingers*. The *rider* pulls the reins this way and that, and the horse turns" (513). The bridle is powerful and controlling: "When you felt it pull, you'd know it was time. You'd know you were going somewhere" (513). The host in "Cathedral," his eyes closed as the blind man's "*fingers rode* my fingers," would have felt like that horse. Collaboration involves loss of control, whether it be from the horse to the rider, a sighted man to a blind one, a writer to his editor, one story to the one that follows and recycles elements from it, or a book like this one that invites its readers to collaborate in the work of putting it together.

Works Cited

Carver, Raymond. *Conversations with Raymond Carver*. Ed. Marshall Bruce Gentry and William L. Stull. Jackson: UP of Mississippi, 1990. Print.

___. *Collected Stories*. New York: Lib. of Amer., 2009. Print.

___. "The Idea." *Northwest Review*, 12.1 (1971–72): 81–84. Print.

Carver, Realism, and Narrative Self-Consciousness___
Vasiliki Fachard

In the arts and in literature, the main tendency among artists from classical Greece onward has been to copy reality. Until recently, this copying was variously bound with philosophical, religious, and aesthetic dogmas; that is, it was based upon, and determined by, unquestioned assumptions regarding the order of the universe and man's place in it. In complying with these imperatives of representation, artists manifested their belief in a higher fixed order, which in turn served as a paradigm and reference for their own creations.

The scientific and philosophical breakthroughs of the modern era undermined many of the assumptions that had shaped art for centuries. As the relationship between faith and art crumbled, along with the prevailing worldview, the notion of "authority" came to be viewed with suspicion or dismissed altogether. What artists had been willing to represent as the real was seen as artifice, a mere construction whose illusory nature must be exposed. In literature, the confident, omniscient narrators of realist authors such as Honoré de Balzac—who dictated, godlike, the action and fate of their characters—gave way to the modern narrative voice: a doubting, introspective one that cannot fathom the characters' minds and motives any more than it can penetrate the mysteries of its own existence. This development, in which "realism" was displaced from a world of unquestioning certainty to the terrain of the subconscious, where multiple interpretative possibilities coexist, allows a story to unfold in an unknowable, indifferent, and disquieting world. Psychoanalyst Sigmund Freud's groundbreaking insights into the human psyche played an important role in this replacement of an orderly (external) universe with another (inner) chaotic one.

Although no theorist or art critic, Raymond Carver was aware of the limits of representation and of the fact that writing is a means of probing—as opposed to copying—reality:

> I like to mess around with my stories . . . revising the work once it's done
> is something that comes naturally to me and is something I take pleasure
> in doing. Maybe I revise because it gradually takes me into the heart of
> what a story is *about*. I have to keep trying to see if I can find that out. It's
> a process more than a fixed position. ("Paris Review" 218)

Carver's insistence on the elusiveness of meaning would seem to place his fiction in the modern or postmodern tradition. Yet Carver has also been called a realist, and rightly so. His painstaking search for the *mot juste* makes him a continuator of the old masters he revered—realists such as Leo Tolstoy and Gustave Flaubert, to name a few—from whom he nonetheless distanced himself, mainly through his repudiation of descriptive exhaustiveness. In this sense, Carver is closer to Ernest Hemingway than to Henry James.

The originality of Carver's fiction lies in its intermediate position between these two traditions, reconciling the influence of the old realist school with the imperatives of a new fiction that purports to give voice to the unconscious by forcing it to crop out of the surface of a text. Carver believed that it was "possible to write a line of seemingly innocuous dialogue and have it send a chill along the reader's spine" (*Collected* 730).[1] He achieves that ideal by exploiting the evocative power of words, by *hinting* while *telling*. The oscillation between these two goals creates the sense of an impending "menace" that is characteristic of Carver's work:

> I like it when there is some feeling of threat or sense of menace in short
> stories . . . For one thing, it's good for the circulation. There has to be
> tension, a sense that something is imminent, that certain things are in re-
> lentless motion, or else, most often, there simply won't be a story. What
> creates tension in a piece of fiction is partly the way the concrete words
> are linked together to make up the visible action of the story. But it's also
> the things that are left out, that are implied, the landscape just under the
> smooth (but sometimes broken and unsettled) surface of things. (732)

This subterranean "landscape" teems with clues or "signals"—the title of one of Carver's tales, incidentally—that Carver invites his readers to pick up and connect. Such signals may consist of incongruous situations, names, or words that disrupt a story's linearity, thus baffling realist expectations. To make sense of these seemingly unaccountable, jarring, and intrusive signals, which are outcrops of the unconscious, readers must connect them and transpose them to another register— what one might, in musical terms, call another "tonality"—where these discrepancies are no longer discordant or semantically dissonant.

Repetitions often act as signals. In "Put Yourself in My Shoes," the repetition of the word *match*—a character keeps lighting his cigarette with a match, throwing it in the fireplace or, incongruously, behind a couch—underscores the importance of weaving together, or *matching*, parts of a story into a more coherent whole. Sometimes repetitions or signals are to be gathered across several stories. In such cases, they serve as connections that echo and refer to each other as if Carver's stories were "somehow eavesdropping on each other, somehow invading their neighboring stories' space" (Runyon 20).

By prompting his readers to harvest these signals, Carver shows his impatience with the limits of straightforward storytelling and of realist fiction. Eager to share with the reader his questioning of the unconscious material he draws upon for his stories, he discloses the mechanics of his fiction, forcing his readers to reflect on the act of writing at the same time that they follow a plotline. This essay will attempt to identify, interpret, and connect these authorial proddings in the stories "Fat," "Neighbors," "The Father," and "Put Yourself in My Shoes."

In the opening lines of "Fat," the first story of *Will You Please Be Quiet, Please?* (1976), a waitress doubling as a narrator "tells" a story-within-a-story to her friend Rita:

> I am sitting over coffee and cigarettes at my friend Rita's and I am telling her about it.
> Here is what I tell her. (3)

The repetition of *tell*, as well as *Rita*, which sounds like "reader," are the first of many signs that the "it" of this story is the act of telling as much as it is a record of the waitress' attraction to an obese customer she serves one day, whom she describes as "the fattest person" she has ever seen. What most impresses her about this customer are his fingers, "They look three times the size of a normal person's fingers— long, thick, creamy fingers" (3). The insistence on the customer's fat fingers prompts the reader to see them as *writing* fingers, an image that, in turn, transforms the fat man into a *narrative* body—a body with an odd voice: "He has this way of speaking—strange, don't you know. And he makes a little puffing sound every so often" (3). The fat man's "strange" mannerism is his use of the royal "we" to refer to himself throughout the story. This strangeness vanishes, however, when one bears in mind that "we" is consistent with the plurality of subconscious narrative voices encased in this body and that manifest themselves in the customer's huffs and puffs. The fat man's multiple-course meal also suggests that the fat man is eating for more than one person.

The regal, gargantuan meal and the fat man about to devour it exert an uncanny attraction on the waitress, who remarks after serving him:

> Enjoy your dinner, I say. I raise the lid of his sugar bowl and look in. He nods and keeps looking at me until I move away.
> I know now I was after something. But I don't know what. (5)

The feeling she is "after" and cannot articulate "comes over" her again when she brings him the Green Lantern Special dessert served with "a big bowl of vanilla ice cream with chocolate syrup to the side," which she goes into the kitchen to see after herself (6). The attraction between the customer and the waitress does not go unnoticed by Rudy, the narrator's partner, who works in the kitchen of the same restaurant:

> Harriet says you got a fat man from the circus out there. That true? . . .
>
> Rudy, he is fat, I say, but that is not the whole story.
>
> Rudy just laughs . . .
>
> Better watch out, Rudy, says Joanne, who just that minute comes into the kitchen.
>
> I'm getting jealous, Rudy says to Joanne. (5, 6)

It is hard to imagine Rudy being "jealous" of an obese stranger whose fingers are "three times the size" of an ordinary human being's until, on another tonality, readers come to view him as a rival storyteller. Rudy, upon hearing Rita's account, also tells a story: "I knew a fat guy once, a couple of fat guys, really fat guys, when I was a kid. . . . Fat, that's the only name this one kid had" (6). Rudy's *rudi*-mentary and obtuse narrative, presents only the "*visible* action of the story," whereas the story of the fat man—enigmatic, disjunctive, yet richly suggestive—offers glimpses into the narrator's unconscious desires.

Unlike the fat man, Rudy the storyteller fails to arouse the interest of the narrator. Everything about Rudy seems insipid and dull when contrasted with the actions and desires of the fat man, which arouse the waitress on some level. Whereas the fat man orders and puts away a feast, Rudy, that evening, seems satisfied only with tea. The narrator's perfunctory preparation of this tea—"I pour the water in the pot, arrange the cups, the sugar bowl, carton of half and half, and take the tray in to Rudy" (6)—further contrasts with the almost sensual serving of a multiple-course meal at the restaurant. Moreover, the tea's orderly preparation recalls Rudy's predictable story, whose linearity the narrator appears to reject in favor of the evocative hints that she culls from all over the rich, corpulent narrative body of her customer.

To win back her favor and draw her into his thin narrative territory, Rudy has no choice but to subdue her, which he proceeds to do in bed, against her will, as the narrator recounts:

I get into bed and move clear to the edge and lie there on my stomach. But right away, as soon as he turns off the light and gets into bed, Rudy begins. I turn on my back and relax some, though it is against my will. But here is the thing. When he gets on me, I suddenly feel I am fat. I feel I am terrifically fat, so fat that Rudy is a tiny thing and hardly there at all. (7)

This occurs shortly after the waitress, drawn to the erotic power of the fat man's narrative, muses, in the shower, on the consequences of mating with him: "I put the water on to boil for tea and take a shower. I put my hand on my middle and wonder what would happen if I had children and one of them turned out to look like that, so fat" (6). Having imaginatively appropriated or, rather, in-corporated the customer's narrative fatness, she now feels "terrifically fat," or powerful enough to resist the sexual domination of the lean Rudy, whose narrative function, in the end, is reduced to "a tiny thing and hardly there at all."

Unsurprisingly, the narrator's story-within-a-story about her customer baffles the realistic expectations of Rita:

That's a funny story, Rita says, but I can see she doesn't know what to make of it.

I feel depressed. But I won't go into it with her. I've already told her too much. (7)

At the end, the narrator of "Fat"—one of Carver's shortest stories—feels she has already said "too much." This excess, it is safe to assume, lies in the subtext, where the reader, unlike Rita, knows how to weave together disparate and peculiar strands into a story about writing a story.

To conclude, Carver's story "Fat" foreshadows his new kind of fiction. The "whole story" lies in a narrator serving the narrative demands of an intriguing fat man as well as of another, unremarkable storyline; in other words, the narrative crux lies in the opposition between an unclear yet richly suggestive narrative and a pedestrian, minimalist one.

The narrator cannot articulate her feelings in the wake of this new perception of things, but her last words show that she has made a discovery: "My life is going to change. I feel it" (7).

In "Neighbors," a couple, Bill and Arlene Miller, agree to look after the apartment of the Stones, who live "across the hall" and are going away for ten days (8). Whenever Bill and Arlene enter the empty apartment, they pry into its every nook and cranny, violating their neighbors' intimacy. They open up cupboards and drawers containing intimate apparel that Bill even tries on, pocket a pill from a bottle of prescribed medicine, and at times forget about the cat and plants that they have been asked to look after. These transgressive visits excite their libido and invariably eventuate in lovemaking, back in their apartment. But this ritual ends when Arlene forgets the key inside the Stones's apartment. Locked out, the distressed couple seek consolation in each other's arms, leaning "into the door as if against a wind, and brac[ing] themselves" (13).

The couple's despair at being locked out appears excessive and puzzling until one finds a connection between "Neighbors" and "Fat," its immediate predecessor and *neighbor* in the collection. The uncanny attraction of the waitress to the fat narrative body of her customer, as well as her subsequent envisaged impregnation by him, recall Bill and Arlene's lust every time they penetrate the premises of their neighbors. The reasons behind these arousals triggered by the fat man's *narrative* body and the neighbors' intimate space, are to be found in a fecund unconscious realm represented by both the fat man's body and by the neighbors' apartment. The unconscious provides erotic stimulation to the characters and, simultaneously, creative energy and material to the writer, whose presence can often be felt behind the character's actions, as in, for instance, Bill's meticulous survey of the neighbors' apartment, which betrays Carver's own meticulous observation: Bill moves "slowly through each room considering everything that fell under his gaze, carefully, one object at a time. He saw ashtrays, items of furniture, kitchen utensils, the clock. He saw everything" (11).

Discerning the author's motivations in the characters' actions helps readers to account for the couple's distress at being locked out. Bill and Arlene's seemingly unaccountable overreaction symbolizes, in fact, the writer's fear that his forays into the unconscious, from which he draws his writing material, are terminated when the key is left behind. This exclusion has depressing consequences for the characters as well as for the writer: Bill and Arlene, like Adam and Eve, may never return to their Paradise, and Carver, shut out from a trove of writing material, fears that he might fall susceptible to writer's block.

"The Father" is the story of a twofold paternity: that of a baby as well as that of a narrative. A mere two pages long, "The Father" opens with the description of a newborn lying "in a basket beside the bed," surrounded by its three sisters, mother, and grandmother. The father is in the kitchen, with his back turned to the family, whom he can hear playing with the newborn. Amidst other comments on the baby's pretty eyes, nose, and fingers, the father suddenly overhears his daughter Alice's insistent query: "But who does he look like, who does he look like?" (33). Her sister Phyllis replies that he "doesn't look like anybody," but the third sister Carol opines that "he looks like *Daddy*." The next question, out of left field—"But who does Daddy *look* like?"—prompts the women to turn to look at the father and elicits the reply "Why, nobody" from the weeping Phyllis. Despite her grandmother's pleas to "hush," Alice repeats that the father looks like "nobody." As the company swing their gaze from the baby to their father, he turns in his chair to show "a face that was white and without expression" (34). This ends the story.

The text yields no explanations on the father's whiteness or lack of expression. But intratextual connections between this story and "Fat" furnish some interpretative clues. The grandmother's comment about the baby's arm being "so fat" will remind readers of the fetus that the waitress in "Fat" imagines when she puts her hand on her "middle" and wonders "what would happen if [she] had children and one of them turned out to look like that, *so fat*" (6; emphasis added). Carver appears to use the events in these two stories to herald—through the evolution of the *embryo* (of a story) into the birth of a baby—the birth of a new kind of fiction.

This metaphor of birth leads readers to establish a parallel between the father and Carver himself, and to see in the father's reaction to his son's birth a reflection of Carver's own feelings about his ground-breaking fiction. Carver's new imperatives for fiction—discrepancies, inconclusive endings, breaches of realist expectations, and reliance on self-reflexive substories—defied prevailing literary conventions. As an artist going against the grain, Carver must surely have had misgivings about the critical reception of his work, and these doubts may well have made him as "white" with anxiety, at times, as anxious as that other creator, the father of the eponymous story. The father's pallor, then, is not a sign of apathy; it symbolizes the insecurity and fears gripping an artist awaiting a critical verdict on his work.

In "Put Yourself in My Shoes," from the same collection, the implicit and explicit functions of language are embodied in the antagonism between Morgan, a professor of literature, and Myers, a writer and Carver's fictional alter ego. Morgan, a staunch defender of realism, champions the conventions that give the illusion of objective reality. Myers, on the other hand, rejects these conventions. He believes that the material of literature springs from a writer's unconscious and that it should not be mediated by the writer but allowed to unfold naturally within the implicit realm of language.

During his sabbatical, Morgan rents out his house to Myers and his wife, Paula. Upon his return, Morgan realizes that his tenants did not observe the terms of the lease: they brought in a cat knowing it was forbidden, unlocked the Morgans' private closet to use their linens, and even broke some dishes. According to Morgan, that is the "real story" of what happened during his absence (114). But another, subtextual story emerges in which the house is also a metaphor for a Jamesian "house of fiction," with Morgan acting as its custodian and the rules of realism as the rental agreement. In breaching the landlord's rules,

Myers and his wife have not only desecrated the physical ground of the professor's house but also his convictions about literary art.

The self-reflexive dimension of "Put Yourself in My Shoes" is suggested by its structure—a sequence of stories told by Morgan and his wife with a view to providing the writer with "grist for the mill" or "raw material" for a story (107, 110). Morgan's worship of realist storytelling, however, is met with derision and insolent laughter by Myers, who, no less insolently, seeks to cut his visit short while Morgan, sensing that he is not prevailing upon Myers, desperately tries to prolong it. At the end of the visit, as Myers drives away from Morgan's premises, he is described as having overcome the writer's block he had at the beginning: "He was silent and watched the road. He was at the very end of a story" (115).

How could Myers create a story by letting someone else do the storytelling? Carver's statement that a story is a "process more than a fixed position" helps to account for this mystery: the process of telling matters more than what the narrative actually tells ("Paris Review" 218). Here, this process is sustained by the lasting clash between Morgan's championing of the realism of the "great masters" and Myers's derisive dismissal of realism in favor of a new kind of fiction (111).

Before Myers and Paula are even let into the house of their hosts, a large dog lunges toward Myers, who falls back, afraid that the dog will "go for his throat" (104). The incident, which Morgan watches from his window, heralds the hostility that awaits them inside the house, a hostility that Morgan initially suppresses in the living room but not in the kitchen, where he can be heard banging the cupboard's door and muttering "a muffled word that sounded like a curse" as he prepares his guests' drinks (106).

Back in the living room, Morgan begins to tell the story of an affair between his colleague and a student. After the adulterous colleague is ordered out of the house by the wife, his son "threw a can of tomato soup" at his father, who was then taken to the hospital in a "quite serious" condition. Myers simply grins at his story. Morgan ascribes

Myers's reaction to his inability to put himself in the victim's shoes: "Think of the story you'd have if you could get inside that man's head" (107). Morgan's belief that a writer can "get inside" his character's head is an assumption of realist fiction, characterized by omniscient and godlike *authors*. (The word *author* comes from the Latin *auctoritas*, from which "authority" is derived.) The realist concept of an *author* is opposed to that of a *writer*, such as Carver, whose characters are not marionettes manipulated by an all-knowing creator but, rather, enigmatic extensions of the voices within the writer. As a spokesman for Carver, Myers cannot *know* what goes on in his characters' minds anymore than Carver himself can know "what the heart of a story is *about*" ("Paris Review" 218). In writing about his characters, Carver/Myers writes about (and hopes to *know*) himself, that is, the subconscious forces within himself that find a voice in a story's characters.

Detached from literary theory, the two wives respond emotionally to the story: Mrs. Morgan deplores that the wife was "betrayed in such fashion after twenty years," and Paula commiserates with the "poor *boy*" and focuses on what he "must be going through" (107). Morgan does not heed the women's responses. He is only concerned with imposing his literary principles upon Morgan—an uphill battle, given that Myers is uninterested in the story. At some point, Morgan has to ask him, "Mr. Myers, are you listening?" (108). To draw a response from Myers, Morgan invites him to switch viewpoints, from the victim's to the mistress': "Put yourself in the shoes of that eighteen-year-old who fell in love with a married man. Think about *her* . . . and then you see the possibilities for your story" (108). This permutation shows that Morgan is not interested in the plight of his colleague but, rather, in the effectiveness of a literary device: *point of view*. In imposing a shift from the colleague's viewpoint to that of his eighteen-year-old mistress, Morgan unwittingly exposes the strings pulled by an author and the artifices of fiction.

Frustrated in his proselytizing, Morgan ultimately taunts Myers with a remark suggesting that he may not be up to the task of telling such a story adequately: "It would take a Tolstoy to tell it and tell it right . . . no less than a Tolstoy" (108). Myers answers, "Time to go," but the women convince him to stay for another round of drinks, prepared by the professor, whom Myers can again hear "curse as he slammed the kettle on the burner" (108).

At this point, a pause occurs in the story, occasioned by the appearance of carolers singing outside. The two couples go to the window and are astonished by Mrs. Morgan's confident prediction that the carolers "won't come here . . . I just know they won't" (109). Her prediction is soon realized: the carolers pass by the Morgans' house without stopping. Mrs. Morgan weeps at the sight, as if she (and her husband) knew but did not wish to reveal the reason for the party's steering clear of their home. The Morgans' effort to conceal some dark secret regarding their house (of fiction) reminds readers of Carver's statement about authorial disclosures in his interview for the *Paris Review*: "You have to be immensely daring, very skilled and imaginative and willing to tell everything on yourself. You're told time and again when you're young to write about what you know, and what do you know better than your own secrets?" (201). Exposing one's secrets is a form of honesty in fiction, a quality that Mrs. Morgan presumably intuited was lacking in her husband's narration of the first story, a story elaborated thanks to those literary conventions that Carver has likened to "tricks" (729). Morgan, also, must have sensed this want in himself, because he entrusts the second telling of the story to a more honest storyteller, his wife:

"We'll let Mrs. Morgan tell this one."
"You tell it, dear. And Mr. Myers, you listen closely," Mrs. Morgan said.
"We have to go," Myers said. "Paula, let's go."
"Talk about honesty," Mrs. Morgan said.

Myers eventually relents and listens to Mrs. Morgan's rendition of her and her husband's visit to a Bauhaus exhibit in Munich "to pay homage to a few of our favorites amongst the old masters" (111). The custodian of a hallowed literary tradition, Morgan venerates past literary masters such as Tolstoy, whom he singles out as a model for the writer. His house, guarded by a dog, is a metaphorical monument to such masters of the past. In desecrating the house, Myers manifests his disregard for the literary tradition that the academic reveres.

While in the museum, Mrs. Morgan forgets her purse, containing more than one hundred dollars, in the ladies' room. A woman named Mrs. Attenborough finds the purse, returns it to the address she found inside, and then drops dead in the Morgans' living room on her way out, prompting Mrs. Morgan to say, "Fate sent her to die on the couch in our living room in Germany" (112). This high-sounding pronouncement causes Myers to burst into laughter and repeat her sentence "between gasps" (112). His mockery once again is consistent with Carver's own rejection of what he calls "literary" or "pseudo-poetic" language (words such as "Fate"), preferring instead the "common language, the language of normal discourse, the language we speak to each other in," which is the hallmark of Carver's fiction ("Fire" 743–44).

Unaffected by the writer's jeers, Mrs. Morgan resumes her story, which ends with the discovery, in the dead woman's purse, of Mrs. Morgan's missing money, "still fastened with the paper clip." Expressing his "keen disappointment" at the stranger's theft, Morgan breaks into a new rage upon hearing Myers giggling: "If you were a real writer, as you say you are, Mr. Myers . . . you would not dare laugh! . . . You would plumb the depths of that poor soul's heart and try to understand. But you are no writer, sir!" (113).

In his anger, Morgan is blind to his own contradiction in calling a dishonest person who has robbed his wife a "poor soul." His request, furthermore, that Myers write about the "poor soul's heart," which he knows nothing about, is at odds with the kind of fiction Carver is "most interested in"—fiction that is "autobiographical to some extent. At the very least it's referential. Stories . . . don't just come out of thin air" ("Paris Review" 200). For the laughing Myers, a character like Mrs. Attenborough, whose psychological "depths" he is asked to plumb, comes "out of thin air": she has landed in their living room by pure accident and has no connection to his life. Slamming his fist on the coffee table to stop Myers's persistent giggling, a furious Morgan embarks on his third and last story, the story that has been gnawing at him since his return from Germany and that is responsible for his cursing in the kitchen: "The real story lies right here, in this house, this very living room, and it's time it was told! The real story is *here*, Mr. Myers" (113).

In proceeding to tell the story of how his former tenants desecrated his house during his sabbatical, Morgan may be unaware that the narrative he is about to unspool differs from the preceding ones in that it exposes some of Morgan's own secrets. His choice to refer to his characters only by letters (Y and Z) fails to conceal the identities of his former tenants, who, along with the reader, know that the accusations are pointed at them:

> Mr. and Mrs. *Y*'s moving into the Zs' house, *invading* the Zs' house, if the truth is to be told. Sleeping in the Zs' bed is one thing, but unlocking the Zs' private closet and using their linen, vandalizing the things found there, that was against the spirit and letter of the lease . . .
> "That's the real story that is waiting to be written."
> "And it doesn't need Tolstoy to tell it," Mrs. Morgan said.
> "It doesn't need Tolstoy," Morgan said. (114)

The first two stories told by the Morgans are remotely connected to their lives, or, to use Carver's words, bear no "lines of reference" to them ("Paris Interview" 200). But the third story touches them more closely, and consequently meets Carver's (and Myers's) requirement that fiction should be "autobiographical to some extent" or, at the very least, "referential" ("Paris Interview" 200). Morgan's further concession that such a real story "doesn't need Tolstoy" to tell it—in other words, that it can be told without resorting to the "tricks" of the old masters—shows a recognition by Morgan of some ideas of the new fiction represented by Myers. At the end of the visit, Morgan thus appears, unwittingly and in spite of himself, to have put himself in the "shoes" of the new writer.

Morgan's confrontation with the writer Myers eventuates in the erosion of Morgan's old certainties about literary art. Myers, however, also profits from this confrontation. His new story was made possible by, and emerges from, his repudiation of Morgan's discourse: His writer's voice is born out of his dialogic confrontation with Morgan and the literary tradition that the academic has defended.

In the four stories discussed above, the conversations about writing heard under the guise of realism reflect the development of the writer's reflections about storytelling as well as his growing awareness of his own place in the literary canon. The narrator/writer's tentative insights into storytelling dropped in "Fat" and his misgivings about creative impotence and about the reception of his work ("Neighbors" and "The Father," respectively) give way in "Put Yourself in My Shoes" to a more lucid view of the mechanics of fiction and to Myers/Carver's confident assertion that a new form of storytelling is required that will prompt readers to look out for signs and signals and to find vestiges of the author's voice in, but also between, the lines.

Note

1. Unless otherwise noted, citations of Carver's works are from *Collected Stories*.

Works Cited

Carver, Raymond. *Collected Stories*. Ed. William L. Stull and Maureen P. Carroll. New York: Lib. of Amer., 2009. Print.

___. "The Paris Review Interview." *Fires*. New York: Vintage, 1991. Print.

Runyon, Randolph Paul. *Reading Raymond Carver*. Syracuse: Syracuse UP, 1992. Print.

Small Good Things: Symbols and Descriptive Details in Carver's Short Fiction_____

Ayala Amir

Symbolism in Carver is one of the more discussed topics in regard to his work and one of the more elusive and fascinating ones. There is the deep connection between form and content in Carver's work by exploring the dynamic that underlies both the symbolic reading of his stories and the attempts of contact and communication undertaken by his characters. The 1983 collection of stories, *Cathedral* is perceived by most critics as a turning point in Carver's career to a fuller, more expanded style. Most of the stories in this collection were written after Carver had overcome his alcoholism and his marital and financial problems. He was in a new relationship with the poet Tess Gallagher and his work had been favorably reaccepted and acclaimed. It was at this time that the influence and involvement of his editor Gordon Lish had lessened. Carver "insisted on complete control of his stories, restricting Lish to standard copyediting."[1] The indication of this change is the inclusion in *Cathedral* of "A Small, Good Thing"—a story that was heavily edited by Lish in *What We Talk About When We Talk About Love*, which Carver now published in its full-length version.

"Where I'm Calling From"—a story in the first person—is based on the time Carver spent at Duffy's, a residential treatment center in Calistoga in the Napa Valley, which in this story is "Frank Martin's drying-out facility" (*Collected Stories* 452). The story begins with an episode that had made a big impression on the narrator: the collapse by a seizure of one of the patients at the center. The distress, the sense of defeat, and the fear of death are strongly conveyed in this episode, which the narrator experiences as a witness, yet is completely involved in. This stance, of an involved witness, also characterizes his relationship with J. P., whom he describes as "first and foremost a drunk," but "also a chimney sweep" (452). J. P. shares with the narrator his life story, which is embedded in "Where I'm Calling From" but without turning it into a frame story that introduces another narrator. The narrator remains the same, and J. P.'s stories are told in the third person, not as they were actually told, but rather as their listener absorbed them in his mind. This choice of narrative voice suggests the role that these stories have in the narrator coming to terms with his own story (a process analyzed by Elliot Malamet). At the same time, it indicates the ability that the listener acquires through J. P.'s stories to overcome his sense of separateness and singularity—an ability that has to do with the role of symbolism in this story. J. P.'s story begins with an episode from his childhood:

> What's J. P. talking about, anyway? He's saying how when he was twelve years old he fell into a well in the vicinity of the farm he grew up on. It was a dry well, lucky for him. "Or unlucky," he says, looking around him and shaking his head . . . J. P. had wet his pants down there. He'd suffered all kinds of terror in that well, hollering for help, waiting and then hollering some more. He hollered himself hoarse before it was over. But he told me that being at the bottom of that well had made a lasting impression. He'd sat there and looked up the well mouth. Way up at the top, he could see a circle of blue sky. Every once in a while a white cloud passed over. A flock of birds flew across . . . In short, everything about his life was different for him at the bottom of that well. But nothing fell on him and nothing closed off that little circle of blue. Then his dad came along with the rope, and it wasn't long before J. P. was back in the world he'd always lived in. (454)

In *Seven Types of Ambiguity*, William Empson explores the many ways by which poetic imagery generates fruitful ambiguity. The image of the boy in the well seems to exemplify this. The well is a locus of anxiety and uncertainty and at the same time of an intense and unique experience, enabling moments of serenity and beauty. J. P., who chooses to launch his life story with this episode, seems to express it by a burning will for life not quite dimmed by the alcoholic's death wish (the luck of falling into a dry well may not be so lucky, says J. P., viewing the event from his standpoint at the drying-out facility).

The boy who cries himself to hoarseness from the depth of the pit is a strong embodiment of the biblical plea in Psalms 130:1 ("Out of the depths have I cried unto thee, oh Lord"), expressing loneliness and outer despair alongside a deep faith in salvation by a higher power. In fact, it is not the sole biblical allusion that springs from this image, as it also alludes to the story of Joseph, thrown into a well by his brothers: a trauma of hate, betrayal, and loss yet the beginning of a glorious trajectory. While Joseph's father could not respond to his plea, J. P.'s father pulled him out with a rope. Yet who's to save him now? The childhood episode suggests a miraculous rebirth from the womb of the earth but is there a second chance for a man who is "first and foremost a drunk"?

We can enumerate at least six qualities in this image: First, it is a rich and ambiguous image that pulls in opposite directions—fear and hope and being at the lowest point of life yet still aspiring to ascend, expressing deep despair as well as faith and trust. Second, it echoes ancient images (in addition to the biblical allusions, folk tales and mythologies abound with wells, and even boys in wells) thus expanding the scope of this story beyond the time-space frame in which it is situated. Third, it is an image that seems to stir our innermost sense of space where, according to French philosopher Gaston Bachelard, lies the most powerful effect of literature. Through space rather than time, Bachelard maintains, our sense of self is formed and our consciousness finds its center. Spaces in which we experienced individual moments of reverie are especially important in that regard, and they are organized along a house's vertical line—from the tower to the cellar. Although the well story about J. P.'s memorable moments in solitude takes place outdoors, it is still situated along a vertical line, reflecting the other powerful image of this story, that of the chimney. The chimney is also a dark yet benign space where you can also see the little circle of blue sky. In this story, it is the locus that stands for J. P.'s love for Roxi, the chimney sweep whose kiss brings good luck, and the place where J. P. had proved his prowess. Herein lies the fourth quality of the well image, which by now can be called a symbol: It is well connected to the invisible net of meanings that underlies the story, giving it, as Malamet has rightly said, a coherency that the narrator's own painful story—full of gaps, lacunae, and avoidances—lacks (69). As much as it opens the story to other mythical or archetypical spaces, it also reflects the actual space where the storytelling takes place— the halfway home—a secluded space, imbued with fear and sense of defeat yet one that offers the fatherly protection of Frank Martin. In that sense, it is truly a place where nothing falls and nothing closes off "that little circle of blue." Finally, the well image—though dry—is connected to the rich and fluid imagery of water sources in Carver's literary scenery: a symbol of death and femininity in the story "So Much Water So Close to Home" and a place where men and boys put to the test their manliness, friendship and morality (again in "So Much Water So Close to Home"[2] and in "Nobody Said Anything" and "The Third Thing That Killed My Father Off").

These qualities of the well image—its ambiguity, cultural resonance, its connection to the spatial organization of the inner life, the way it coheres into the story's net of meanings and actual reality and to Carver's imagery in general—could even be expanded and filled with other possibilities. In all of them, however, we tend to interpret it as a symbol rather than merely a concrete element of the story's plot or atmosphere. And as such, it is prolific, generating more and more meanings and interpretations.

The adjective *prolific* was used as a noun by the poet William Blake in *Marriage of Heaven and Hell*: "One portion of being is the Prolific, the other the Devouring" (155, Plates 16–17) "Under 'prolific,'" Hazard Adams comments, "comes the symbol, which points to nothing beyond it . . . but instead generates from itself food for 'devouring'—interpretation" (19). Just these few words quoted from Blake convey some of the immense importance that the Romantic poets attributed to the symbol and its active, generative, and creative force. For Goethe, "Symbolism transforms an object of perception into an idea, the idea into an image, and it does it in such a way that the idea always remains always infinitely operative and unattainable so that even if it is put into words in all languages, it still remains inexpressible" (141; no. 1113). It was Goethe who first formulated the distinction between symbol and allegory to be later developed by Coleridge. While "allegory," Coleridge suggests, "is but a translation of abstract notions into a picture-language, which is itself nothing but an abstraction from objects of the senses," a symbol

> is characterized by a translucence of the special in the individual, or of the general in the special, or of the universal in the general; above all by the translucence of the eternal through and in the temporal. It always partakes of the reality which it renders intelligible; and while it enunciates the whole, abides itself as a living part in the unity of which it is the representative. (437)

The Romantic conception of the symbol versus allegory persisted into the twentieth century with Yeats ("A symbol is indeed the only possible expression of some invisible essence, a transparent lamp about a spiritual flame; while allegory is one of many representations of an embodied thing. [116]). And D. H. Lawrence:

> You can't give a great symbol a "meaning" any more than you can give a cat a "meaning." Symbols are organic units of consciousness with lives of their own, and you can never explain them away, because their value is dynamic, emotional, belonging to the sense-consciousness of the body and the soul, and not simply mental. (157)

In the twentieth century we have also come to know not only Freudian symbolism, which reveals in images in subconscious contents of the psyche but also the collective images of Jung and Bachelard, evoking archaic layers of experience.

This brief review of highlights in the history of the symbol can give us an idea of how inexhaustible this term is—as much as the object it

---

comes to present. Not often does Carver's symbolism meet the Romantic demands: "Popular Mechanics" could be considered an allegory rather than a symbolic story (though quite a powerful one). With its bare, abstract quality, its faceless people, and its theatrical mise-en-scène, it forms a modern fable about divorce and the price children pay for it. Still, Carver does reach the dynamism and inexhaustible power of the Romantic symbol in images such as the well symbol, whose range of possible interpretations was not exhausted in the above discussion. The title story of *Cathedral* presents a symbol that resonates the highest inspirations of humankind and likewise the symbol of the bread in "A Small, Good Thing" is anything but small. However, more dominant than these resonant symbols that appear in his later, fuller writing are Carver's homemade symbols such as the ashtray in "A Serious Talk," the bridle in a story of the same name, the car in "What Is It?" or the hooks in "Viewfinder." Made of everyday objects, they still call for a symbolical reading that sheds light on the meaning of the story.

In that sense Carver seems to follow the tradition of the modernist short story and the example of writers such as James Joyce whose stories in *Dubliners* waver between the symbolic and the concrete. However, the tension between these two poles is more acute in Carver, as the symbolic tends to clash with the more dominant impression—especially in his early writing—of a painfully factual reality, which, like life (at its worst) and unlike stories, points to no meaning beyond the literal one and cannot be integrated into a meaningful whole.

Carver's critics have expressed this tension in various ways using different labels to denote the layer that goes beyond the literal one—allegory, symbol, and mostly metaphor. Metaphors formulate the unformulated, says Marc Chénetier, and therefore Carver resists them. Yet "one gets a clear sense of allegorical treatment" (187), because overall situations are constructed metaphorically. For Daniel Lehman, the characters' lack of insight is responsible for the sense of futility and a "post-modern" atmosphere, while the text's "rhetoric" is meaning-conducive and permits a symbolic reading. In the first two collections, where symbolism compensates for the lack of psychological depth, it is effective, while in the later stories, with their more fully developed and rounded characters, symbols tend to be artificial and not as powerful as in the early prose (Lehman 43–57). A similar view is taken by Arthur Bethea. Opposing the postmodern view of Carver, he insists on the existence of a signifying process despite the character's bewilderment (7–8, 40–50). Arias-Misson views Carver's metaphor as steering clear of psychological or dramatic illumination yet providing "a passage though an apocalyptic moment, an unsuspected transcendence of the text" (628). According to Claire Fabre-Clark, Carver's use of clichés weaves a metaphoric net, despite the text's literalness, (177–79), while Kirk Nesset posits that Carver does not fully deplete the metaphors he uses because they suggest an awareness, steadiness, and unity of vision that his world does not allow (44–47).

The tension between the literal and the metaphoric, or symbolic, is connected to both Carver's unique place in the realist tradition and to the themes that run through his oeuvre. In fact, this tension is the exact contact point between these two levels of form and content, rhetoric and thematics. In order to clarify this argument, let us concentrate on the elements in Carver's stories that do not lend themselves as easily to symbolic reading: pieces of furniture, cars, cigarettes, leftovers, small gestures, and pointless dialogues. Readers who have noticed their existence refer to them as "unexplained and disquieting symptoms" (Chénetier 174); or as "physically present tokens of silence and secretiveness," of "absence," which engulf the characters who are emotionally repressed (Karlsson 147). Carver himself addressed these bewildering objects that seemingly have no function in the story, arguing that:

> I see these objects as playing a role in the stories; they're not "characters" in the sense that the people are, but *they are there* and I want my readers to be aware that *they're there*, to know that this ashtray *is here*, that the TV *is there*. (Gentry and Stull 107. Emphases added.)

Carver's insistence that readers should realize that things are "here" or "there" is, I think, his own perception of a concept the French thinker Roland Barthes first described in "The Reality Effect" (1968). In the article, Barthes connects the rise of the realist tradition (both in literature and in historiography) to the emergence of unnecessary, superfluous detail that has no function in the story's plot, symbolic network, or even atmosphere. This "scandalous" (11), singular, visual detail that sticks out of the text's fabric disturbs our sense of unity and our expectation that every detail, at least in the constructed system of fiction, would fall into place and serve a function. Yet, Barthes does assign this detail a function, though outside the text's signifying system. He treats it as a residue of the (fictional) reality that the text presumably represents. Its purpose is to announce that "that has been." It validates, as it were, like a photograph or an historical exhibit, the "reality" that the realist stories aspire to convey. Barthes's argument is brilliant and appealing yet elusive; he actually supplies no criteria with which to determine the necessity or superfluity of details. Indeed, Barthes's opponents have easily found functions for the details he produces as examples for unnecessary, meaning-resistant details (a barometer in a Flaubert story, a knock on a small door in Michelet's historical account). Readers who try to apply Barthes's distinction in reading text often waver between the tendency to exempt some details from any symbolic role, simply deciding that "they were there" and the feeling that they do, indeed, point to some hidden level beyond the story's factual reality. Such are, for example, the peacock or the cast of teeth in Carver's "Feathers." They are disturbing and bewildering, but it is possible to give them a function in this story, and some readers have actually done so. Letting details be, leaving them in their opaque singularity is a challenge for any reader. Most of us prefer to see them (in Coleridge's words) as "translucent," echoing other meanings and building the text's unity, and we easily "devour" them (in Blake's words) by interpretation.

The challenge that Carver's work presents to the signifying impulse of his readers is what connects them to his characters. Many of these characters are in liminal, in-between situations. They are between lives, jobs, and stories, as Boxer and Phillips have observed. They are unemployed ("Preservation," "Mr. Coffee), separated from their wives and children ("Viewfinder," "Why Don't You Dance?"), in temporary housing ("Careful," "Chef's House"). They are, in other words, out of any functional system, redundant, disconnected from any unifying network that would give significance to their lives. The form of the short story—which, as writer Frank O'Connor suggests has "an intense awareness of human loneliness" (19)—supports this impression by avoiding to situate these characters in any explanatory context. Moreover, often these characters insist on their singularity and separateness. Returning to "Where I'm Calling From," the narrator, in the liminal space of the halfway home, describes himself as between relationships—separated from his wife yet not fully committed to his girlfriend and her "mouthy" teenager son. When his girlfriend finds out that she might be sick, they celebrate it with a bout of drinking that leads to their decision to hospitalize him in the rehabilitation center. After the girlfriend's departure, he never hears from her again: "If she has something wrong with her, I don't want to know about it" (463). His difficulty in participating in other lives is also evident in his remark regarding J. P.'s stories. J. P. "rambles on" (*Collected Stories* 455) and it relaxes him because "It's taking me away from my own situation" (457). Although terrified by the prospect that the seizure episode presents to him, he refuses to acknowledge the analogy between himself and others. The insistence to cling to his separateness and singularity is also evident in moments of happiness. Remembering the morning he spent with his wife in bed while his landlord was painting the house outside his window, he recalls feeling "a wave of happiness" that "I'm not him—that I'm me and that I'm inside this bedroom with my wife (465)." As much as this memory is of peace and happiness, it reveals the narrator's insistence on the line dividing inside and outside, himself and others.

However, J. P.'s story does have a transformative power. When he becomes acquainted with J. P.'s wife in person, acknowledging—after hearing J. P.'s story—her strength and beauty, he asks her to kiss him the way she had kissed J. P. on the night they met at his friend's house. Thus, the episode from J. P.'s story (including the triangle of two men and a woman) is reconstructed. He puts himself in J. P.'s shoes, and through this kiss enters into another person's story, and at the same time performs it for J. P., evoking for him this constitutive moment. What allows it is the process he undergoes while listening to J. P.'s story, whose symbolic structure revolves around the well image. This image—connecting light and darkness, life and death, the low and the high, the general and the particular, the past and the present—enables the listener with a connection as well. As the "drunk" "rambles on," a symbolic undercurrent runs through the episodes, which makes them echo his own situation. For a moment (it is rarely more than a moment in Carver's stories), he is able to break through his separateness and he is set to repeat in a phone call to his girlfriend the desperate yet trustful call of the boy out of the depth of the well.

Two other symbols—the cathedral and the bread—have the same quality of not only signifying but taking an actual role in the characters' reach for a connection. It is a culmination of a process, suggested by Moshe Ron (189–90), that began in Carver's early stories, where a character encounters another character who is revealed to be a mirror image, either wanted ("Fat") or unwanted ("Viewfinder," "Why Don't You Dance?"). While the core of the early stories is merely the encounter, the later ones present a moment of recognition and even contact. No wonder that in the two stories where Carver allows this contact to evolve into a moment of catharsis he turns to two of the most prominent symbols of western culture. In both stories, these symbols never become allegories, since the sublime objects they point to are inseparably integrated into the actual, concrete, even banal, reality of the story. The cathedral is truly, in Goethe's words, a transformation of an idea into an image—an idea that "remains always infinitely active and unapproachable in the image." Constructing this image with another person, enabling a blind man to feel the movement of his hand that draws a cathedral allows the narrator of "Cathedral" to activate this symbol of infinity, making it, in Lawrence's words "dynamic, emotional, belonging to the sense-consciousness of the body and the soul" (157). Similarly, the bread that a baker shares with the bereaved parents whose feelings he unintentionally hurt in "A Small, Good Thing," suggests the ultimate symbol of the Host[3] (Note that the word *symbol* was adopted from the Greek and connected in Christianity with the sacraments [Adams 17]). It is a symbol that practically contains (in Coleridge terminology) the eternal in the temporal, involving (again, in Lawrence's terms) the body and the soul. Yet, in both stories, the theological resonance of the Christian symbols is translated into the realm of human relations. This is, according to philosopher Emmanuel Levinas, the realm where a person can truly break through his/her closed off totality and reach infinity.[4]

Connecting Carver's symbolism with the theme of human contact might suggest though too clear-cut a distinction between symbols and descriptive details, or reality effects, in terms of their function in the story's thematics. I wish to conclude this article with an attempt to soften the boundaries between these two terms. True, many details in Carver's stories seem singular and redundant, and an analogy is drawn between them and the closed-off singularity and redundancy of the characters. The way these details disturb the text's unity simulates the difficulty these characters have in connecting themselves to a wider circle of connections and meanings. At the same time, the unnecessary details remain open for interpretation. They raise a constant hesitation as to whether they can still be integrated into the story's whole. Thus, rather than closing off the text by blocking interpretation, they activate the reader and might serve as point of contact with the text—a process that reflects the flickers of hesitant connection that Carver's characters do experience. The story that illustrates this dynamic beautifully is "Errand"—one of Carver's last stories and the one that comes to symbolize his soon-to-come death. In this story, where he retells the episode of Chekhov's death, he focuses on a side, fictional character, a servant who comes to clear away the empty glasses of champagne that Chekhov's doctor let his patient drink before his death. The servant notices the cork that has popped out of the bottle and has fallen on the floor, and the story ends with him bending to pick it up. The cork is a detail that appears in Chekhov's biography and in his wife's memoirs. As such, it is a residue of the reality of Chekhov's death that definitely produces a reality effect. Carver, who admired Chekhov, picked up this detail and invested it with his creativity and imagination, the way readers tend to do with such details. He thus turns the cork into that "small, good thing" that allows him entrance into the reality of the dead, beloved Chekhov. It is not only through interpretation and symbolic reading then that readers enliven a text in the reading process. Both symbols and "unnecessary" details have this open, dynamic quality and partake in the engaging reality that stories evoke for their readers.

Notes

1. As indicated by Stull and Carroll in their notes to Carver's texts in *Collected Stories* 974.
2. Bachelard, who devoted a book to each of the four elements, connects the water image with femininity and death; see *Water* 86.
3. As many critics have noticed, among them Stull in "Beyond Hopelessville."
4. Thanks to Mira Amir for sharing her insights to "Cathedral" with me.

Works Cited

Adams, Hazard. *Philosophy of the Literary Symbolic*. Tallahassee: UP of Florida, 1983. Print.

Amir, Ayala. *The Visual Poetics of Raymond Carver*. Lanham: Lexington, 2010. Print.

Arias-Misson, Alain. "Absent Talkers." *Partisan Review* 49.4 (1982): 625–28. Print.

Bachelard, Gaston. *The Poetics of Space*. Trans. Maria Jolas. Boston: Beacon, 1964. Print.

___. *Water and Dreams: An Essay on the Imagination of Matter*. Trans. Edith R. Farrell. Dallas: Dallas Inst. for Humanities and Culture, 1983. Print.

Bathes, Roland. "The Reality Effect." *French Literary Theory Today: A Reader*. Ed. Tzvetan Todorv. Cambridge: Cambridge UP, 1982. 11–17. Print.

Bethea, Arthur F. *Technique and Sensibility in the Fiction and Poetry of Raymond Carver*. New York: Routledge, 2001. Print.

The Bible. 1611. 2nd vers., 10th ed. Champaign: Project Gutenberg, 1990s. eBook. King James vers.

Blake, William. "The Marriage of Heaven and Hell [1790]." *The Complete Writings of William Blake*. Ed. Geoffrey Keynes. New York: Random, 1957. Print.

Boxer, David, and Phillips, Cassandra. "'Will You Please Be Quiet, Please?': Voyeurism, Dissociation, and the Art of Raymond Carver." *The Iowa Review* 10.1 (1979): 75–90. Print.

Carver, Raymond. *Collected Stories*. Ed. William L. Stull and Maureen P. Carroll. New York: Lib. of Amer., 2010. Print.

Chénetier, Marc. "Living On/Off the 'Reserve': Performance, Interrogation, and Negativity in the Works of Raymond Carver." *Critical Angles: European Views of Contemporary American Literature*. Ed. Marc Chénetier. Carbondale: Southern Illinois UP: 1986. 164–90. Print.

Coleridge, Samuel Taylor. "The Statesman's Manual." 1816. *The Complete Works of Samuel Taylor Coleridge*. Ed. W. G. T. Shedd. Vol. I. New York: Harper, 1984. Print.

Empson, William. *Seven Types of Ambiguity*. New York: Noonday, 1955. Print.

Fabre-Clark, Claire. "The Poetics of the Banal in *Elephant and Other Stories*." *New Paths to Raymond Carver: Critical Essays on His Life, Fiction and Poetry*. Ed. Sandra Lee Kleppe and Robert Miltner. Columbia: U of South Carolina P, 2008. 173–86. Print.

Gentry, Marshall Bruce, and Stull, William (eds.). *Conversation with Raymond Carver*. Jackson and London: UP of Mississippi, 1990. Print.

Goethe, Johann Wolfgang. *Maxims and Reflections*. 1872. Trans. Elisabeth Stopp. London: Penguin, 1998. Print.

Karlsson, Ann-Marie. "The Hyperrealistic Short Story: A Postmodern Twilight Zone." *Criticism in the Twilight Zone: Postmodern Perspectives on Literature and Politics*. Ed. Danuta Zadworna-Fjellestad and Lennart Björk. Stockholm: Almqvist, 1990. 144–53. Print.

Lawrence, D. H. "The Dragon of the Apocalypse" [1930]. *Selected Literary Criticism*. Ed. Anthony Beal. London: Heinemann, 1955. Print.

Lehman, Daniel W. "Raymond Carver's Management of Symbol." *Journal of the Short Story in English* 17 (1991): 43–57. Print.

Levinas, Emanuel. *Totality and Infinity: An Essay on Exteriority*. Trans. Alphonso Lingis. Dordrecht: Kluwer, 1991. Print.

Malamet, Elliott. "Raymond Carver and the Fear of Narration." *Journal of the Short Story in English* 17 (1991): 59–72. Print.

Nesset, Kirk. *The Stories of Raymond Carver: A Critical Study*. Athens: Ohio UP, 1995. Print.

O'Connor, Frank. *The Lonely Voice: Study of the Short Story*. London: Macmillan, 1965. Print.

Ron, Moshe. Epilogue. *Last Stories*. By Raymond Carver. Tel Aviv: Hakibbuthz Hameuchad, 1998. 181–95. Print. In Hebrew.

Stull, William L. "Beyond Hopelessville: Another Side of Raymond Carver." *Philological Quarterly*, 64.1 (1985): 1–15.

Yeats, William Butler. "William Blake and His Illustrations to the *Divine Comedy* [1903]." *Essays and Introductions*. London: Macmillan, 1916. Print.

Short Cuts: Robert Altman's Take on Raymond Carver_____

Peter J. Bailey

The late Gore Vidal is credited with the assertion that Robert Altman's *Short Cuts*, inspired by nine of Raymond Carver's short stories and one of his poems, is "The Great American Novel." His characterization is cited here not from a belief that it has any claim to accuracy (it seems, to the contrary, generically nonsensical), but because it typifies critical attempts to present *Short Cuts* as a more effective and coherent adaptation of Raymond Carver's fiction than it actually is. The question, then: Does *Short Cuts,* as Vidal and the film's producers maintained,[1] make of Carver's stories a coherently plotted, Carveresque filmic novel, or does Altman's film undermine Carver's literary purposes sufficiently as to largely dilute his stylistic and thematic presence? Before we seek to resolve that debate, however, we need first to delineate the counter-arguments of it.

The affirmative side has been expressed best by Tess Gallagher, Carver's widow and literary executor, whose enthusiastic endorsement of the movie quite appropriately pervades the "Special Features" disk of Criterion's DVD package of the movie. Gallagher argued persuasively that the meeting of "two geniuses" in a film adaptation cannot be expected to leave the literary source unchanged; Carver has his artistic signature, Altman has his, and *Short Cuts* is, necessarily, going to be an commingling of those signatures rather than an unaltered reproduction of either of them. "I was relieved when he translated the stories to Los Angeles," Gallagher also acknowledged, "because I knew that [Altman] would be adding self, adding his own vision to the stories, that it wouldn't be just Ray" (*Luck*). The transplanting of Carver country from the Pacific Northwest to Southern California constitutes the most extreme divergence in Altman's film, one that Gallagher commended for having the effect of contesting the clichéd notion that all of Carver's fiction is set in trailer courts among the Northwest's working poor. (Ironically, all but two of the stories Altman chose to work from in *Short Cuts*—"Will You Please Be Quiet, Please" and "A Small, Good Thing"—are narratives depicting characters in economically straitened circumstances; accordingly, their translation into the Los Angeles middle classes transforms or reconfigures them in very significant ways.) Gallagher also appreciated the intersecting of Carver's narratives in the film: "Seeing the stories intertwined, seeing the way in which they began to reverberate off each other—that hadn't happened before. To see them sharing the same time frame, to see characters interacting, a character from one story appearing in another story and impacting on the characters in that story—that was very exciting" ("Moving Pictures"). Approaching the adaptation from a poet's generously aesthetic perspective, Gallagher proved herself in relation to Altman's film anything but the "dragon lady" she dreaded becoming—the widow whose only purpose was to protect Carver's work and reputation ("Moving Pictures"). Although I differ with Gallagher's argument for the dramatic effectiveness of the changes that Altman/ Barhydt introduced into *Short Cuts*, no one can deny the movie's very substantial success in presenting Raymond Carver's work to a nonliterary audience of filmgoers.

Those who have expressed more reservations about the effectiveness of Altman's adaptation have sometimes been characterized as "Carver purists"—as viewers for whom any substantial variations from Carver's texts border on the heretical. Roger Ebert, whose critical review of *Short Cuts* for the *Chicago Sun-Times* will for our purposes typify the argument that the adaptive balance Gallagher extols is missing, contends not that adaptations must never alter the material they are working from, but that excessive transformations sometimes sacrifice the sensibility of the original. Ebert minced no words: "The movie is based on short stories by Raymond Carver, but this is Altman's work, not Carver's, and all the film really has in common with its source is a feeling for people who are disconnected—from relatives, church, tradition—and support themselves with jobs that never seem quite real."

Ebert continued, "Altman has made this kind of film before, notably in 'Nashville' (1976) and 'The Player' (1992). He doesn't like stories that pretend that the characters control their destinies, and their actions will produce a satisfactory outcome. He likes the messiness and coincidence of real life, where you can do your best, and some days it's just not good enough. He doesn't reproduce Raymond Carver's stories so much as his attitude." I suspect that Ebert would find the same "attitude" expressed in his characterization of Altman's skepticism about the potentiality of effort to alter human circumstances articulated in Carver's comment in his "Fires" essay, where he wrote, "We had great dreams, my wife and I. We thought we could bow our necks, work very hard, and do all that we had set our hearts to do. But we were mistaken" (22).

Similarly skeptical attitudes toward American cultural promises are at play in both artists' works, certainly, but, at the risk of seeming to be a "Carver purist," I'm going to argue here that the dissimilarities in Carver's and Altman's artistic and philosophical visions ensured that, however effective *Short Cuts* might be as a stand-alone film, Altman's adaptation of Carver's stories results in a confusion of filmic intentions, in a movie in which Altman's cinematic signature regularly relegates Carver's to, at best, the status of cosigner. Altman insisted that *Short Cuts* "wasn't a verbatim retelling of Carver's works, but rather a cinematic interpretation of their essence" (Berardinelli), but it's arguable that shifting the social strata of the characters while intertwining their narratives leaves not much of Carver's essence behind. My point is not to disparage *Short Cuts* so much as it is to illuminate how Carver's and Altman's divergent visions dictated that the resulting movie veers far from Carver's stories when Altman is invoking issues closest to his heart. In order to make that case, I'll resort to detailed comparisons of the stories (their conclusions in particular) and Altman's filmed versions of them, to Altman's and his crew's comments about their movie and Carver's comments on his art of the short story and, finally, to a BBC "Moving Pictures" special features segment that, in seeking to document Altman's fidelity in *Short Cuts* to the text of Carver's "Jerry and Molly and Sam," instead ends up dramatizing how thoroughly dissimilar they are.

One of the patterns in the Altman/Frank Barhydt screenplay that seems particularly significant in the subordination of Carver's artistic vision is its consistent penchant for blurring substantial Carver themes and truncating the endings of the Carver stories it appropriates. Admittedly, those omissions are in part products of the inclusion in *Short Cuts* of nine Carver stories and a poem,[2] the sheer number of excerpts necessitating the movie's truncation of many of Carver's narratives. Bill and Arlene Miller in "Neighbors," the first story in the 1993 Vintage Contemporaries edition of *Short Cuts: Selected Stories*, agree to feed the cat and take care of the apartment of neighbors they perceive as living a "fuller and brighter life" than do the Millers. "The Stones were always going out for dinner," Carver's narrator comments, "or entertaining at home, or traveling about the country somewhere in conjunction with Jim's work" (13). Altman's version does little with the story's clear suggestion that by occupying the Stones's apartment the Millers are imaginatively embedding themselves in lives they perceive as "fuller and brighter" than theirs. Both the story and film do make much of the erotic charge that Bill and Arlene get from snooping in their neighbors' place; what the movie ignores is Bill's sudden perceptual experience while casing the apartment: "He looked out the window and then he moved slowly through each room considering everything that fell under his gaze, carefully, one object at a time. He saw ashtrays, items of furniture, kitchen utensils, the clock. He saw everything" (17).

In his essay "On Writing," Carver acknowledged his debt to Flannery O'Connor and her notion of "writing as discovery" (*Fires* 16); I'd nominate this scene from "Neighbors" as an instance of discovery on the parts of both the protagonist and author. What Bill Miller seeks to discover here is a sense of life as lived by people more satisfied than he and his wife are with their existences; years before Bub's alcohol-and-pot-facilitated attempt in "Cathedral" to enter the perspective of a "blind man," Carver is trying out the notion, so ironically treated in his other stories, that human beings can see things differently, that they can gain new experiences and insights from their perceptions. In that same essay, Carver cites a favorite fragment from Chekhov: "And suddenly everything became clear to him." "I find these words," he added, "filled with wonder and possibility. I love their simple clarity, and the hint of revelation that's implied" (14). Carver, these citations from "On Writing" suggest, was ultimately more modernist than post-modernist: The unchangingness of his working-class background had rendered him deeply skeptical of conventional beliefs in experiences of transformation, of lives born anew, and yet even his early fiction contains moments like this one in "Neighbors" in which surfaces potentially lead the perceiver toward insights, toward at least "the hint of revelation." In "Neighbors," the moment of potential illumination comes to very little: After one of his and his wife's plundering visits, Bill inadvertently locks the key in the apartment, and he and Arlene are consequently expelled back to their own unhappy lives across the hall. Carver leaves it to the reader to decide how Bill's experience of seeing "everything" in that apartment might affect his subsequent interactions with the world.

In Altman's *Short Cuts*, Honey Bush (Lili Taylor) and Bill Bush (Robert Downey Jr.) agree to water the plants and feed the cat and fish of their African American neighbors while they're away, and Bill immediately decides that the arrangement takes advantage of them. He suggests that Honey grab some drinks and that they, in retaliation, begin a month-long party in the apartment. Instead, they hold a cannabis and beer bash for friends in the apartment and later use the neighbors' silk-sheeted bed as a backdrop for the enactment of sadistic scenarios featuring Honey directed by Bill. An apprentice makeup man, Bill scatters red dye on the sheets and makes up Honey to look as if she has been brutally assaulted; his faked lunges at her excite him as he photographs her with a butcher knife nestled in her armpit. There's a slightly vexed moment at the Fotomat when Bill's photos of bloodied

Honey get switched with those of another customer, Gordon Johnson (Buck Henry), but because his photos of an actual abused dead woman are even more grotesque than Bill's, the exchange of folders gets made and, as far as *Short Cuts* is concerned, Bill and Honey suffer no consequences for their highly un-neighborly occupation of the apartment.

It's a very rare Carver story in which "suddenly everything became clear to him," but the potentiality of change, growth, and transformation imbue his stories with tension that those deterministic narratives dramatizing the immutability of the characters' class-based fates ("Gazebo," "Are These Actual Miles?," "Sacks," and "A Serious Talk") generally lack, and all the stories in which protagonists' lives are changed by sudden, unexpected events clearly suggest that Carver thought that such experiences and their aftereffects were the very stuff of short stories. He thought so, clearly, because the story form allowed him to delineate, in narratives in which such experiences happen, the repercussive consequences of life-transforming events. (Asked by *Paris Review* interviewers whether he is religious, Carver responded, "No, but I have to believe in miracles and the possibility of resurrection. No question about that. Every day I wake up, I'm glad to wake up. That's why I like to wake up early. In my drinking days, I would wake up at noon or whatever and I would usually wake up with the shakes" [Simpson and Buzbee 206–07].) Carver's ambivalence about the possibility of altered human perceptions changing the world around the perceiver pervades his stories and essays. In "Fires," he wrote, "I'd had, I realized later, an insight. But so what? What are insights? They don't help any. They just make things harder"(24). One of his most resonant fictional dialogues embodying this conflict between affirming individual insights and the suspicion that "they just make things harder" takes place in "So Much Water So Close to Home."

Claire's husband, Stuart, returns from a fishing trip with his two buddies (Gordon Johnson, Vern Miller) with an account of how they continued to fish for two days after they'd discovered the corpse of a woman floating in the river. Never a writer given to crafting stories from a female point of view, Carver works hard to show the shock Claire experiences at learning that her husband is capable of such pitilessness, and much of the story is devoted to her conflicted meditations upon what she should or must do in response to Stuart's bewildering self-revelation. Despite the horrific nature of Stuart's indifference to this body, Claire is initially convinced that his act of human obliviousness won't alter their lives: "Look at what has happened," she contemplates. "Yet nothing will change for Stuart and me. Really change, I mean. We will grow older, both of us. . . . And certain things around us will change, become easier or harder, one thing or the other, but nothing will ever be really different. I believe that. We have made our decisions, our lives have been set in motion, and they will go on until they stop. But if that is true, then what? I mean, what if you believe that, but keep it covered up until one day something happens that should change something, but then you see nothing is going to change after all. What then?" ("So Much Water" 78–79). One version of a response to "what then" is the *What We Talk About When We Talk About Love* version of "So Much Water," which ends with Claire submitting to her husband's erotic desires, masochistically identifying herself as another hapless victim of male aggression as she gives in to him by affirming that, "I can't hear a thing with so much water going"[3] (88). In Carver's original, extended version of the story, Claire gives in much less readily. While she is attending the drowned woman's funeral, which she must drive alone a long distance to reach, she "imagine[s] her journey down the river, the nude body hit by rocks, caught at by branches, the body floating and turning, her hair streaming in the water. Then the hands and hair catching in the overhanging branches, holding, until four men come along to stare at her. I can see a man who is drunk (Stuart?) take her by the wrist. Does anyone [at the funeral] know about that? What if these people knew that? I look around at the other faces. There is a connection to be made of these things, of these events, of these faces, if I can find it. My head aches with the effort to find it" (89). The story is seemingly about nothing other than that ache and the interior conflict it symptomatizes.

Claire never completely discovers how to sufficiently articulate her devastating identification with the victim in order to allow those other than her husband to be affected by it, how to persuade them to alter their behavior in the light of it. Stuart may never understand what the fishermen's treatment of the body has told Claire about his unconscious attitude towards her, but in her refusal to submit to his erotic advances and by moving out of their bedroom into a spare room, she leaves him in no doubt that she has been permanently changed by this event. The story's closing line (Claire tells him, "For God's sake, Stuart, she was only a child") may suggest that her rebellion continues, or it could be interpreted as indicating that her identification with the victim is beginning to wane with time because "she was only a child" and Claire isn't. However we read that sentence, it points to the conflicted attitude much of Carver's fiction (and poetry) expresses toward human expression, his ever-evolving stance on the issue about whether "connection[s] to be made of these things" have any meaning and whether the articulation of them ultimately has a value or effect. In "So Much Water," Claire is irremediably changed by her experience, and she seeks to communicate that change to others; in a poem titled "Distress Sale," a family has moved all of its possessions onto the front lawn of their house to sell them (the situation dramatized in "Why Don't You Dance?"), and Carver responds:

> What's going on here? Can no one help them?
> Must everyone witness their downfall?
> This reduces us all.
> Someone must show up at once to save them,
> to take everything off their hands right now, every trace of the life before
> this humiliation goes on any longer.
> Someone must do something.
> I reach for my wallet and that is how I understand it:
> I can't help anyone. (38–39)

One of the givens of adaptation analysis is that prose passages like the one invoking Claire's thoughts at the funeral are nearly impossible for directors to convey on film without resorting to voiceover narration. While film is superior at conveying human acts, the axiom runs, fiction is superior at representing the interior life of characters. Accordingly, it would be unfair to criticize Altman for not dramatizing the depth and complexity of the conflict that Claire experiences over the void of human sensibility her husband's and the other fishermen's behavior exposes. It can fairly be asked, nonetheless, how does he handle this material?—if his re-presentation of the "So Much Water" narrative isn't depicting Claire's painful realization about her husband and her conflict over what to do about it, what is it about?

When Stuart (Fred Ward) informs Claire (Ann Archer) of the body they had left floating while they fished, she expresses angry incomprehension at their insensitivity; she doesn't know, as the viewer does, that while eating breakfast at a diner before setting out on their trip, Stuart and friends Gordon (Buck Henry) and Vern (Huey Lewis) harass the waitress (Lily Tomlin) serving them by duping her into bending over to retrieve butter containers so that they can gaze upon what her short skirt reveals. Doreen realizes what they're up to, and insults them; they giggle. Once they're on the river, discussing whether to fish or report the body, they take a vote, which turns out to be in favor of having a drink. Gordon suggests that "if the current takes it away, it's not our problem."

Ever since the 1970 film *M*A*S*H*, Altman earned a reputation for his sympathetic depictions of misogynistic males and for placing female characters (and actresses) in humiliating circumstances. Why, then, commit himself to filming a Carver story that takes a remarkably nuanced and sympathetic stance toward its female narrator? After Stuart and Claire argue about the fishing event (she concludes it by saying, "You're making me sick"), there are three more scenes terminating the film's treatment of "So Much Water": Claire reads the name of the victim to Stuart from the newspaper, informing him that Carolyn Avery was raped and smothered to death. Then Claire appears at the funeral for the victim, and because her husband's name has been in the papers in coverage of the event, she only pretends to sign the guest register. That evening, she and Stuart go to dinner at the home of Ralph (Matthew Modine) and Marian Wyman (Julianne Moore), and once all four are thoroughly inebriated, Claire (who has decked herself and Marian in clown outfits stored in her "Claire the Clown" station wagon), sings Stuart a song about a scene on a river: "One day [while I was] sitting by the woods, a little man by the river stood, he saw a girl come floating by, and he heard her cry, 'Help me, help me, help me!' she said." Stuart interrupts her song: "He couldn't help her—she was dead." So much for Altman's adaptation of "So Much Water So Close to Home."

Altman devotes so little time to this story once the originating fishing scene has been elaborately shot that it's difficult not to conclude that in some instances he construed Carver's stories as sources of plots and little else. That is, Carver's stories are sources of situations for the film to exploit, not templates of individual characters' psychic processes acted out in the context of human crises. Actor Tim Robbins (Gene Shepard in *Short Cuts*) came up with the idea of giving Claire the occupation of a clown ("Conversation"), and consequently, Ann Archer spends most of the movie in greasepaint and a lime-colored wig. That occupation generates effective scenes outside the "So Much Water" plot, but turning the one female character in the movie with a significant ethical conflict into "Claire the Clown" seems to suggest how little consideration went into the ways in which the movie's various plots interact with each other. Or, more precisely, it indicates that Altman shared little of Carver's conviction that events can have lasting consequences, and therefore he could use Carver's narratives without worrying much about what repercussions evolve in the texts because he was ultimately more interested in what happens than in what it means. As Altman explained in "Collaborating with Carver," his introduction to Carver's *Short Cuts: Selected Stories*, "I look at all of Carver's work as just one story, for his stories are all occurrences, all about things that just happen to people and cause their lives to take a turn. Maybe the bottom falls out, maybe they have a near miss with disaster. Maybe they just have to go on, knowing things they really don't want to know about one another. They're more about what you don't know than what you do know, and the reader fills in the gaps, while recognizing the undercurrents" (7).

Altman's notion that Carver's stories are "more about what you don't know than what you do know" returns us to the postmodernist/modernist disparity between the two artists, a disparity that is corroborated by substantial comments on their work offered by the filmmaker and author. In the documentary on the film, Altman discussed the characters in *Short Cuts*, disavowing any responsibility, as either screenwriter or director, for knowing why they act as they do. "If we were able to explain any of these characters, any of the twenty-two of them, it probably wouldn't be interesting enough to make stories out of them," he asserted. "It's the very fact that the things that happen to them happen to them, and that they are inexplicable, because I think that's more truthful to the way things really are. And, I don't think we have any explanations. I mean, I've been doing this for thirty years and I'm still getting the same flak from the critics—they say, 'why did they do that, you didn't explain why.' Well, I don't know why" (*Luck*). Of course there are some characters in *Short Cuts* whose behavior has reasons the audience can draw inferences about by "recognizing the undercurrents."

Jerry Kaiser (Christopher Penn) cleans pools for a living, a job that sometimes allows him to peep at beauties swimming nude in pools he'd never be invited into; his wife, Lois (Jennifer Jason Leigh) makes sex phone calls for cash, using words with her clients that titillate Jerry but are never included in their lovemaking, which is often suspended by her need to care for their children; an African American in a jazz club offers her $200 for a blow-job, and after rejecting the offer, she tells her husband, "I could have used that money, Jerry."[4] Consequently, when he encounters a young woman in Griffith Park, Jerry is ready to vent his frustrations with women via a rock. Nonetheless, inexplicability of character and motive pervade *Short Cuts* much more markedly than reasons do, the movie never indicating, for instance, if it's something about Southern California that makes many of the protagonists "pathological liars" (Sherri Shepard's favorite term for her husband, Gene) whose dishonesty manifests their basic contempt for and antipathy towards other human beings.

In "On Writing" Carver didn't discuss character so much as setting for fiction, but the contrast between his artistic premises and Altman's nonetheless clearly emerge. Blurring somewhat the distinction between the world he wrote in and the one he wrote about, Carver explained:

> To write a novel, it seemed to me, a writer should be living in a world that makes sense, a world that the writer can believe in, draw a bead on, and write about accurately. A world that will, for a time anyway, stay fixed in place. Along with this, there has to be an essential belief in the correctness of that world. A belief that the known world has reasons for existing and is worth writing about, and is not likely to go up in smoke in the process. This wasn't the case with the world I knew and was living in. My world was one that seemed to change gears and directions, along with rules, every day. (26)

Although it's difficult to know what "the correctness of that world" meant to Carver—the world in which he was living, of working dead-end jobs and raising demanding children, in which he felt nothing but "unrelieved responsibility and permanent distraction" (24)—was clearly the antithesis of "correct." Permeating this statement about "a world a writer can believe in," is the assumption that writing is about illuminating a place's reasons for existing, about accounting for the fact that, "for a time anyway, it remains fixed in place."

Carver's comments here all-too-aptly point to the stunning irony of transplanting Carver Country to Southern California: There's nothing about the place, as Altman presents it, that "a writer can believe in." His depiction in *Short Cuts* of southern California opens with helicopters spraying malathion over the suburbs to combat an infestation of medflies; the film ends with an earthquake that "isn't the big one," and that therefore slides by as inconsequentially as does everything else. (One death is attributed to the earthquake, but that was actually inflicted by Jerry with his rock. Just more proof, if we needed it, that justice doesn't exist here.) Admittedly, that world doesn't "go up in smoke," but a question that dogs so much of postmodern art was nonetheless provoked for some reviewers by the movie: If the place is as empty of meaning as *Short Cuts* projects it as being, is it, in Carver's terms, "worth writing about"? One approach to generating an answer to that question would be to ask, who lives there?

In the film, Gene Shepard is a motorcycle cop who uses his job to conceal his numerous affairs from his wife and who pulls women motorists over for no reason other than to harass and intimidate them into giving him their phone numbers. Betty Weathers (Frances McDormand) is separated from helicopter pilot Stormy Weathers (Peter Gallagher) and is sleeping with both Shepard and Wally the airline pilot so regularly that her son, Chad, can't keep their names straight; when she takes Chad off to Tahoe for a weekend with Wally, Stormy breaks into the house they shared and takes a chainsaw to all of her possessions. Tess Trainer (Annie Ross) is a jazz singer whose trombone-playing husband died of a drug overdose; she feels so sorry for herself that when her daughter, Zoe (Lori Singer) tearfully informs her of the death of a neighbor's child, Tess responds, "I'll be damned—kids! It's a cryin' shame, baby—[his mother] must feel like shit." Tess then returns to the jazz club bandstand to continue wailing out her boozy ballads of personal loss and self-pity, and Zoe heads home to commit suicide. What these characters have in common is that none of them derives from Carver stories—Altman and Barhydt created them all. "There were no ironies in the [Carver] stories," Barhydt explained in an interview, "in the sense that you're looking down on the characters, thinking, 'Those poor schmucks, they don't know what they're doing.' None of that. I mean, you're very quickly brought to understand, as a careful reader would, that their problems are my problems, in a sense, and I think we were consistent with that" ("Moving"). The reader's/viewer's problems involve betraying loved ones, chain-sawing ex-wives' furniture in paroxysms of vengeance, and being too self-involved to acknowledge a daughter's grief, much less to mourn the death of a child?

In the film, that child is Casey Finnigan (Zane Cassidy)—Scotty in Carver's story. Altman asserted that the "clothesline" narrative of *Short Cuts*, the one that pervades the movie from beginning to end, is the story Carver called "A Small, Good Thing." And, with one intrusive exception, it is also the Carver story least drastically altered by the adaptation. Casey's mother (Andie MacDowell) sends her son off to school and goes to a bakery to order a birthday cake with a baseball motif for him. While she's at the bakery, Casey is hit by a car driven by a hit-and-run driver—in the film, by Doreen, the diner waitress, who tries to give Casey a ride home and ensure that he isn't injured before agreeing to leave him. Returning home, Casey is able to tell his mother what happened before he passes out. Ann and Howard (Bruce Davison) take their son to the hospital, where Dr. Ralph Wyman assures them that Casey is not in a coma and should wake up soon. He doesn't regain consciousness, and when his parents go home for brief respites from the hospital, they receive elliptically threatening phone calls occasionally invoking their son's name ("mighty Casey has struck out"), sending them racing back to his bedside in case there has been any change. Both the story and film present highly nuanced depictions of the parents' terror as they wait, with diminishing hopes, for their son's promised recovery. Carver invokes Ann's desperate desire to be a woman in a long coat she sees out a window getting into a car: "She wished she were that woman and somebody, anybody, was driving her away from here to someplace else, a place where she would find Scotty waiting for her when she stepped out of the car, ready to say Mom and let her gather him in her arms" (103–4). Altman dramatizes

Ann's tenuous psychic condition by having her obsessively repeat Dr. Wyman's assurances as if they were a mantra when she is asked how Casey is: "He has a head injury—a little clot and some swelling, but they don't have to operate. We're a little worried because he won't wake up." Ultimately rejecting Dr. Wyman's reassurances, she whispers to her son, "We love you, Casey. Wake up now. Cas-ey . . . ." His eyes blink open, but only as a symptom of the brain occlusion that kills him.

In the midst of a sleepless night following the boy's death, Ann realizes that the phone calls must be the work of Mr. Bitkower (Lyle Lovett), the baker who prepared the birthday cake for Casey that was never picked up. Here, Carver and Altman are on exactly the same page: radically different perceptions of the same circumstance generate wildly divergent and incongruous responses. Bitkower doesn't know that the cake wasn't collected because the child it was intended to celebrate is hospitalized; he perceives the Finnigans as another example of the feckless customers from over the years who fail to keep their promises.[5] The Finnigans rise early the next morning to confront Bitkower at his bakery; his irritability vanishes in reaction to the rage, then grief, with which they assault him. He apologizes for the phone calls, offers them coffee and muffins—"Eating is a small, good thing at a time like this"(121), he explains—and he then finds himself confiding in them the hardships of a life devoted to producing celebratory provisions for others. Carver's narrator takes over the interaction:

> Although they were tired and in anguish, [the Finnigans] listened to what the baker had to say. They nodded when the baker began to speak of loneliness, and of the sense of doubt and limitation that had come to him in his middle years. He told them what it was like to be childless all these years. To repeat the days with the ovens endlessly full and endlessly empty. The party food, the celebrations he'd worked over. Icing knuckle-deep. The tiny wedding couples stuck into cakes. Hundreds of them, no, thousands by now. (121)

Perhaps Carver chose narration here in order to evade the potential sentimentality of an extended monologue; nonetheless, it's clear that the story's ending asserts the value of the human candor of this conversation, its truthfulness fueled by the extremity under which the three have met. After writing so many stories in which characters fail completely to communicate with anyone at all, Carver late in his career crafted narratives implicitly affirming what Mrs. Webster tells Carlyle in "Fever": "'Go on . . . I know what you're saying. You just keep talking, Mr. Carlyle. Sometimes it's good to talk about it. Sometimes it has to be talked about. Besides, I want to hear it. And you're going to feel better afterward'" (246). And so "A Small, Good Thing" closes: "They listened to him. They ate what they could. They swallowed the dark bread. It was like daylight under the fluorescent trays of light. They talked on into the early morning, the high, pale cast of light in the windows, and they did not think of leaving" (121).

Altman shot a *Short Cuts* scene in which Bitkower settles the Finnigans in seats at his bakery and tells them, "I shouldn't have made those calls. I'm very sorry. . . . I'm just a baker. That's really all I do. I have nothing outside of my work here. That doesn't excuse what I did. . . I guess what it comes down to is I don't know how to act anymore." As in Carver's story, the baker's confession is his effort to match the terrible reality of their experience with a comparable honesty of his own as a form of apology. The scene is necessary to bring closure to the narrative since the boy's death is a tragic event that resolves none of the story's themes. Consequently, it's highly indicative of the divergence between their visions that Altman filmed the scene Carver wrote but omitted it from the final release of *Short Cuts*: It exists only in the deleted scenes segment of the Criterion Collection supplementary disk. In Altman's film, the baker settles Howard and Ann in their seats, and we cut to the Fotomat scene in which Honey Bush and Gordon Johnson get their folders confused. After we get brief glimpses of the grotesque photos they recover from each other, we cut back to the bakery where Ann asks Bitkower to show her Casey's birthday cake.

He considers this for a few moments, but then tells her, "You can't—I threw it away." Because we never see the frames of film in which Bitkower extends his apologies and sympathies to the Finnigans, we would be justified in thinking the baker is reverting to his rude behavior in saying he threw away the cake rather than, as the scene in the context of his apology and kindness implies, that he'd determined that it would be too painful for Ann to see it and therefore tells her he disposed of it. Altman clearly decided against the Carver ending affirming communication in extremity as the only resolution for a story of tragic loss; by having the bakery scene interrupted by the photos mix-up and then closing on the "I threw it away" line, it's difficult to know exactly what to make of the culmination of the clothesline narrative of *Short Cuts*. Perhaps Barhydt's explanation is apposite: "There is redemption in his stories that isn't in the movie, but it's because the movie is ongoing. It's because there is no narrator, it's because these people are living the kinds of lives they're living which don't permit them to evaluate, which is true, I think, to how things usually are" ("Moving"). As Barhydt implied, however, it's not true to how Carver stories are.

The narrative of "A Small, Good Thing" is regularly interrupted by other *Short Cuts* narratives, of course, but, based on movie reviews, the most controversial intrusion is the appearance at the hospital of Howard's father, Paul Finnigan (played by Jack Lemmon), whom Howard hasn't seen since his parents' divorce when he was a teenager. Paul is drawn to the hospital, apparently, because he failed to visit Howard there once during his teen years because he was embroiled in a one-day sexual dalliance with his wife's sister, which culminated in the marriage's termination and Paul's complete withdrawal from the family.

He has chosen Casey's hospitalization as the perfect occasion to re-enter his son's life and to introduce himself to the boy and Ann, neither of whom he has ever met. His primary objective seems to be to rationalize to Howard the circumstances of his disappearance, and, as in "Sacks," which inspired his monologue, the son experiences only demoralization. In "Sacks," father and son, Les, meet in an airport that Les is passing through, and their conversation takes place in a lounge over drinks. There, the father's adultery partner is a door-to-door sales-woman whom he invites into the house and with whom he subsequent-ly begins a protracted affair. The gist of the story is that Les's father views his son as "an educated man" who should, if informed of the entire background, be able to explain to his father how he managed to compromise himself and destroy his marriage. But Les, more em-barrassed than enlightened by the confession, provides no illumina-tion, and his father angrily responds, "You don't know anything, do you? You don't know anything at all. You don't know anything but how to sell books"(45). Sometimes, "insights just make things harder" ("Fires" 24) and sometimes there are no insights at all.

The controversy that this scene in *Short Cuts* elicited has to do with whose fault it is that Paul shows up when he does. (As Ann asks How-ard, "So why does he pick now?") Sheila O'Malley, posting on *The Sheila Variations* blog on August 8, 2011, was impressed: "Lemmon (like he was so able to do in his later roles) plays a man rigidly and *willfully* unself-aware, behaving from a place of panic, self-preserva-tion, and a highly decayed sense of the charm he once had. The time to divulge this story is long past due, and nothing will change the damage he did so many years ago. . . . He is so without ANY clue whatsoever that it is excruciating to watch, but some people in life are like that." Sheila's admiration for Lemmon's performance was not shared by Vin-cent Canby in his *New York Times* review of *Short Cuts*: "Jack Lem-mon, so fine in *Glengarry Glen Ross*, nearly stops *Short Cuts* for the wrong reasons. Mr. Altman allows him to go on at embarrassing length in a soppy monologue that has a perfunctory sound to it, something extremely rare in this director's work."

These disparate readings result less from disparate perceptions of Lemmon's performance as from the critics' competing perceptions of the character's/scene's motives: for Sheila, Paul Finnigan's dreadful un-self-consciousness is the point, his complete obliviousness to the inappropriateness of unburdening himself of all this to Howard while Howard's son lies in intensive care being exactly what the scene and Bruce Davison's pained, nearly wordless reaction to the monologue conveys. Canby worried, instead, about the interruption of the film, of the fact that Lemmon's monologue distracts the viewer from the tension the film has so effectively built up over Casey's condition. Altman very much wanted a sense of simultaneity to be one of *Short Cuts'* effects, the camera's rapid cutting from scene to scene, story to story, giving viewers the sense that in life tragic/comic/ordinary/brutal things are all happening at the same time without any connection among them. The risk that that cumulative dramatization runs is melodrama—the impression left with the audience that the filmmaker/screenwriters are less placing incongruous plot elements in random juxtaposition with each other than willfully piling them on. Paul Finnigan seems more the product of screenwriters overplaying their hands than he does a persuasively constructed, sincere (if deranged) father who has ignored his son for thirty years until this very day. The Paul Finnigan monologue moves the interweaving of Carver plots from exemplifying the randomness of actuality that Altman sought to create by "scrambling" these narratives toward its becoming an over determined meta-story dispensed by a postmodern *deus ex machina*.

Admittedly, some of the interpenetrating of plots works very effectively in Altman's film. On the afternoon of the day she hits Casey, Doreen tells her daughter, Honey, "If I'd been driving faster, I'd have killed him. Imagine—how could you get over that? You couldn't." As far as *Short Cuts* is concerned, Doreen won't have to try to get over that because she will never know that two days after the accident, Casey dies of his injuries. To cement the point, Altman has Doreen and her husband, Earl (Tom Waits), drunkenly celebrating another reconciliation in their hopelessly vexed, alcoholic marriage while simultaneously the Finnigans arrive at the bakery to tell Bitkower their son died. The absurdity of Stormy Weathers chain sawing Betty's furniture is broadened by the arrival at the house of a vacuum salesman (derived from Carver's story, "Collectors"); he claims that Mrs. Weathers has won a complimentary carpet cleaning and, accordingly, he vacuums while Stormy saws. At the end of a day on which they have been arguing about Carolyn Avery and the fishing trip, Stuart and Claire bring his catch from the river to a barbecue at the house of Dr. Ralph and Marian Wyman, who have been violently arguing about whether Marian engaged in drunken sex with an artist at a party two years earlier. Although the individual members of the couples jab cryptically at their mates from within their respective marital conflicts, the four stay up all night, drinking, hot-tubbing, and resolving nothing.[6] These characters and most of the others in *Short Cuts* are serially pictured reacting to the earthquake in the film's closing minutes, and perhaps that scene more than any other exemplifies the problem with the movie's interpolation of Carver's plots: It reminds viewers who have read Carver's early stories how isolated his characters are, how seldom other people (other than spouses) figure in his protagonists' conflicts. They're just not well-suited to survive their translation into communal Los Angelinos.

Since the title of the story "Jerry and Molly and Sam" doesn't include the protagonist, Al, it might seem a counterargument for the isolation of Carver's heroes, but not so. Jerry is a bartender Al hardly knows, Molly is a young woman he meets in Jerry's bar and for whom he buys a pizza, and Sam is a dog he'd had as a boy—they're more projections of his tenuous psychological condition than they are characters. This is also the story that the BBC's "Moving Pictures" chose to emphasize the convergences between Carver's vision and Altman's film.

In Carver's story, Al is worried about losing his job in the aerospace industry, but this is only one of many symptoms of his burgeoning personal crisis. "Al was drifting," the narrator explains, "and he knew he was drifting, and where it was all going to end he could not guess at. But he was beginning to feel he was losing control over everything. Everything. . . . What was he going to do with his life? he wanted to know" (123). He drops by the apartment of Jill, with whom he's having an affair, begging her, "Hold. I'm falling. Tell you, Jill, skating on thin ice. Crash through any minute. . . . Serious" (131).

The film's Gene Shepard (Robbins) we've already met: He's an ero-tomaniac with anger management issues who uses his cop's badge as a pretext for meeting and harassing women, and he shares with the Carver of "Fires" a frustration verging on psychopathy with his role as husband and father of children. The toothpick Shepard chews incessantly remains stuck in his jaw even when he's French kissing his mistress, Betty. What Al and Gene have in common is a penchant for projecting their troubles on the family dog, Suzy—female in Carver, male in Altman. Waking up after oversleeping at Betty's house, necessitating a new battery of lies at home, Gene mumbles darkly about Suzy, who has piqued his ire by chewing on his belt, peeing on the bed, and yapping at Gene whenever he's home. Al meditates on the sister-in-law who gave his kids Suzy while hitting him up for loans, such as "the one just a few months ago to make her car payment—her car payment, for God's sake, when he didn't even know if he'd have a roof over his head—made him want to kill the goddam dog" (124).

Gene lures Suzy out of the house, puts him in the side box of his motorcycle and drops him off in a suburban neighborhood, leaving him with one of the few truthful things he says in the film: "Run away, Suzy—we don't want you anymore. Run away." Truthful for Gene only—the children are apoplectic with grief when Gene returns home, and the next morning, Gene and Sherri's connubial relations are interrupted by their daughter, awakened early by her brother's weeping over Suzy. In uniform, Gene returns to the neighborhood and, on the pretext that the dog is dangerous, he takes Suzy from the boy who has adopted him, admonishing the boy's father (Vern of the fishing excursion), "Every animal has a rightful owner, sir." Back home, the children are ecstatic, and Sherri wraps Gene in a deeply erotic kiss of appreciation. "I hear people say," Frank Barhydt comments in *Moving Pictures*, "'well, [the characters of *Short Cuts*] are all losers. There's nobody in there you can like, really. Well, on the contrary, there isn't anybody I dislike, even Gene Shepard, because he's complex."

The *Moving Pictures* segment imports all of Gene's complexity from the story from which Tim Robbins reads excerpts juxtaposed with clips of his performance in the Gene Shepard scenes. Al's psychic crisis (which he experiences in isolation from others in the story save for his mistress) renders him incapable of acting consistently, of making decisions to which he can commit himself. He worries about where he can leave Suzy, realizing that, "Held up to public view, without all the facts being in, it'd be a shameful thing to be caught abandoning a dog" (127). Shepard manifests no awareness whatever that he's even capable of acting shamefully, and he devotes no energy to choosing a neighborhood of abandonment. Al drops Suzy off in a neighborhood in which he and his family previously lived—one in which, he believes, they were happier. He's surprised that this first act of "getting things in order" brings with it no sense of relief, and when he sees the traumatic effect Suzy's disappearance has on his children, "He saw his whole life a ruin from here on. If he lived another fifty years—hardly likely—he felt he'd never get over abandoning the dog. He felt he was finished if he didn't find the dog. A man who would get rid of a little dog wasn't worth a damn. . . . He knew he must somehow retrieve the dog, as the night before he knew he must lose it" (134–35).

Robbins reads that "He knew" line, of course, but his performance manifests no self-consciousness on Shepard's part that he's contradicting himself—he's just retrieving Suzy for the kids because they raised such a fuss and because Sherri is at wits' end with their unhappiness. (He shows no consciousness, either, of how his wife and children would feel had they known how Suzy had vanished.) Al knows he is, as he puts it, "a weathervane," and as he looks for Suzy in the neighborhood where he left her, he asks himself, "Is there still a chance for me?" When he locates Suzy, he and the dog look questioningly at each other, and she walks around the fence and out of sight. As Robbins reads the last paragraph with dramatic finality: "[Al] sat there. He thought he didn't feel so bad, all things considered. The world was full of dogs. There were dogs and there were dogs. Some dogs you just couldn't do anything with" (137). Has Al realized that Suzy is only a dog, unrelated to his problems, and he can let her wander away? There clearly are ironies in Carver's stories, and this is one of them: Al thinks he's talking about Suzy, but he's actually enacting once again his impulse towards tergiversation, toward perversely adopting the behavior opposite to what he committed himself five minutes earlier. "Jerry and Molly and Sam" is about the deep psychological trouble Al is in, neurotically projected upon a pet named Suzy; its adaptation in Altman's *Short Cuts* is about the fact that its screenwriters are interested in what characters do without exploring the psychic motives of their actions. Gene Shepard is all surface: an LAPD uniform, mirrored sunglasses, a toothpick, a sneer, and an only slightly concealed feeling of contempt for everyone but himself. What do we know about Gene Shepard from the film's depiction of him? He didn't like Suzy because the dog chewed his belt and peed on the bed.

As Altman generously acknowledged in the *Moving Pictures* segment, "Raymond Carver is always going to be the literary star, and this film is never gonna be. But that's all right—I'm not going to compete with Raymond Carver."

Notes

1. This is the argument closing the documentary *Luck, Trust, and Ketchup: Robert Altman in Carver Country*, which suggests that "Altman broke the frames of these stories, allowing the characters to interact in unexpected ways, and in doing so, perhaps created the novel Carver was denied the time to write."

2. In fact, ten Carver stories are employed—although "Sacks" isn't included among the stories included in the *Short Cuts* collection published by Vintage Books, Jack Lemmon's monologue at the hospital to his son is taken directly from that Carver story.

3. The Vintage edition of *Short Cuts* uses the extended versions of Carver's stories rather than the *What We Talk About When We Talk About Love* versions edited by Gordon Lish. For an excellent discussion of the various versions of Carver's stories and the role editor Lish played in making him more of a minimalist than

Carver ever wanted to be, see Carol Sklenicka, *Raymond Carver: A Writer's Life* (New York: Scribner, 2009), 352–84.

4. This scene derives from "Vitamins," the film's only borrowing from that very substantial story.

5. Gordon Lish's edit of the story, "The Bath," closes on this dark irony: in the story's last line, the reader understands that the baker is making the phone calls, angered by the couple's failure to pick up the cake he'd prepared.

6. It isn't at all clear whether Dr. Ralph Wyman's mood or behavior this night are affected by his having been told at the hospital this afternoon that he's "a miracle worker" for saving one family's son or by his failure to order surgery for Casey, which might have saved him. He mentions neither case to his wife. In Carver's story, both of the hospitalized sons die, and it's difficult to guess what point Altman and Barhydt were making by revising that outcome, save, perhaps, affirming that "it's how things usually are."

Works Cited

Altman, Robert. Introduction. "Collaborating with Carver." *Short Cuts: Selected Stories*. By Raymond Carver. New York: Vintage, 1993. 7–12. Print.

Berardinelli, James. Rev. of *Short Cuts*, dir. Robert Altman. *Reelviews*. James Berardinelli, n.d. Web. 13 Feb. 2013.

Canby, Vincent. "Review/Film Festival: Short Cuts; Altman's Tumultuous Panorama." *New York Times: Movies*. New York Times Co., 1 Oct. 1993. Web. 13 Feb. 2013.

Carver, Raymond. "Fever." *Where I'm Calling From*. New York: Atlantic Monthly P, 1988. Print.

___. "Distress Sale." *Fires 38–39*. Print.

___. "Fires." *Fires 19–24*. Print.

___. *Fires: Essays, Poems, Stories*. New York: Vintage, 1984. Print.

___. "On Writing." *Fires 13–18*. Print.

___. "Sacks." *What We Talk About When We Talk About Love*. New York: Knopf, 1981. Print.

___. *Short Cuts: Selected Stories*. New York: Vintage Contemporaries, 1993. Print.

___. "So Much Water So Close to Home," *What We Talk About When We Talk About Love*. New York: Knopf, 1981. Print.

"Conversation between Robert Altman and Tim Robbins." *Short Cuts*. Dir. Robert Altman. Criterion Collection, 2008. DVD. Disc 2.

Ebert, Roger. Rev. of *Short Cuts*, dir. Robert Altman. *rogerebert.com*. Chicago Sun-Times, 22 Oct. 1993. Web. 13 Feb. 2013.

Luck, Trust, & Ketchup: Robert Altman in Carver Country. 1996. Dir. John Dorr and Mike Kaplan. EZTV. *Short Cuts*. Dir. Robert Altman. Criterion Collection, 2008. DVD. Disc 2.

"Moving Pictures." BBC Television. 1993. *Short Cuts.* Dir. Robert Altman. Criterion Collection, 2008. DVD. Disc 2.

O'Malley, Sheila. *The Sheila Variations.* Sheila O'Malley, 9 July 2009. Web. 13 Feb. 2013.

Short Cuts. 1993. Dir. Robert Altman. Perf. Tim Robbins and Lily Tomlin. *Criterion Collection*, 2008. DVD. 2 disks.

Simpson, Mona, and Louis Buzbee. "Raymond Carver." *The* Paris Review *Interviews,* Ed. Philip Gourevitch. Vol. 3. Edinvurgh: Canongate, 2008. 206–07. Print.

To Write and Keep Kind: A Portrait of Raymond Carver. 1992. Prod. Jean Walkinshaw. Perf. Studs Terkel, Maryann Burk Carver. KCTS Seattle. *Short Cuts.* Dir. Robert Altman. Criterion Collection, 2008. DVD. Disc 2.

What's Postmodern about Raymond Carver?[1]

Françoise Sammarcelli

Asking what is postmodern about Raymond Carver may sound paradoxical, as Carver has frequently been associated with the realist tradition, with a return to representation in the 1980s, or even more specifically with what some critics dubbed "dirty realism." Indeed his texts focus on ordinary, unheroic characters who try to come to terms with such prosaic problems as unemployment, indebtedness, alcoholism, divorce, or adultery. In stylistic terms, Carver's terse stories also evince no apparent rhetorical sophistication, and they conspicuously avoid metaphors and tropes. The power of language appears to be limited both on the lexical and syntactical levels as Carver followed the advice of his teacher John Gardner, who taught him to use "common language, the language of normal discourse, the language we speak to each other in," as Carver noted in his essay "Fires" (*Collected Stories* 743). Likewise, Carver's stories seem to refrain from using metafictional or narcissistic literary strategies such as self-reflexivity, thus implicitly rejecting postmodernist aesthetics.

Yet, on closer scrutiny one finds that this obvious simplicity is deceptive. Though Carver is wary of "formal innovation" and defines experimentation as being too often "a license to try to brutalize or alienate the reader" (*Collected Stories* 729), his fiction also questions the notions of plot and characters, and his work contains elements that can be considered experimental or postmodern. Admittedly, critics have often disagreed as to the meaning of the term *postmodern* and its usefulness for the study of contemporary literature. As literary scholar Charles Molesworth once remarked, "For every ten critics who have tried to define postmodernism, there are a hundred who have been dissatisfied with the efforts" (Molesworth 9). British critic David Lodge, in his book *The Modes of Modern Writing* (1977), lists such literary elements as permutation, discontinuity, randomness, excess, and short-circuit as characteristics of postmodern texts. As to literary scholar Ihab Hassan, he considers that postmodernist art "cancels" or "deprecates itself," becoming a "self-reflexive game" that refuses interpretation (*Paracriticisms* 21), while literary theorist Linda Hutcheon emphasizes parody and a narrative "narcissism" that calls attention to a story's own techniques and constructs. According to novelist and short-story writer John Barth, postmodern art should "rise above the quarrel between realism and irrealism, formalism and 'contentism,' pure and committed literature" (Barth 70).

In spite of their diverging views, most theorists agree that postmodern literature investigates the nature, the limits, and the possibilities of language and involves a new attitude toward representation and self-referentiality. Molesworth is probably right when he states that postmodernism challenges one's habits of reading and does not raise questions of totalization—that is, postmodernist artists dismiss the idea that the personal can be made to represent the universal (Molesworth 10–12). Bearing in mind the variations in Carver's aesthetics and strategies—the lean stories of the first collections contrasting with the longer, more "universal" and humanist-sounding texts of the later volumes—this essay will contend that his writing is not devoid of a postmodern dimension, insofar as it evinces an interest in fragmentation, an unexpected reflexivity, an awareness of intertextuality, and experimentations with gaps and silences in order to engage the reader's active collaboration.

Fragmentation and the Effects of Discontinuity

In his influential introduction to the book *The Postmodern Condition* (1979), French philosopher Jean-François Lyotard tried to answer the question "what is postmodern?" He emphasized the postmodern "incredulity toward metanarratives," which leads to the prevalence of fragments (Lyotard xxiv). This is consonant with Carver's aesthetics, and much critical attention has been paid to the effects of fragmentation in Carver's texts, especially in his earlier collections. Such a short text as "Viewfinder," for instance, consists of five sections that are visually separated by white space. Likewise, the short story "The Bath" contains thirteen sections, while nine sections make up the nine pages of the story "So Much Water So Close to Home." Typography and the textual layout create blanks that invite the reader to consider paragraphs as fragments—discursive islands emerging from an ocean of mystery.

Indeed, not only are many stories divided into short units, but a sense of continuity is also missing in individual sentences. Carver relies on juxtaposition or parataxis, arranging clauses or phrases independently, sometimes even without the customary connectives. Carver scholar Claire Fabre has eloquently commented on Carver's strategy and has underlined the author's tendency toward the "fragmentation of a sequence into distinct units with the logical links themselves removed from their usual positions" (38). Moreover, this unconventional use of coordinators (placing conjunctions such as *and* or *but* at the beginning of sentences) is combined with restricted punctuation and a recurrent use of periods to produce abrupt juxtapositions and create an effect of arbitrariness. Witness the beginning of "Neighbors": "Bill and Arlene Miller were a happy couple. But now and then they felt they alone among their circle had been passed by somehow" (*Collected Stories* 8). Thus, Carver's syntax mirrors the predicament of his characters experiencing a general feeling of disconnection.

This strategy, which can be observed on the syntactic level, is reinforced semantically by effects of absurdity or incoherence within many passages, as is exemplified by the fourth section of "So Much Water So Close to Home" (*Collected Stories* 275–76). During a fishing trip, Claire's husband and his friends have found the naked body of a murdered girl in a river and have not immediately reported their ghastly discovery. The text conveys Claire's disorientation at their decision by mixing a dialogue that is at cross-purposes between husband and wife (she talks about murderers from the past; he resents her disapproval of his behavior) and normally unutterable statements such as the following: "I look at the creek. I'm right in it, eyes open, face down, staring at the moss on the bottom, dead" (*Collected Stories* 276). The dead cannot speak, but this passage seems to complete Claire's identification with the young victim.

In other stories, a twisted logic is often at work, as in the last lines of "Gazebo": "'Duane,' Holly goes. / In this, too, she was right" (*Collected Stories* 239). This is also evinced in the opening lines of "The Third Thing That Killed My Father Off":

> I'll tell you what did my father in. The third thing was Dummy, that Dummy died. The first thing was Pearl Harbor. And the second thing was moving to my grandfather's farm near Wenatchee. That's where my father finished out his days, except they were probably finished before that. (*Collected Stories* 280)

In the example from "Gazebo," Duane responds to Holly's calling his name as if it contained some discursive truth, but readers do not know what the deictic pronoun *this* refers to. In the latter example, the declarative first sentence written in the future tense ("I'll tell") announces a narrative or an answer to a question. Yet the second sentence, devoted to the "third thing," only provides an enigmatic clue that is not immediately elaborated upon. Instead, the rest of the paragraph lists two other "things" and, moreover, the last sentence is ambiguous, with the appositive clause qualifying the accuracy of the entire account. Nothing is quite what it seems to be.

Interestingly, in Carver's longer stories, flashbacks contribute to the text's fragmentation and the reader's disorientation with a shift of focus: Who is the protagonist in "Where I'm Calling From"? What is the point of the father's confession to his estranged son in "Sacks"? What is the significance of the memory of the night at Alfredo's in "Menudo"? In "Sacks" the son's inattention to the father's tale debunks the narrative's dynamics and breaks up the embedded story into fragments. Yet memories sometimes blur the limits between past and present by superimposing layers of emotional experience, as is the case in the story "Furious Seasons."

Ultimately, one cannot ignore the various images of disconnection and dismemberment contained in Carver's stories. If the violent end of "Popular Mechanics" pertains to the unnamable (as this essay will later show), the last section of "The Compartment" is more explicit: Myers, estranged from his family, is traveling by train in Europe but, after a stop in Strasbourg, he cannot find his compartment anymore and realizes that "they must have uncoupled his car while the train was in the yard" (*Collected Stories* 401). More emphatically, the scene with the cut ear in "Vitamins" not only stuns the protagonist but also reorients the action of the story. This ghastly trophy that a soldier brought back from Vietnam can then be seen as a metaphor for disjunction, also representing the difficulty of communication in Carver's fiction (*Collected Stories* 436–38). In other words, the refusal of metaphors as ornaments and of most figures of speech (such as hyperbole, chiasmus, and so on) does not prevent Carver from using *structural* metaphors— that is, presenting abstract concepts in place of other, more concrete ones. Thus, the dynamics of fragmentation relate Carver's texts to a major trend in postmodern literature.

Narrative Self-Reflexivity

Another element typically associated with postmodern fiction is reflexivity or self-consciousness. Now, when studying the system of representation in Carver's work, one could object that his short stories do not exhibit a primary interest in exploring their own linguistic or imagistic processes. Nonetheless, one finds numerous traces of such an interest, though expressed in varying forms, throughout Carver's career. As the title of his collection *What We Talk About When We Talk About Love* makes clear, Carver's stories actually tell about language and about the rules or mechanics of storytelling. In the collection's title story, not only do Mel, the heart surgeon, and his second wife Terri argue about "love," but Carver stages their linguistic interaction and disagreement:

When the conversation revolves around heroism and knights in armor, Terri corrects Mel's mistake by saying he confuses vassals and vessels, which makes him angry (*Collected Stories* 318).

Carverian characters are often shown discussing the meaning of words and their power. The end of "Why Don't You Dance" underscores this questioning, as the girl who has visited a strange garage sale with her boyfriend feels that she cannot put her experience into words: "She kept talking. She told everyone. There was more to it, and she was trying to get it talked out. After a time she quit trying" (*Collected Stories* 227). Conversely, words can be dangerous, as if naming things can make them more real: "You *wouldn't call* this a coma, then?" the father of a hospitalized boy desperately asks in "The Bath." But the doctor's choice of words fails to reassure the distraught parents: "No, I *don't want to call* it that," hence the mother's response: "It's a coma. . . . A kind of coma" (*Collected Stories* 254; emphasis added).[2]

Like the reader, these characters often seem to wonder if language can adequately designate things and these texts—by focusing on individual words, their spelling, and even typography—indirectly speculate on the nature of representation, thereby defamiliarizing the banal. Any crisis therefore provides a context in which the tiniest element of the narrative may be challenged. Thus, in "So Much Water So Close to Home," Claire writes out a note for her son, ending with "Love, Mummy," but deep emotional disturbances are echoed in her sudden doubts: "I look at the word 'Love' and then I underline it. Then I see the word *backyard*. Is it one word or two?" (*Collected Stories* 277). Often considered quite uncharacteristic of Carver, the story "Blackbird Pie" even focuses on the material aspect of a letter the narrator has received. Claiming he does not recognize his wife's handwriting, he argues that she cannot have written the letter. This highly self-conscious narrator seems to deny that signs or words may refer to an extra-textual reality. His own frequent use of italics enhances the distance between his narrative and his experience, framing fiction within fiction.

Fiction itself thus comes under scrutiny. Even highly condensed stories, such as "Popular Mechanics," sometimes seem to stylize the rules of mimetic fiction. One could argue that they bare the device, both dramatizing a crisis and showing the dynamics of representation. "Popular Mechanics" is an ambiguous title, potentially referring to a common service and a do-it-yourself magazine, but also suggesting some complex (and cruel) reflexivity: the phrase could designate the mechanics of bodies, feelings, and impulses; the textual mechanics themselves; or the dynamics of reading. Indeed, the story "Popular Mechanics" stages a violent fight between the parents of a baby. The father is leaving and wants to take the child away with him, and the mother tries to stop him. The verbal fight soon turns into a physical one, as in a game of tug-and-pull, so that both parents are likely to lose the baby by refusing to let go of him. If the title hints at some generalizing appreciation, readers may then wonder to what extent it is exemplary.

A playful metafictional dimension cannot be dismissed, as several texts reflect on the activity of storytelling, often with comical effects. Thus "Put Yourself in My Shoes," from *Will You Please Be Quiet, Please?* (1976), stages a couple, Myers and his wife, who decide to pay a visit to the Morgans, whose house they once rented. They are unexpectedly treated to several gloomy anecdotes. Edgar Morgan is keen on telling stories that, in his view, are just the kind of material that Myers, a writer "between stories" (102), could use to stimulate his imagination: "Now, *there's* a tale for you, Mr. Myers. . . . Think of the story you'd have if you could get inside that man's head" (*Collected Stories* 107). Morgan continues, "Put yourself in the shoes of that eighteen-year-old coed who fell in love with a married man. Think about her for a moment, and then you see the possibilities for your story. . . . It would take a Tolstoy to tell it and tell it *right*" (*Collected Stories* 108). The Morgans' pompous rhetoric—"Fate sent her to die on the couch in our living room in Germany" (*Collected Stories* 113)—and Myers's amused response to it draw the reader's attention to clichés about writing and psychology. Thus Carver *quotes* conventional phrases but does not rely upon them. Morgan concludes that Myers is not a real writer because he cannot help but laugh instead of attempting to "plumb the depths of that poor soul's heart and try to understand" (*Collected Stories* 113). Morgan ultimately insists on the damage done by the Myers during their stay in the house: this turns out to constitute the "real story" that is waiting to be written, according to the outraged owners. During their ride home Myers's wife insists these people are "just crazy," but Myers may have found something else in this strange encounter, as the last sentences intimate: "He was silent and watched the road. He was at the very end of a story" (*Collected Stories* 115).

Significantly, if one encounters several writer figures among the protagonists or even the minor characters, they are not presented as successful creators but rather disenchanted if not disreputable individuals.[3] If characters' names are to be trusted as consistent across stories, it seems that Myers, who first appears in "Put Yourself in My Shoes," published in 1971, reappears in "Kindling," printed in 1999, in which he still cuts a rather poor figure. In this posthumously published story, a divorced Myers takes terse notes but has no illusion about the value of his prose while his lodger Bonnie plans to write about him in her own notebook. It is therefore worth comparing their respective productions and self-assessments: "At the top of a blank white page he wrote the words *Emptiness is the beginning of all things*. He stared at this, and then he laughed. Jesus, what rubbish! He shook his head" (*Collected Stories* 657). On the other hand, Bonnie "closed her eyes and thought about what she was going to write. 'This tall, stooped— but handsome!—curly headed stranger with sad eyes walked into our house one fateful night in August'" (*Collected Stories* 658). The narrator does not openly take sides with either of them, but the reader may be tempted to find Myers's self-deprecatory thoughts more in keeping with Carver's own aesthetics than Bonnie's confident prose.

Ultimately, the writer may be seen as a scavenger, as the story "Intimacy" suggests. The story draws a disquieting picture of its protagonist: "You know why you're here. You're on a fishing expedition.

You're hunting for material," the narrator's former wife asserts (*Collected Stories* 563). She blames him for remembering only the "hard times" and recycling only "the low, shameful things" of their life together (*Collected Stories* 563). Significantly, the text mostly consists of the woman's bitter monologue, while the fascinated writer kneels down and holds the hem of her dress. Yet even this vibrant indictment does not preclude some unexpected wordplay—"My eggs in one basket, she says. A tisket, a tasket. All my rotten eggs in one basket" (*Collected Stories* 564), which ironically echoes a children's rhyming game ("a-tisket a-tasket / a green and yellow basket").

The rules of the game have changed but not much hope is left. In that respect, James Packer, the bingo player and retired accountant of "After the Denim," whose wife is seriously ill, may actually be considered as an alternative figure of the author as he modestly fights life's hardships with his needle and embroidery and injects romance into a drab reality: He "stabbed at the eye with a length of blue silk thread. Then he set to work—stitch after stitch—making believe he was waving like the man on the keel" (*Collected Stories* 272).

Thus, whereas realist writers tend to use language as a transparent medium, the narratives of a crisis or its aftermath in Carver's stories are not devoid of a self-conscious quality that they share with postmodern texts.

Telling a story sometimes involves inquiring into the fallacy of storytelling. "The Lie" provides a brilliant example of this investigation, insofar as it offers a casual *mise en abyme* of a performance, and questions the nature of truth and illusion. What is it that prompts the "willing suspension of disbelief"? Should the husband trust his wife or the neighbor who denounced her? The text unravels as an ambiguous combination of telling and not telling—significantly, the nature of the fault is never revealed (*Collected Stories* 329–31)—deceiving and showing (readers find that the wife has undressed while talking to the suspicious husband). Can the husband resist this teasing game? Mixing erotic attraction and narrative seduction, the text ends on the wife's lulling words to her mesmerized husband:

> "Little Pasha," she said. "Come up here, dumpling. Did it really believe that nasty lady, that nasty lie? Here, put your head on mommy's breast. That's it. Now close your eyes. There. How could you believe such a thing? I'm disappointed in you. Really, you know me better than that. Lying is just a sport for some people." (*Collected Stories* 331)

Readers may close their own eyes, but escape and easy consolation are not to be found in Carver's stories. Rather memory is called for, and not just because of the Scheherazade-like accents of this particular narrative.

Although Carver never expressed any concern about the difficulty of producing original works, the meaning of some stories is conditioned by literary or biblical references, drawing attention to the presence of intertextuality and parody in Carver's prose, as in postmodern fiction. Thus, when reading "Popular Mechanics," the reader is subtly made aware of the biblical references underlying the story. The theme of the judgment of Solomon is never made explicit but can be detected as if in a negative image, since the edifying conclusion brought about by the king's sentence strikingly contrasts with the parents' mad determination in the story. In the biblical episode, two women claim to be the mother of a child and the king settles the dispute by suggesting they should split the baby in half, which forces the women to reveal their true feelings when the child's real mother opts to rescind her parental rights rather than risk her child's life. In the end, her renunciation is rewarded. On the contrary, the parents pictured in Carver's text seem impervious to their child's suffering and go on fighting to keep him at all costs. As to the writer, Carver keeps his compact prose under tight control by paring down all unnecessary details.

More ironic intertextual connections can be traced in Carver's stories, though readers must take full responsibility for uncovering and interpreting them. Thus, when studying the image of the letter lying on the floor that the protagonist does not dare to pick up in the story "Collectors," literary scholar Claudine Verley has pointed out motifs potentially borrowed from American poet Edgar Allan Poe (the purloined letter) and novelist Henry James (the figure in the carpet). Likewise, the complex relationship between brother and sister and the effects of temporal deconstruction in "Furious Seasons" may evoke William Faulkner's acclaimed stream-of-consciousness novel *The Sound and the Fury* (1929). This is perhaps to say that some precious links have to remain secret—or that intertextuality is both a dynamic and never-ending game between text and reader.

When one concentrates on explicit references, things are not much simpler. Contrary to what one might expect when considering the cultural background and limited education of most of Carver's protagonists, Carver's narrators are not unaware of their literary heritage or the burden of memory. They sometimes indulge in literary allusions or call for the reader's recognition of generic conventions. Thus several texts include references to Ernest Hemingway, Rainer Maria Rilke, Leo Tolstoy, and Anton Chekhov, whose death "Errand" purports to narrate. If Tolstoy, the author of *War and Peace*, is consistently presented as a successful writer, a national icon confidently expatiating on theories of the soul, he sometimes seems to provide a counter-model for some Carverian protagonists. Conversely, Chekhov, for whom Carver professed a great admiration, is both conjured up and imitated in "Errand," a tribute to Chekhov's art of brevity and intensity. Echoing Chekhov's interest in small prosaic details, this story adopts the point of view of minor characters (thus, the young hotel employee who brought champagne to the dying man's room cannot help being fascinated by the cork that has fallen on the carpet) and retains a detached tone.

With the exception of "Errand," these intertextual references mainly serve to introduce a playful note. Characters are also readers, as in "Nobody Said Anything" or "Bright Red Apples"; some even take reading classes, like the women met by the narrator of "Night School," one of whom equivocally complains that she would like to read "Hemingway and things like that" but their teacher has them "reading stories like in *Reader's Digest*" (*Collected Stories* 74). Rather than embellishing the scene, these literary allusions seem to further blur the distinction between high and low cultures, while sometimes contributing to an uncanny or incongruous effect. Thus "Collectors" presents Aubrey Bell, a vacuum-cleaner salesman, casually referring to such authors as W. H. Auden, Rilke, and Voltaire. But Bell is more concerned with demystifying biographical details and what takes place behind the scenes of literary creation: Readers thus learn that "W. H. Auden wore slippers all through China" (*Collected Stories* 79), and that "Rilke lived in one castle after another: (*Collected Stories* 81), in keeping with the postmodern tendency to debunk literary authority. As Claudine Verley has remarked, the motif of usurpation underlies "Collectors" (Verley 105), in which the salesman eventually leaves with a letter addressed to the narrator, and many other stories that deal with exchanged roles or even inheritance, such as "Harry's Death."

An interesting case could be made for some of the early stories, which have not drawn much critical attention, owing to their not being included in the major collections. Among these texts that are less easily categorized, it is worth examining "The Aficionados" and "Poseidon and Company," both published in the literary magazine *Toyon* in 1963. Set in an unidentified foreign country, "The Aficionados" can be read as a parody of Hemingway, whose influence Carver often acknowledged. The elliptic dialogue between the man and the woman, who both remain unnamed but seem to have been in love, obliquely echoes those between Brett Ashley and Jake Barnes in Hemingway's novel *The Sun Also Rises* (1926). The text hints at a ritual (like that of the fiesta in Hemingway's novel) and its title may lead readers to expect scenes of heroic bullfighting, whereas the arena turns out to be the stage of a human sacrifice: The text literalizes the image of heartrending love as the woman cuts out the man's heart and "holds it up to the lustrous sun" (*Collected Stories* 638). Surprisingly, a more explicit fragment entitled "From *The Augustine Notebooks*" stages its characters' awareness of the dangers of bad literary imitation: "If we just wouldn't look or act or even talk like broken-down Hemingway characters. That's what I'm afraid of" (*Collected Stories* 648). When these characters point to their own artificiality, the text transgresses the limit between narrative levels, which corresponds to the short circuits that Lodge identified as a hallmark of postmodern texts in his book *The Modes of Modern Writing*.

Carver's story "Poseidon and Company," a mere page and a half long, plays with suggestion while adopting the perspective of a blind boy living by the sea. The title of the story indirectly warns that the use of mythological references will not be conventional and, while the story does not specify the temporal and spatial location, the mention of the gods and several clues, including the children's names, Aias and Achilles, are meant to stimulate the imagination and allow readers to tentatively picture a scene from ancient Greece. The blind boy seems to register every sensation and he "remembers every song he's heard, every story handed down at night around the fire" (*Collected Stories* 639). Does the story stage a poet's apprenticeship, while the other boys are playing war, with Achilles "yelling loudest of all"? Is it young Homer the evening wind finds "dizzy with memory and idea," perhaps ready to tell the story of the Trojan War (*Collected Stories* 640)? At any rate, the text itself seems to perform the dynamics of poetic creation insofar as it appropriates the data of individual experience to reactivate the spell of narrative, but it also indulges in the typical Carverian play with gaps and ellipses.

The Power of the Unsaid

Silence has often been discussed by scholars intent on defining facets of postmodernism. According to critic Ihab Hassan, the central movement of postmodernism seems to be toward an ultimate condition of silence, or "moving toward a vanishing point," as noted in his 1971 book *The Dismemberment of Orpheus* (7). He defines silence as one of the ends of postmodernism. Though Carver does not push this logic to such extremes, he relies on the power of the unsaid in order to create a sense of mystery and unease, as numerous critics have observed and he himself famously acknowledged:

> What creates tension in a piece of fiction is partly the way the concrete words are linked together to make up the visible action of the story. But it's also the things that are left out, that are implied, the landscape just under the smooth (but sometimes broken and unsettled) surface of things. (*Collected Stories* 732)

Typically Carver achieves his goal by erasing traces of psychology, dismissing motivation for his characters: Readers do not know why Bill puts on women's clothes in "Neighbors" or what Jerry's laconic answers conceal in "Tell the Women We're Going." As literary scholar Arthur Saltzman put it, in Carver's writings "dialogues are brief, hedged, and in the shadow of what they need to be about" (Saltzman 7). One of the dialogues between Bill and Jerry in "Tell the Women We're Going" epitomizes Carver's method:

> Bill was thinking how Jerry was getting to be deep, the way he stared all the time and hardly did any talking at all.
> Bill moved in his chair and lighted a cigarette.
> He said, "Anything wrong, man? I mean, you know."
> Jerry finished his beer and then mashed the can. He shrugged.
> "You know," he said.
> Bill nodded. (259)

The story is told from Bill's perspective and the reader shares his curiosity about Jerry but not his apparent understanding when he nods. The beginning of the story insists on the close connection between the two men, who have grown up and done many things together. Yet, as the plot unravels, the dynamics of colloquial English and the use of repetition ("you know") gradually introduce a sense of defamiliarization:

Though words are exchanged between the two men, Jerry remains a riddle.

Thus Carver experiments with contextual effects, both in descriptions and dialogues, and his reluctant narrators frustrate readers' expectations by leaving major information out: "Show me how much," the protagonist of "Viewfinder" enigmatically requests from the photographer who has come to sell him a picture of his house (*Collected Stories* 230). The use of the verb "show" combined with the elliptical "how much" prevents readers from making sense of the command, but sets off the intensity of the character's injunction. Carver exploits negativity to frustrate readers' expectations, a fitting strategy in a text that confronts its protagonist with "a man without hands" (228). This adds to the "unfurnished" aspect that literary scholar Marie-Christine Lemardeley-Cunci identified in her study of "Boxes." As Carver put it, when emphasizing the role of speed and tension in fiction, "Get in, get out. Don't linger. Go on." (*Collected Stories* 728).

According to critic Marc Chénetier, Carver's stories are "suspended between unclear, enigmatic origins and . . . pre-seismic endings" (168). Depriving the reader of conventional endings, this aesthetic of inconclusiveness connects Carver with postmodernism if one accepts the notion that postmodern theory emphasizes openness rather than closure. One senses that something (but what?) is about to happen to these characters: "My life is going to change. I feel it," the narrator of "Fat" claims (*Collected Stories* 7). "Anything could happen," as Bill comments in "Neighbors" (*Collected Stories* 13). In Carver's longer stories this may take the form of silent epiphanies, as in "Cathedral," in which the protagonist apparently learns something vital from his blind guest) or the less famous story "Fever," in which Carlyle suddenly feels "something come to an end" (*Collected Stories* 496), not to mention the ambiguous transformation at the end of the story "Will You Please Be Quiet, Please?"

While redefining the ways in which the exchange between text and reader takes place, these reticent endings also task the reader with finding resolution to the characters' conflict. In "Popular Mechanics," which starts with the end of a marriage, the narrator focuses on the characters' actions but refrains from openly showing their consequences, hence the remarkably terse statement "in this manner, the issue was decided" (*Collected Stories* 303). It is then up to the reader to imagine the resolution of the crisis that the deictic "this" only pretends to disclose. Likewise, "Tell the Women We're Going," the story of a friendship between two men that leads to tragedy, resorts to simple generic words to amplify the horror of the ending. Indeed after the men have chased two girls in the mountain, it is difficult not to visualize a scene of murder: "He never knew what Jerry wanted. But it started and ended with a rock. Jerry *used* the same rock on both girls" (264; emphasis added).

Even when seemingly striking less violent chords, many stories end on suspended actions or unexpressed feelings. Thus "Viewfinder," from *What We Talk About When We Talk About Love*, demonstrates the impact of the unsaid, as the story freezes the motion of the protagonist, who stands on the roof of his house, no longer talking or calling, but screaming:

"I don't know," I heard him shout. "I don't do motion shots."
"Again!" I screamed, and took up another rock. (230)

Is the man going to throw the rock at the photographer? At any rate conventional reading is under attack, and perhaps the reader is framed like the picture.

More generally, Carver creates ruptures on the surface of the text by overemphasizing neutrality with the insistent pronoun *it* and recurrent indefinite forms such as "something or the omnipresent "thing"—the latter even works its way into titles such as "I Could See the Smallest Things," "A Small, Good Thing," "One More Thing," or "The Third Thing That Killed My Father Off." While mimicking the limited linguistic skills of some narrators, the use of this device implies that what matters most often remains unsaid: "You see, there are things" the divorced father states in "Sacks" (*Collected Stories* 249).

This strategy also helps draw attention to the way meaning is constructed, or rather to the fact that no stability is to be guaranteed to these extrapolated meanings. One should therefore not be surprised to find "things" associated with images of fall, as in the end of "Vitamins": "I knocked some stuff out of the medicine chest. Things rolled into the sink. . . . I knocked down some more things. I didn't care. Things kept falling" (*Collected Stories* 440). The narrator of "One More Thing" almost makes fun of the reader by pointing to the enigmatic depth of "things" in a self-cancelling effect when he is finally about to leave: "He said, 'I just want to say one more thing.' / But then he could not think what it could possibly be" (*Collected Stories* 326).

This relates Carver to the postmodern insistence on disorder. As Ihab Hassan observes, "Giving up control and the attempt to impose order on chaos, the [postmodern] author has the reader participate in the creative activity" (*Paracriticisms* 21). Owing to this denial of organizing or totalizing powers, readers are invited not only to share in the focalizers' predicament, but also to fill in the blanks and pay a renewed attention to their own role in constructing meaning.

When all is said, Carver's fiction proves more complex and self-conscious than many critics focused on the return to representation and realism would have us believe. Carver resorts to fragmentation in texts often endowed with reflexivity; he plays with intertextuality and parody; and relies on gaps and silences to arouse his readers' curiosity. Not unlike the ideal postmodernist writer referred to by John Barth, he "neither merely repudiates nor merely imitates his twentieth-century modernist parents or his nineteenth-century premodernist grandparents" (Barth 70). Of course one should not exaggerate the presence of these postmodernist techniques in Carver's stories, but acknowledging them helps one to better appreciate the uncanny effect and the unique quality in his voice.

Notes

1. For the sake of coherence this issue will be addressed exclusively in regard to Carver's fiction, leaving out his poetry. When there are two versions of the same story, this essay usually quotes from the first, shorter version.

2. The longer version of this story, "A Small, Good Thing," exploits more or less the same effect (*Collected Stories* 407).

3. In that respect and more generally, it seems that several educated protagonists (whether teachers or writers) do not fare better than the less articulate ones, caught as they are in a web of uncontrollable events (see Ralph Wyman in "Will You Please Be Quiet, Please?," Carlyle in "Fever," or the husband in "Blackbird Pie").

Works Cited

Barth, John. "The Literature of Replenishment: Postmodernist Fiction." *Atlantic Monthly* 245.1 (1980): 65–71. Print.

Carver, Raymond. *Collected Stories*. Ed. William L. Stull and Maureen P. Carroll. New York: Lib. of Amer., 2009. Print.

Chénetier, Marc. "Living on/off the Reserve: Performance, Interrogation, and Negativity in the Works of Raymond Carver." *Critical Angles: European Views of Contemporary American Literature*. Carbondale: Southern Illinois UP, 1986. 164–70. Print.

Fabre, Claire, and Serge Chauvin. Short Cuts*: Raymond Carver, Robert Altman*. Paris: Didier Erudition CNED, 1999. Print.

Hassan, Ihab. *The Dismemberment of Orpheus: Toward a Postmodern Literature*. 2d ed. Madison: U of Wisconsin P, 1982. Print.

___. *Paracriticisms: Seven Speculations of the Time*. 1975. Champaign: U of Illinois P, 1985. Print.

Hutcheon, Linda. *Narcissistic Narrative: The Metafictional Paradox*. 1980. London: Methuen, 1984. Print.

Lemardeley-Cunci, Marie-Christine. "Du poème à la fiction: les nouvelles démeublées de Raymond Carver." *Profils américains*. Ed. Claudine Verley. Montpellier: Université de Montpellier, 1993. 71–81. Print.

Lodge, David. *The Modes of Modern Writing: Metaphor, Metonymy and the Typology of Modern Literature*. Ithaca: Cornell UP, 1977. Print.

Lyotard, Jean-François. *The Postmodern Condition: A Report on Knowledge*. 1979. Trans. Régis Durand. Manchester: Manchester UP, 1984. Print.

Molesworth, Charles. "Contemporary Strategies of Representation." *TLE* 5 (1987): 9–19. Print.

Saltzman, Arthur M. *Understanding Raymond Carver*. Columbia: U of South Carolina P, 1988. Print.

Verley, Claudine. "'Collectors': la lettre sur le tapis." Short Cuts*: Raymond Carver, Robert Altman*. Ed. Claudine Verley. Paris: Ellipses, 1999. 99–108. Print.

RESOURCES

Chronology of Raymond Carver's Life_____

1938	Raymond Clevie Carver, Jr. is born on May 25 in Clatskanie, Oregon, the first child of Ella and Clevie Raymond Carver, a sawmill worker who drinks too much.
1941	Clevie Raymond, or C. R. as he's known, finds a promising new job as a saw filer for Cascade Lumber in Yakima, and the whole family moves to a broken-down house without an indoor toilet in a poor section of town.
1943	Carver's brother, James Franklin Carver, is born on August 18.
1950	Carver's parents buy a house in a middle-class neighborhood the same year that he begins junior high school in Yakima. The house is close enough for him to walk to the Yakima Public Library, which he visits weekly.
1953	Carver begins a part-time job as a delivery boy for a local drug store. He also takes a creative writing correspondence course.
1955	C. R. decides to move the family to a bigger house in a better Yakima neighborhood, but to do so he sells their house and goes back to renting. That same year Carver finds summer employment at a Union Gap grocery store near the donut shop where his mother works as a waitress. There he meets and begins dating a counter girl named Maryann Burk, the fourteen-year-old daughter of a Yakima schoolteacher.
1956	After Carver graduates from Yakima High School, he follows the family to Chester, California, where he joins his father as a sawmill worker. He conspires to move back to Maryann and Yakima in November.
1957	Carver, who returns to his job at the drug store where he worked as a sophomore, marries Maryann on June 7 in an Episcopal church. She is already pregnant with their first child, Christine LaRae, who will be born on December 2. Ironically, Carver's father is in the psychiatric ward of the same hospital undergoing electroshock therapy for severe depression. Carver visits them both on the day his child is born.

1958	Carver moves his young family to Paradise, California, in the Sierra Nevada foothills and begins taking college courses at Chico State in the California State University system, some twenty-five miles west. A second child, Vance Lindsey, is born on October 19.
1959	The commute between home and school becomes too much, and the Carvers move to Chico in the summer. That fall he finds the first of his mentors in creative writing professor John Gardner, who tells his students on the first day that none of them is serious enough to become a writer.
1960	With fellow student Nancy Parke, Carver co-founds and co-edits *Selection*, a literary magazine at Chico State. He takes classes during the school year and works during the summer in a sawmill in Eureka, where the Carvers relocate. That fall, after transferring to Humboldt State College, which was more conveniently located, he finds his second mentor in creative writing professor Richard Cortez Day, who becomes a friend as well.
1961	Carver's short story "Furious Seasons" is published in the second issue of *Selection*—his first creative work to appear in public. At Humboldt State, the campus literary magazine *Toyon* publishes another of his stories, "The Father," in its spring issue. The Carvers move temporarily to Blaine, Washington, to live on property owned by the Burk family, but they return to California and rent a house in Arcata, where they both take classes at Humboldt State.
1962	*Carnations*, Carver's first play, is performed at Humboldt in May but is poorly received; his poem "The Brass Ring" is published in the September issue of the literary magazine *Targets*, the first of his poetry to make it into print. At Humboldt State, Professor Thelwell Proctor encourages him to read Chekhov.
1963	In a breakthrough year, Carver's short story "Pastoral" is published in the higher-circulation *Western Humanities Review*, and a revised version of "Furious Seasons" appears in the well-known literary magazine *December*. It later earns a mention among the year's "distinctive stories" in *Best American Short Stories 1964*. After receiving his BA in English from Humboldt State, Carver follows Richard Day's advice and accepts a fellowship to study a semester at the famed Iowa Writer's Workshop. Earlier, as *Toyon* editor, he had published

three of his own stories, with one of them—"The Aficionados"—
a Hemingway parody under the pseudonym John Vale. He leaves
Maryann and the children that summer to work as an assistant at the
University of California, Berkeley, library.

| 1964 | Maryann's father dies in January and she takes the children to the funeral in Blaine while Carver stays behind to keep up with classes at the Iowa Writers' Workshop. Later the family relocates to Sacramento, California, ostensibly to be closer to C. R. and Ella. Carver has a hard time finding a job that will allow him to write. He eventually watches the children by day and works as a janitor at Mercy Hospital by night while Maryann waitresses. |

| 1966 | Carver, who is accepted into the library science program at Western Michigan University but decides not to enroll, sits in on a Dennis Schmitz poetry workshop at Sacramento State College and finds another mentor. |

| 1967 | A bad year for the Carvers. Because of Carver's objections, Maryann is forced to turn down a job traveling for the *Parents Magazine* Cultural Institute and instead tries to keep up by selling encyclopedias door-to-door for the Institute. The couple files for bankruptcy protection and leaves their rented home to live rent-free at the Riviera Apartments, which Maryann manages after quitting her job. C. R. dies on June 17 as Carver is en route to Iowa City to enter the library science program there, and he flies back to California for the funeral. Carver decides not to enter the program after all, and he begins working as a textbook editor for Science Research Associates (SRA) in Palo Alto, California. *December* editor–publisher Curt Johnson introduces Carver to Gordon Lish, who coincidentally is working for a different textbook company in the area. |

| 1968 | The English Club of Sacramento State College publishes Carver's first book, *Near Klamath* (poems). Carver collates the pages of the twenty-six-poem chapbook, which does not sell well, even priced at fifty cents. Maryann, who had transferred to San Jose State College, receives a fellowship to study abroad. Though Carver prefers Italy, the director talks them into Tel Aviv by promising extra money. That summer, the Carvers fly to Israel, but it turns out to be a "miserable" experience for all of them. When they return to the states they decide |

to live with relatives in Hollywood, where the Carvers hope to find work as actors. But Carver ends up selling movie theater programs instead.

1969	Carver is relieved when SRA offers him the position of advertising director and the family moves to San Jose. Carver meets *Kayak* editor George Hitchcock and works the trimming machine at Hitchcock's collating parties for the little magazine. He also hears from Lish, now working as the fiction editor for *Esquire* magazine, who asks Carver to send some of his work.
1970	The Carvers move again—this time to Sunnyvale, a suburb of San Jose. Carver receives the National Endowment for the Arts Discovery Award for Poetry, and Hitchcock publishes Carver's first full collection of poems, *Winter Insomnia*. Meanwhile, "Sixty Acres" appears in *The Best Little Magazine Fiction 1970*, and Lish accepts "Neighbors" for publication in *Esquire*—but not without some heavy editing and a slight change in title. Carver loses his SRA job, but the NEA grant helps the family get by.
1971	"Fat" is published in *Harper's Bazaar*, and Carver places a story in *The Best Little Magazine Fiction 1971* ("A Night Out"). As a visiting lecturer at the University of California, Santa Cruz—which prompts another move by the Carver's—he becomes the founding advisory editor of the school's literary magazine that survives now as *Quarry West*.
1972	The Carvers purchase a house in Cupertino, California, after Raymond receives a Wallace Stegner Fellowship at Stanford University and a visiting lecturer appointment at the University of California, Berkeley. At one party Carver gets sick drunk with Charles Bukowski, and students will later tell how incredibly much Carver drank. While attending a workshop in Montana, Carver has a love affair with Diane Cecily, a graduate student and university employee. His drinking increases and he becomes more violent with Maryann.
1973	An appointment as visiting lecturer at the Iowa Writers' Workshop, where he was once a student, finds Carver going to Iowa City alone and living in the same campus housing as another hard-drinking writer and fellow lecturer, John Cheever. Five of his poems are included in the anthology *New Voices in American Poetry*, and "What

Is It?" makes the *O. Henry Prize Stories 1973* collection. Though he quits the Berkeley appointment, he tries to teach at both Santa Cruz and Iowa, flying back and forth.

1974   A visiting appointment at the University of California, Santa Barbara, is cut short because of Carver's decline into alcoholism, which precipitated a DUI arrest this year. Yet he places another story in the *O. Henry Prize Stories* annual ("Put Yourself in My Shoes") and finds another small-press supporter in Noel Young of Capra Press, who will publish many of his works in limited editions.

1975   "Are You a Doctor?" is chosen for the *O. Henry Prize Stories 1975* volume. But Carver is jobless and his alcoholism leads to the first of many stints at an alcoholism treatment center, and his illness and philandering put a strain on his marriage.

1976   Capra Press publishes Carver's poetry collection, *At Night the Salmon Move*, and with Lish's engineering, his first big-press book is published: *Will You Please Be Quiet, Please?* (McGraw-Hill). Another honor comes his way when "So Much Water So Close to Home" makes the *Pushcart Prize* anthology for that year. But Carver is hospitalized four different times for acute alcoholism, and his illness and erratic behavior leads to a separation from Maryann. He goes to Duffy's to "dry out."

1977   *Furious Seasons and Other Stories* is published and Carver receives a Guggenheim Fellowship. He moves to McKinleyville, California, and Maryann joins him there in the summer after he quits drinking, though their relationship remains tense. Carver backslides, but quits drinking for good on June 2 with the help of Alcoholics Anonymous. In autumn at a writer's conference in Dallas he meets poet Tess Gallagher, who will share the bulk of his sober life with him.

1978   Carver goes to Plainfield, Vermont, to teach at Goddard College, while Maryann stays behind. That summer at a literary conference in El Paso, Texas, he meets Gallagher again and their relationship quickly grows. They decide to live together.

1979   While Gallagher teaches at the University of Arizona, Carver defers an appointment as a visiting writer at Syracuse University so that he can concentrate on his writing.

1980	The awards keep coming, with Carver receiving a National Endowment for the Arts Fellowship in fiction. Carver and Gallagher live in Port Angeles, Washington, during the late spring and summer, but they move to Syracuse, New York, in the fall. Both of them join the Syracuse faculty, with Gallagher serving as coordinator of the creative writing program and Carver as an appointed professor of English.
1981	With Lish's editing, *What We Talk About When We Talk About Love* is published to wide acclaim by Knopf, with the title story appearing in *The Pushcart Prize* anthology for that year. "Chef's House" is published in the *New Yorker* and Carver's essay on writing, "A Storyteller's Shoptalk" (also known as "On Writing") is published by the *New York Times Book Review*.
1982	Carver and Maryann divorce. In the fall, Carver and Gallagher are commissioned to write a screenplay about the Russian writer Fyodor Dostoevsky. It's never produced. Later that year, Carver's early mentor, John Gardner, dies in a motorcycle accident not long after including "Cathedral" in *Best American Short Stories 1982*.
1983	*Fires: Essays, Poems, Stories* is published by Capra Press and *Cathedral* is published by Knopf. "Where I'm Calling From" appears in *Best American Short Stories 1983*, while "A Small Good Thing," Carver's initial version of "The Bath," appears in the *Pushcart Prize* anthology and is named the top story in *O. Henry Prize Stories 1983*. But the biggest news comes from the American Academy and Institute of Arts and Letters, which names Carver one of its first Mildred and Harold Strauss Livings award recipients. The award, thirty-five thousand tax-free dollars a year for five years, comes with a condition: no teaching.
1984	For three-fourths of the year, Carver and Gallagher live in Port Angeles at Sky House, the home she had built, returning to Syracuse in the fall so she could teach and fulfill her obligations.
1985	Carver buys his own house in Port Angeles so that each writer has a space in which to write. Capra Press publishes *Dostoevsky: A Screenplay* in the fall, and *Poetry* magazine takes some of Carver's poems for the first time.

| 1986 | *Ultramarine* is published by Random House. Carver guest edits *Best American Short Stories 1986* and co-edits (with Tom Jenks) *American Short Story Masterpieces*, which is published the following spring. |

| 1987 | After traveling through Europe with Gallagher during the spring and summer, Carver, a lifelong smoker who said in a 1977 interview that he was "beginning to feel like a cigarette with a body attached to it," is diagnosed with lung cancer and a large portion of his left lung is removed. "Boxes" is included in *Best American Short Stories 1987*. |

| 1988 | *Where I'm Calling From* is published by Atlantic Monthly Press, and the awards keep coming. "Errand" is included in *Best American Short Stories 1988* and named top story in *O. Henry Prize Stories 1988*, and Carver is inducted into the American Academy and Institute of Arts and Letters. But the cancer is back, detected in his brain, and Carver undergoes treatments back in Washington. Subsequently, the cancer returns to his lungs. Carver and Gallagher make the most of their remaining time, collaborating on writing projects, fishing together, and getting married in Reno on June 17. Carver dies at age fifty on August 2 in his Port Angeles home, with Gallagher by his side. |

Works by Raymond Carver_____

Short Fiction
Will You Please Be Quiet, Please?, 1976
Furious Seasons and Other Stories, 1977
What We Talk About When We Talk About Love, 1981
Cathedral, 1983
Where I'm Calling From: New and Selected Stories, 1988
Elephant and Other Stories (UK), 1988
Short Cuts: Selected Stories, 1993
Raymond Carver: Collected Stories, 2009

Poetry
Near Klamath, 1967
Winter Insomnia, 1970
At Night the Salmon Move, 1976
Where Water Comes Together with Other Water, 1985
Ultramarine, 1986
In a Marine Light (UK), 1987
A New Path to the Waterfall, 1989
All of Us: The Collected Poems, 1998

Drama
Dostoevsky: A Screenplay (with Tess Gallagher), 1985
Carnations: A Play in One Act (ed. William L. Stull), 1992

Mixed Genre
Fires: Essays, Poems, Stories, 1966–1982,1983
No Heroics, Please: Uncollected Writings (ed. William L. Stull), 1992
Call If You Need Me: The Uncollected Fiction and Other Prose (ed. William L.
  Stull), 2001

Bibliography

Aldridge, John W. *Talents and Technicians: Literary Chic and the New Assembly-Line Fiction.* New York: Scribner's, 1992. 1–43. Print.

Amir, Ayala. *The Visual Poetics of Raymond Carver.* London: Lexington, 2010. Print.

Bethea, Arthur F. *Technique and Sensibility in the Fiction and Poetry of Raymond Carver.* New York: Routledge, 2001. Print.

Birketts, Sven. "The School of Gordon Lish." *An Artificial Wilderness: Essays on 20th-Century Literature.* Ed. Sven Birkerts. New York: Morrow, 1987. 251–63. Print.

Bloom, Harold, ed. *Raymond Carver.* Broomall, PA: Chelsea House, 2002. Print.

Campbell, Ewing. *Raymond Carver: A Study of the Short Fictioni.* New York: Twayne, 1992. Print.

Carver, James. *Memories of Ray.* San Francisco: Sore Dove, 2007. Print.

Carver, Maryann Burk. *What It Used to be Like: A Portrait of My Marriage to Raymond Carver.* New York: St. Martin's, 2007. Print.

Carver, Raymond, and Bob Adelman. *Carver Country: The World of Raymond Carver.* New York: Scribner's, 1990. Print.

Chénetier, Marc. "Living On/Off the 'Reserve': Performance, Interrogation, and Negativity in the Works of Raymond Carver." Critical Angles: European Views of Contemporary American Literature. Ed. Marc Chénetier. Carbondale: Southern Illinois UP, 1986. 164–90. Print.

Clarke, Graham. "Investing the Glimpse: Raymond Carver and the Syntax of Silence." *The New American Writing: Essays on American Literature Since 1970.* Ed. Graham Clarke. New York: St. Martin's, 1990. 99–122. Print.

Fachard, Vasiliki, ed., "Special Issue: Raymond Carver." *Journal of the Short Story in English*, Spring 2006. Web. 12 Feb. 2013.

Gallagher, Tess. *Soul Barnacles: Ten More Years with Ray.* Ed. Greg Simon. Ann Arbor: U of Michigan P, 2000. Print.

Gentry, Marshall Bruce, and William L. Stull. eds. *Conversations with Raymond Carver.* Jackson: UP of Mississippi, 1990. Print.

Goodheart, Eugene. *Pieces of Resistance.* Cambridge: Cambridge UP, 1987. Print.

Grant, Paul Benedict, and Katherine Ashley, eds. *Carver across the Curriculum: Interdisciplinary Approaches to Teaching the Fiction and Poetry of Raymond Carver.* Newcastle upon Tyne: Cambridge Scholars, 2011. Print.

Halpert, Sam. *Raymond Carver: An Oral Biography.* Iowa City: U of Iowa P, 1995. Print.

___. *When We Talk about Raymond Carver.* Layton, UT: Gibbs Smith, 1991. Print.

Hansen, Ron, and Paul Skenazy, eds. Spec. Raymond Carver issue of *Quarry West* 31 (1993). Print.

Hemmingson, Michael. *The Dirty Realism Duo: Charles Bukowski and Raymond Carver on the Aesthetics of the Ugly*. Rockville, MD: Borgo, 2008. Print.

Kirszner, Laurie G., and Stephen R. Mandell. *The Wadsworth Casebook Series for Reading, Research and Writing: Cathedral*. Beverly, MA: Wadsworth, 2003. Print.

Kleppe, Sandra Lee, and Robert Miltner, eds. *New Paths to Raymond Carver: Critical Essays on His Life, Fiction, and Poetry*. Columbia: U of South Carolina P, 2008. Print.

Lainsbury, G. P. *The Carver Chronotope: Inside the Life-World of Raymond Carver's Fiction*. New York: Routledge, 2004. Print.

Lonnquist, Barbara C. "Narrative Displacement and Literary Faith: Raymond Carver's Inheritance from Flannery O'Connor." *Since Flannery O'Connor: Essays on the Contemporary American Short Story*. Eds. Loren Logsdon and Charles W. Mayer. Macomb: Western Illinois U, 1987. 142–50. Print.

Lopez, Ken. "Raymond Carver: A Collection." Catalog. *LopezBooks*. Ken Lopez Bookseller, 2007. Web. 12 Feb. 2013.

May, Charles. "Chekhov and the Modern Short Story." *A Chekhov Companinon*. Ed. Toby W. Clyman. Westport, CT: Greenwood, 1985. 147–63. Print.

McSweeney, Kerry. *The Realist Short Story of the Powerful Glimpse: Chekhov to Carver*. Columbia: U of South Carolina P, 2007. Print.

Meyer, Adam. *Raymond Carver*. New York: Twayne, 1995. Print.

Miltner, Robert, and Vasiliki Fachard, eds. *The Raymond Carver Review*. Kent State University, Winter 2007. Web. 12 Feb. 2013.

Nesset, Kirk. *The Stories of Raymond Carver: A Critical Study*. Athens: Ohio UP, 1995. Print.

Newman, Charles. *The Post-Modern Aura: The Act of Fiction in an Age of Inflation*. Evanston, IL: Northwestern UP, 1985. Print.

Robison, James C. "1969–1980: Experiment and Tradition." *The American Short Story, 1945-1980: A Critical History*. Ed. Gordon Weaver. Boston: Twayne, 1983. 77–109. Print.

Rubenstein, Suzanne. *Raymond Carver in the Classroom: "A Small Good Thing."* Urbana, IL: National Council of Teachers of English, 2005. Print.

Runyon, Randolph Paul. *Reading Raymond Carver*. Syracuse, NY: Syracuse UP, 1992. Print.

Saltzman, Arthur M. *Understanding Raymond Carver*. Columbia: U of South Carolina P, 1988. Print.

Scobie, Brian. "Carver Country." *Forked Tongues? Comparing Twentieth-Century British and American Literature*. Eds. Ann Massa and Alistair Stead. London: Longman, 1994. 273–87. Print.

Sklenicka, Carol. *Raymond Carver: A Writer's Life*. New York: Scribner, 2009. Print.

Smith, Allan Lloyd. "Brain Damage: The Word and the World in Postmodernist Writing." *Contemporary American Fiction*. Eds. Malcolm Bradbury and Sigmund Ro. London: Edward Arnold, 1987. 39–50. Print.

Stull, William L., and Maureen P. Carroll. *Remembering Ray: A Composite Biography of Raymond Carver*. Santa Barbara: Capra, 1993. Print.

Zhou, Jingqiong. *Raymond Carver's Short Fiction in the History of Black Humor*. New York: Peter Lang, 2006. Print.

About the Editor _____

James Plath is Professor of English at Illinois Wesleyan University, where he teaches journalism, American literature, film studies, and creative writing. The recipient of the university's highest award for teacher-scholars, he also spent a semester teaching at the University of the West Indies in Barbados as a Fulbright scholar in 1995.

In addition to publishing critical articles on Raymond Carver, Plath has written essays on John Updike, Ann Beattie, Norman Mailer, John Steinbeck, Ernest Hemingway, and F. Scott Fitzgerald for such publications as the *Journal of Modern Literature*, *Journal of the Short Story in English*, the *Hemingway Review*, the *F. Scott Fitzgerald Review*, and the *Mailer Review*.

Plath's essays have also appeared in a number of creative and critical anthologies, among them *The Cambridge Companion to John Updike*, *Hemingway in Context*, *John Updike and Religion: The Sense of the Sacred and the Motions of Grace*, *Hemingway and the Natural World*, *Critical Insights: John Updike*, *French Connections: Hemingway and Fitzgerald Abroad*, *Rabbit Tales: Poetry and Politics in John Updike's Rabbit Novels*, and *Hemingway Repossessed*. He is also the author/editor of *Remembering Ernest Hemingway*, *Historic Photos of Ernest Hemingway*, and *Conversations with John Updike*.

As a Hemingway scholar, Plath was invited to deliver keynote addresses at the Museo Ernest Hemingway and the Instituto Internacional de Periodismo José Martí in Havana, Cuba. A co-founder of the John Updike Society, Plath has served as society president and has been an editorial board member of the *John Updike Review* since 2009.

Contributors

James Plath, who wrote his dissertation on *The Painterly Aspects of John Up-dike's Fiction* in the eighties, has often explored the connection between writers and art. Among his publications are essays on "Fishing for Tension: The Dynamics of Hemingway's Big Two-Hearted River" (Hemingway and Cezanne), "*Le Torero* and 'The Undefeated': Hemingway's Foray into Analytical Cubism," and "Verbal Vermeer: Updike's Middle-Class Portraiture." His art-related chapbook of poems, *Courbet, on the Rocks*, was published in 1994.

Chad Wriglesworth is assistant professor of English language and literature at St. Jerome's University, which is federated with the University of Waterloo in Ontario, Canada. His teaching and research interests focus on relationships between twentieth-century American literature, environmental humanities, and religious studies. He is currently working on a literary-environmental history of the Pacific Northwest titled *Geographies of Reclamation: Writing and Water in the Columbia River Basin.* He serves on the editorial board for the *Raymond Carver Review* and has recently published work on *Carver in Western American Literature* and *New Paths to Raymond Carver: Critical Essays on His Life, Fiction, and Poetry*.

William L. Stull is professor of English at the University of Hartford in Connecticut. He has published critical editions of works by Raymond Carver, including *Those Days: Early Writings* (1987), *Carnations: A Play in One Act* (1992), *All of Us: The Collected Poems* (1996), and *Call If You Need Me: The Uncollected Fiction and Prose* (2000). In collaboration with Maureen P. Carroll, he has edited *Remembering Ray: A Composite Biography of Raymond Carver* (1993) and the Library of America edition of Carver's *Collected Stories* (2009). In the latter volume, Stull and Carroll included their archival reconstruction of a previously unavailable Carver manuscript that has since been separately published as *Beginners: The Original Version of* What We Talk About When We Talk About Love (2009).

Maureen P. Carroll has practiced law in Connecticut and New York for twenty-five years. She has taught as an assistant professor of theology at the College of the Holy Cross and adjunct professor of humanities at the University of Hartford. In collaboration with William L. Stull, she has edited *Remembering Ray: A Composite Biography of Raymond Carver* (1993); co-authored literary articles on Carver and Tess Gallagher; and edited *Raymond Carver: Collected Stories* (2009), which published for the first time in English the restored versions of seventeen stories by Carver, titled *Beginners: The Manuscript Version of* What We Talk About When We Talk About Love. The latter collection has been separately published as *Beginners* in more than ten languages.

Enrico Monti is senior lecturer in English and translation studies at the Université de Haute-Alsace in Mulhouse, France. He received his PhD from the University of Bologna (Italy) and has published various articles on literary translation and contemporary American literature, specializing in the works of Raymond Carver, Richard Brautigan, and William Gass. A member of the editorial board of the *Raymond Carver Review*, Monti's Carver scholarship focuses primarily on the editorial hand of Gordon Lish in Carver's fiction, drawing from his own archival research on the subject.

Kirk Nesset is the author of two books of fiction, *Mr. Agreeable* and *Paradise Road*, as well as *Alphabet of the World: Selected Works by Eugenio Montejo* (translations) and *The Stories of Raymond Carver* (nonfiction). *Saint X*, a book of poems, is forthcoming. He was awarded the Drue Heinz Literature Prize in 2007 and has received a Pushcart Prize and grants from the Pennsylvania Council on the Arts. His work has appeared in the *Paris Review, Kenyon Review, Southern Review, American Poetry Review, Gettysburg Review, American Literature, Ploughshares, Agni, Prairie Schooner*, and elsewhere. He teaches at Allegheny College in Meadville, Pennsylvania, and serves as writer-in-residence at Black Forest Writing Seminars (Freiburg, Germany).

Matthew Shipe earned his PhD in English and American literature from Washington University in 2007. He wrote his dissertation on John Updike's short fiction, and his work has appeared in *Philip Roth Studies, Perspectives on Barry Hannah* (2007), and *Roth and Celebrity* (2012). He is currently a lecturer in the Department of English and the Center for Humanities at Washington University in St. Louis.

Claire Fabre holds a teaching and research position at the Université de Paris XII in France and is on the editorial board of the *Raymond Carver Review*. She has published articles on Raymond Carver, David Foster Wallace, Nicholson Baker, and Grace Paley, and has contributed a chapter on Patricia Eakins for *Reading Patricia Eakins* (2002), as well one on Carver's poetics of the banal for *New Paths to Raymond Carver: Critical Essays on His Life, Fiction, and Poetry*. Her work focuses on the relationship between literature and stereotypy following the path opened by Roland Barthes, with new projects devoted to Mary Caponegro, Christine Schutt, and Laura Kasischke.

Robert Miltner is associate professor of English at Ohio's Kent State University Stark, and he is Kent Campus coordinator and is on the poetry faculty of the Northeast Ohio MFA in Creative Writing program. He is the author of *Against the Simple*, winner of a Wick poetry chapbook award, and his collection of prose poems, *Hotel Utopia*, selected by National Book Award finalist Tim Seibles as winner of the Many Voices Project book award (2011). Miltner is co-editor, with Sandra Kleppe, of *New Paths to Raymond Carver* (2009) and with Vasiliki Fachard, of *Not Far From Here: The Paris Symposium on Raymond Carver* (2013). He edits the *Raymond Carver Review* and *Quickly*.

Randolph Paul Runyon, professor of French at Miami University of Ohio, is the author of *Reading Raymond Carver* (1992). His work on Carver has also appeared in *New Paths to Raymond Carver* (2008), the *Journal of the Short Story in English*, and *Q/W/E/R/T/Y*. Among his other books are *Order in Disorder: Intratextual Symmetry in Montaigne's Essays* (forthcoming in fall 2013), *Intratextual Baudelaire* (2010), *La Fontaine's Complete Tales in Verse: An Illustrated and Annotated Translation* (2009), *Ghostly Parallels: Robert Penn Warren and the Lyric Poetic Sequence* (2006), *The Art of the Persian Letters* (2005), and *In La Fontaine's Labyrinth* (2000).

Vasiliki Fachard studied French and comparative literature in the United States and Paris. After finishing her PhD and teaching at the State University of New York at Albany, she moved to Lausanne, Switzerland, where she works as an independent scholar. Fachard was the guest editor of a *Special Issue on Raymond Carver* published in 2006 by the *Journal of the Short Story in English*. She is co-editor of the *Raymond Carver Review* and of the forthcoming collection of essays from a 2008 conference, *Not Far from Here: The Paris Symposium on Raymond Carver*.

Ayala Amir earned her PhD at the Hebrew University of Jerusalem and taught at the department of comparative literature there for many years. She is currently a lecturer in the department of literature at Bar Ilan University and is teaching coordinator at the Open University, both in Israel. Her book, *The Visual Poetics of Raymond Carver* (2010) examines Carver's use of the eye-of-the-camera technique and the tensions that structure his visual aesthetics. Amir has also published articles on narrative study, modern and postmodern fiction, and the interconnections between literature and the visual arts.

Peter J. Bailey is the author of *Reading Stanley Elkin*, *The Reluctant Film Art of Woody Allen*, and *Rabbit (Un)Redeemed: The Drama of Belief in John Updike's Fic-tion*. He has published in *Contemporary Literature*, *Critique*, *Modern Fiction Studies*, *Postscript*, *Review of Contemporary Fiction*, and the *John Updike Review*. Bailey teaches American literature, fiction writing, and film studies at St. Lawrence University in Canton, New York, where he is Frank P. Piskor professor of literature. He is co-editor, with Sam B. Girgus, of the forthcoming *Companion to Woody Allen*.

Françoise Sammarcelli is professor of American literature at Paris Sorbonne University and head of the Sorbonne Research Center on Text and Image. She has published extensively on American fiction—including several articles on Raymond Carver—as well as on literary representation, intertextuality, and intersemiotics. A former editor of the *French Journal of American Studies* (RFEA), she has been a member of the editorial board of the *Raymond Carver Review* since 2008. She is the author of a book on John Barth (1998) and the editor of two collections of essays: *Image et Mémoire* (Picture and Memory) (2009) and *L'Obscur* (Obscurity) (2009). She recently organized an international conference on "Visual Texts, Textual Pictures" at the Sorbonne in 2012.

Index